OUR *Secret* RULES

Why We Do the Things We Do

JORDAN WEISS, MD

SQUAREONE
PUBLISHERS

Cover Designer: Phaedra Mastrocola
Typesetter: Gary A. Rosenberg
Editor: Helene Ciaravino

Square One Publishers
115 Herricks Road
Garden City Park, NY 11040
(516) 535-2010
www.squareonepublishers.com

Library of Congress Cataloging-in-Publication Data
Weiss, Jordan.
   Our secret rules : why we do the things we do / Jordan Weiss.
      p. cm.
Includes index.
   ISBN 0-7570-0010-X (pbk.)
   1. Conduct of life. I. Title.
   BF637.C5 W45 2003
   158—dc21

                                                    2002012940

Printed in the United States of America

10   9   8   7   6   5   4   3   2   1

Contents

How to Use This Book

This book was designed to help you uncover and understand your secret rules—the internal rules that, consciously or unconsciously, guide everything you do, from making decisions about your health to falling in love. Thus, *Our Secret Rules* is divided into ten chapters, each of which highlights a major area of your life. Although you may wish to read through each chapter of the book, if you prefer, you can turn only to those sections that explore the issues of greatest concern to you. Chapter 1, for instance, examines your secret rules regarding money, while Chapter 2 looks at work and career.

Within each chapter of *Our Secret Rules*, you will find ten hypothetical situations. After reading a given situation, you will be asked how you would respond to the scenario. Three possible answers—labeled A, B, and C—are provided. Importantly, the answer choices are not the secret rules. Rather, they are markers that will guide you in determining your rule, which is explored in an analysis that follows.

After selecting the answer that best reflects your true feelings, read the analysis that corresponds to your choice. After a few introductory thoughts, the first two paragraphs of each analysis explore answer A; the second two paragraphs, answer B; and the remaining two paragraphs, answer C. Therefore, it is not necessary to read all of the paragraphs included in each analysis.

You will notice that many of the analyses include questions designed to help you further understand your secret rule. Many also make statements that come from a "devil's advocate" perspective. This material is not meant to judge you or persuade you to change your opinion. It is simply aimed at helping you establish if your rule is firm, and if it's a healthy one for you. If you find yourself easily doubting your decision or switching from your original answer, you have identified a life area that could be causing you conflict and anxiety.

Some of the hypothetical situations are very realistic and might even parallel your own experiences. Others will require you to stretch your mind and use your imagination. In either case, when selecting an answer, try to be true to your personality and beliefs. Choose the answers that align most closely with who you are at the present time, even if you don't judge them to be the most politically correct, wise, or kind responses. The goal is to uncover those unspoken rules that you actually believe and follow. Be fully honest with yourself, and you'll be better able to understand your secret rules and, if necessary, to modify them as a means of living a happier and more satisfying life.

Introduction

We humans are an orderly lot. We have rules regulating any and every aspect of behavior. There are rules that we learn during the very first years of life, such as rules for basic survival and rules that govern family behavior. Then there are rules we apply to friendship, school, work, courtship, and marriage. And don't forget about all those rules that apply to activities such as playing sports, driving cars, eating meals, tipping at restaurants, crossing streets . . . rules, rules, rules! Over the course of our early years, we gather thousands of rules. You'd think that by the time we hit adulthood, if we'd just follow the patterns created by all of the rules, we'd have everything under control. We'd know the necessary things about life and how best to achieve our goals. That sounds logical enough! But, of course, it's never quite that simple.

WHAT'S THE BIG SECRET?

Why do bright and thoughtful people who know the rules of life find it so difficult to bring work, family, relationships—all of it—together successfully? Why do so many of us feel disappointed? How is it possible, in this age of enlightenment, therapy, and untold numbers of self-help books, that we continue to feel stressed and unfulfilled?

Perhaps the problem lies in the conflict between our stated rules and the rules that actually govern our lives. We think we know our own rules because we can articulate various goals, preferences, and values. But, as this book will explain, underneath our stated goals, preferences, and values is a deeper truth—the one encompassing our *secret rules*. Each one of us has our own set of secret rules that influences us to some degree, on some—usually unconscious—level.

A person's secret rules may not agree with society's rules, be consistent with the culture's routine, or sit well with family beliefs. And when real life doesn't harmonize with these secret rules, stress, anger, and disappointment result. Interestingly, the vast majority of individuals never identify and study their secret rules, and therefore never resolve the conflicts caused by friction between their present lives and what their secret rules demand.

Secret rules aren't that simple, either. Some are good for us, and some are bad for us. We don't listen closely enough to some of them, while we unconsciously let other secret rules dominate our lives. You see, over the course of our early years, we accept many established rules and make them part of our secret rules. Some of these work well with our natures, but others do not. Therefore, we hold secret rules that run contrary to what would be best for our lives.

So, there are the secret rules that we formed after certain experiences, but that ultimately prove unhealthy. And then there are the healthy secret rules that we simply ignore, because they are uncomfortable to obey. As a result, life becomes further riddled with anxiety.

Let me emphasize the point that while some of our secret rules are directly influenced by culture, religion, and family, we formulate many other secret rules according to our own experiences, natures, and desires. These are the most powerful rules, for they are designed internally and are true to our most fundamental selves. If we can identify these most basic rules, we can follow the healthy secret rules more closely and eliminate the unhealthy ones, ultimately achieving happier, healthier lives. Isn't it about time you stopped feeling so stressed out and let down?

CAN I REALLY REDUCE MY CHRONIC ANXIETY?

A vast number of people can reduce the disappointment and anxiety in their lives just by analyzing their secret rules and making a commitment to do something about them. By taking the time simply to listen to yourself while searching for your secret rules, you will begin to recognize the capacity you have to control your life. That will *certainly* reduce your anxiety. After figuring out what you truly think and observe—as opposed to what you accept, follow, assume, or pretend—you can craft a more fulfilling, more productive life. It all starts by asking yourself several probing questions designed to get to the heart of your beliefs and behaviors. We'll do that over the next ten chapters.

It helps to look at a few examples. Take, for instance, a secret rule that many of us have but to which many of us don't consciously admit: Never face any truth about yourself or your family that might be painful. Perhaps the word *denial* springs to mind. Another related and harmful secret rule is as follows: Anything that allows us to forget emotional pain is acceptable and necessary. Because of such secret rules, some parents refuse to have their children assessed for special education. Because of such secret rules, some people continue to overeat, abuse alcohol, and the like. Now what if you shine a light on these rules and truly face them? Then you have a better chance of realizing the absurdity and danger of such rules! Imagine how different life could be if you realized the futility of these secret rules—how much they hurt you and those you love. So sometimes secret rules need changing. We can work on that.

Consider a man who lives his life according to—and raises his children to believe in—the basic American values of equality and personal freedom. For years, the man finds it easy to claim belief in these values because they are never really challenged. One day, though, his daughter comes home with a wonderful partner—a man who is of a different racial background. The couple has a very healthy relationship. They announce that they are considering marriage. All of a sudden, the father finds himself getting angry. He has a bad attitude toward his daughter. He wakes up with tension knots and stress headaches every morning. On the outside, this man knows he would sound like a terrible bigot if he discouraged the marriage, so he tries to bury these tensions that are so unfamiliar and ugly to him. But one day it all explodes and he refuses to support such a union. His secret rules—rules he never really thought about, and never really had to think about before—are now manifesting as he tries to prevent the marriage.

If this man were to examine his deepest secret rules about equality and freedom, he would find that his perspective needs changing. If he were to be a hundred percent honest with himself, he wouldn't let the anxiety consume him, nor would he explode with mean-spiritedness. Instead, he would steadily work to change the habits and attitudes that have been lurking below his stated values. And how much better off would he be if he had read *Our Secret Rules* before the whole situation occurred? He'd be prepared! First, the father must discover and throw out his old rule that runs contrary to equality and freedom among all people. Perhaps his culture influenced his secret rules; perhaps he is just uncomfortable with change or the unfamiliar. Whatever the case, by identifying his secret rules and realizing that they are inappropriate, he has the freedom to form a new secret rule that says, "A person should not be characterized, judged, accepted, or rejected according to his ethnic background." Eliminating prejudice towards others by adjusting secret rules is a win-win situation. Every time we ask ourselves if we really need that rule about that group or person, we change ourselves *and* the world in which we live.

Remember, there are very good secret rules too. Sometimes your secret rules spur you on to better things. In the early 1900s, what happened to a wife and mother who wanted to bring her talent into the business world? Her secret rule said, "You have a God-given talent. Use it to do as much as you can in this world." At that time, however, society's rules answered, "If you are a good woman, you will remain a full-time housewife and not invade the man's work world." The result was a great deal of internal conflict and confusion for such a woman. Fortunately, enough women who struggled with this issue began following their secret rules and eventually changed society, despite the initial prejudice and emotional pain. Now, collectively, as a nation, we have looked at our secret rules regarding women and have concluded that equality between genders makes the world a better place—and simply makes sense.

So there is a great deal of benefit to be gained from identifying your secret rules and taking action to adjust them, where necessary. You will make life more effective and enjoyable for yourself, your loved ones, and the world at large. And this book will guide you through a large part of the self-examination, prodding you on when the going gets tough and patting you on the back when you need a little support.

WHAT IS THE DIFFERENCE BETWEEN RULES AND LAWS?

A personal rule is a statement that prescribes a certain way you are supposed to be. It is a statement defining the behaviors that you expect yourself to live by. If you don't follow a rule, as used in this context, there are negative consequences. The consequences range from mild feelings of irritation to profound feelings of failure. Personal rules can be fostered from the outside, in the form of religious requirements or family expectations, for example. But ultimately, you command yourself to obey these rules. After all, you can break as many social taboos as you desire and still feel powerful and triumphant, but if you break your own rules, you will pay dearly in the deepest of ways—guilt, loss of self-respect, and internal anger.

A law is different from a rule. While a behavior that is expected or demanded of you is called a *rule*, a behavioral requirement that is clearly expected or demanded in society's arena is called a *law*. The consequences of breaking a law are legally mandated from outside the self or family. Also, there are cultural customs that have the *force* of laws, and guilt or exclusion are used to enforce such value systems.

The bottom line is that the negative consequences of breaking a federal, state, or even cultural law come from external sources. Meanwhile, the source of the punishment for breaking one of your own rules is primarily internal. By breaking your own rules, you can put yourself in jail long before the law does. After breaking a personal rule, you may even judge that you have lost the right to happiness, ultimately punishing yourself.

Your secret rules are so powerful that, in breaking one, you may determine that you are not entitled to love, prosperity, or harmony. A rule such as "Only weak people cry!" may convince you that emotions are bad and must be avoided at all costs. Your rules may even make you value money over love or law or country. They may hold that only the educated, wealthy, and beautiful are entitled to the best things that life has to offer. That's why it is so important to assess your personal rules, and change the ones that can very well make life miserable. And for the record, unjust or inappropriate laws can be changed when enough people listen to their secret rules and start to effect change on the social, state, and federal levels.

It is also important to realize that *secret* rules are more powerful that any other rules. Yes, we even have levels of rules in our lives. There are rules we follow according to laws, rules we follow according to tradition, and the like. But our secret rules are the rules we follow according to ourselves. They are the primary forces directing behavior and action. That's why an addict will sometimes destroy himself rather than face the truth about his condition. His secret rule, "Avoid what might be very painful to face," dominates over the more obvious rule that says, "If you cannot function without relying on a substance, then you are addicted to it. You need help."

A few more examples might help. A woman who repeatedly finds herself in relationships with abusive and unloving men follows a secret rule, "It's acceptable for love to hurt; the contact and attention make the pain worth it," over the more general rule that states, "Your love relationship should be productive and life-enhancing." She tolerates and even expects disrespect because her secret rule continually allows her to do so. Furthermore, consider how a good cop who feels forced to violate his own ethical code will often bring an end to his suffering by "accidentally" making mistakes that lead to his own arrest. The policeman subconsciously seeks to punish himself because he knows how fundamentally wrong it is to break his secret rules that cry out, "Your integrity is more important than material profit."

At the outset of this journey, you may find it difficult to distinguish general rules, influenced by laws and by culture, from your secret rules. Sometimes, the two seem very similar, and sometimes they actually are identical. But for the most part, secret rules are more numerous and situation-dependent than external laws and rules.

ARE MY SECRET RULES ESSENTIALLY ABOUT MY PERSONAL LIMITATIONS?

It is our secret rules set against the background of natural abilities and native culture that make us who we are. For example, you may have an inherited talent to play concert-level piano, but it is your rules about the value of music and the meaning of success that drive you to excel at playing the piano. Sometimes the word "rules" sounds like a series of limitations, but this is a misunderstanding, for the term is not synonymous with restrictions or limitations. Remember, a rule is not a law. Your rules give direction and meaning to your life. They motivate, excite, and support you.

Your secret rules should not be a matter of limitation. Rather, they should be a matter of direction. In other words, the world as you see it *or as you think it ought to be* determines your set of rules. Your personality is a function of your rules. The self that you know contains a collection of rules about how life is supposed to be. Therefore, it behooves you to know as much as you can about your own secret rules, to make sure the direction in which you are going is actually the one you want to pursue.

So do your best to wipe away old stigmas about "rules" from the get-go. Think of the questions that you are about to answer over the next few chapters as an adventure in self-study. You are figuring out about the real you, not about what you can't or shouldn't do. More than anything else, self-knowledge means freedom—from unnecessary anxiety, disappointment, conflict.

There is no way to prepare yourself for everything that occurs over the course of your life. You are forced to make difficult choices very quickly, based on your secret rules. Suppose that by knowing what many of your secret rules are, you were able to avoid certain unhappy or even harmful experiences? Knowing your secret rules, then, may be much more important than you ever imagined.

Hypothetical, interesting, even frustrating scenarios can be posed in order to test your secret rules and therefore get you to learn more about yourself. The following ten chapters contain a series of questions and analyses that you should really think about if you want to operate as happily, healthily, and successfully as you can. These questions will help you identify who you are and how you can better live your life. Happiness is attained through choices, and choices are made according to your secret rules. Getting down to the secret rules that govern the way you respond will help you become truer and kinder to yourself. All you have to do now is take a little time to get to know yourself a whole lot better. Make a difference that will last a lifetime by uncovering your secret rules.

1. *Money*

MONEY IS CREDITED WITH ALMOST magical properties. Much like Aladdin's lamp, it can transform peasants and paupers into princes. How many people throughout the ages have given their lives and taken many more lives in the pursuit of wealth?

Unfortunately, we are often judged by the amount of money we have. So many of us covet it, need it, and want more of it. Money is a great source of tension in many people's lives. As a psychiatrist, it is hard to escape the conclusion that many of the problems described as *psychiatric* are really *financial*. The spouse who desperately wants to terminate a bad marriage may stay simply because it's too expensive to get out. And then there's the societal pressure to send the children to top schools and buy a house with at least three bedrooms. We can become obsessive over financial gain. Our culture teaches us that we can never have enough money. Yet as a result, many children hardly know their parents, and many professionals suffer from anxiety-induced heart disease by the time they are middle-aged. Is a large amount of money worth our health and immediate happiness? Is the financial security of the future worth the quality of the present?

Money may sound like a cure-all, but is it? Perhaps you think you already know your rules when it comes to money. Maybe you think you already know where finances fall on your priorities list. However, the following questions will bring some tough issues to the foreground. They will help you figure out how you really view money and its benefits.

1. Congratulations! You just won the lottery and are scheduled to receive $500,000 annually for the next twenty years. No more "nothing job" for you! You can do everything that you've always wanted to do. Before winning the lottery, you had not planned to attend your high school reunion, but now you think you will. Many of your old friends will be there, as well

as that "in" crowd which always rejected you. Will you tell your former class-mates that you struck it rich?

A. Yes, I will tell them that I am a rich person.

B. No, I will dress my usual way and won't say anything about the change in my financial circumstances.

C. I will don expensive clothing and jewelry, but I won't discuss anything about the lottery.

What should people think about you, with respect to your financial success? Should they know your status? Do you care? A lot depends, of course, on what *you* think about you. This question reveals whether or not financial status is a key part of your identity. The secret rule behind answer A is quite simple: *It is important that people know I am a financial success.* Even more powerfully, it says that you *need* to be seen as a success. You *need* to be somebody. There is nothing wrong with wanting people to know you have financial security. It is not wrong to be proud of your successes or your fortune. But if you chose this response immediately above the others, know too that you have some pent-up feelings about accept-ance and acknowledgement. You feel more worthy of praise and admira-tion when you have more money in your pocket.

Perhaps it is time to take a deeper interest in your self, not your wallet. It is undoubtedly a challenge to avoid placing heavy attention on your financial worth. Yet often, people who base their identities and con-fidence on money are not very happy people. Does that sound like you? Are you always feeling the pangs of financial competition? Would you see yourself as suddenly smarter and more attractive if you received a large sum of money? That's a lot of pressure to put on yourself. The only way to free yourself is to try to change your patterns. Find things about *you*—not your bank account—that are rewarding, fun, and special. De-velop these aspects of yourself, so that you feel less like proving yourself and more like sharing yourself.

Choice B points to the following secret rule: *It is neither necessary nor wise to let others know about my monetary fortune.* Is this because you are comfortable with your true self? If you are really at peace with who you are, sudden money would not change you much. You have already achieved a level of self-acceptance that others can only envy. You are to be commended because you have developed your identity according to your own fulfillment, not the fulfillment of others' expectations.

However, there are other possibilities for choosing B, as well. Are you afraid that people will hit you up for a loan, or that you will make others feel jealous or intimidated? If that question strikes a nerve, the next question to ask yourself is whether you are afraid of money and how it will change you. Are you afraid of becoming false or phony because of your newfound money? Are you actually afraid of being isolated? Money is energy and can be used for making life better or worse—it is all up to you. If you decide not to reveal your wealth out of fear, acknowledge that you are a private person. Your secret rules must allow for that privacy, or else you will feel vulnerable and anxious. Also note the power that money has over you. If you feel yourself getting increasingly tense as your bank account grows, it's time to work on your perspective. You want to deal with fortune in a healthy and happy way. Be wary of changing a positive into a negative by obsessing over what people will now want from you. Be strong enough in yourself not to cover up and just to be you.

If you selected answer C, your secret rule reveals the importance you place on envy: *I want people to envy me, not to know me.* You want to strut your stuff without explanation. The "oohs" and "aahs" make you feel important. Hey, admiration feels good. But is it so important that people think you are financially special? And if you are going to wear it on your sleeve, why not be honest and say where the wealth came from? Your answer shows that you don't necessarily feel worthy of the money—perhaps you are embarrassed that you didn't earn it—and therefore will maintain a pretense. You don't care to share your whole story with others. Instead, you just want them to know the good parts. If you subscribe to this rule, your life is bound to be full of pretense and tension. It takes a tremendous amount of energy to edit your life in order to make it sound or look good. You are caught in a harmful pattern, convincing yourself that your life is only as good as others perceive it to be.

If you are sensitive to how others have felt about you in the past, put that behind you. You have continued to grow and to shine. If they have been misguided about who you are, that's their loss. Is it really a compliment if your mysterious money—displayed in pricey objects—impresses them? Choosing answer C shows that you focus on the superficial and may overvalue the admiration of others. What matters most, of course, is that you like yourself. Once you become confident in who you are and let other people into your life, you will find that socializing can be fun and enjoyable—no strings attached.

2. While at a party where almost everyone is dressed to the nines, you are approached by a man who is shabbily dressed, loud, boisterous, and displays terrible manners. He begins to discuss the stock market. This man tells you what will be hot in the NASDAQ very soon and is emphatic that if you are smart, you will listen to him. After hearing his advice, you politely excuse yourself and walk away thinking, "I ought to lend this guy a few bucks to get some decent clothes and a place to stay." A few days later, you are amazed to find that his predictions came true. The stock he suggested has skyrocketed! You call the host to find out who the man was, only to learn that he is a hotshot billionaire who made more money in one day than you have ever made in your whole life. Considering this experience, which of the following rules about "rich people" do you feel is most accurate?

A. Rich people look either wealthy or eccentric.

B. Rich people don't have any particular look or attitude.

C. Rich people know what they are talking about.

Do you believe there is something special or unique about wealthy people? Is it true that wealth can be discerned by looks, behavior, or spoken knowledge? If you are rich, does that mean you are naturally wise or intelligent? Answer A reveals preconceived notions of the rich: *Money is linked with a certain physical appearance.* Perhaps it's in the way rich people dress. Maybe it's in the way they carry themselves. And I guess, therefore, less wealthy people are supposed to look their particular way, too. Think about the complications of this approach. It requires constant judgment that is based on shallow observation. How can we truly know about somebody by looking at him?

Do you find the need to put people into categories in order to relate to them? If you chose answer A, you probably do. This may help you respond to a person in a pinch, but you are likely to mess up along the way. When you were surprised that the above-mentioned man was a billionaire—because he looked like a bum—did you immediately change your secret rule to suit him? Did you think, "Well, ordinarily a rich man would dress with sophistication. But this sloppy guy was rich too. So I guess rich people can look eccentric." If you did that, you rely heavily on stereotypes and generalities. You start looking at part of the person, not the whole. You also become harder on yourself, as you make personal demands to remain in a category that you see as desirable. It might help to rewrite your rule by resolving not to make significant generalizations based on a person's initial appearance.

The secret rule behind choice B states, *I don't pass judgment on people according to how they look or carry themselves.* Good for you! It is certainly a mark of character to see beyond surface-level details. With that perspective, you can learn more profound lessons in life. You are not caught up in generalizations or stereotypes. If you trust your instincts and can truly look beyond stereotypes, then your life is probably quite fulfilling.

But sometimes we lie to ourselves. In order to be politically correct, we pretend to be blind to any differences among individuals. Meanwhile, we're taking silent notes. While you may not assign a special "look" to wealth, check out the other areas of your life. Do you rely on *any* signs to aid you? Are you able to notice certain markers that would actually help you in some situations? For example, an open-minded person may speak calmly and smile a lot. A liar might shift his eyes a lot and talk quickly. Do not allow the secret rule under discussion to keep your from discerning who is a true success and who is a phony. Being nonjudgmental does not mean being naïve. Know the company you keep.

If you selected answer C, your secret rule reveals that you place a lot of faith in the moneyed class: *Wealthy people are successful, which means they are smart.* Often, wealthy and successful people are viewed as sages well outside their professional fields. Do you give a person more credence simply because of financial success? Do you look up to rich people as smarter or better than you? Would being richer make *you* smarter and more reliable? In truth, making money doesn't make you smart or wise or kind. Although that sounds like a simple and obvious statement, many of us need to be reminded of it. Some people can get wealthy by a stroke of luck. Others have limited insights that serve them well. And still others do possess true skill that allows them to make it big.

Examine your rule carefully. You might devalue yourself and others by placing too much confidence in someone based on his annual income. As a personal challenge, try observing more about a person's character. Does this person seem to have a knowledgeable vocabulary and a fluency in the field? Does he seem confident without being arrogant? Is he too pushy? Learning to be a better judge of character based on the subtleties of life—not clothing and etiquette—will serve you well. Money does not equal intelligence.

3. Your mother is desperately ill and needs a life-saving procedure. Her insurance plan will not cover that procedure, and neither she nor you has enough funds in the bank to pay for it. Moreover, you don't have any friends or contacts who could offer financial help. You do have an option, however. You have an opportunity to carry a small package containing something illegal—but definitely not drugs—across the United States border. If you agree to do it, the amount of money you make will cover the treatment. Keep in mind that, if caught, you could be sentenced as a smuggler. What will you do?

A. I will smuggle the package so that I can afford that crucial treatment for my mother.

B. I will not smuggle the package or do anything else illegal for money, even for the sake of my mother's health.

C. I will not smuggle the package, not because it's illegal but because I am afraid of what will happen to me. If I get caught, it will make things even worse.

The specific issue at hand is whether or not you would do something shady in a desperate financial situation. This question asks how heavily you weigh consequences when it comes to family and financial matters. If you chose answer A, your secret rule is as follows: *Financial ethics take a far second to the care of my family.* You would risk bending your usual code—and even sacrificing your own standing—for love of your family members. It is quite clear that you do not value the law over the heart. Such self-sacrificing behavior can make you feel alive and fulfilled. However, it can also create many painful, residual conflicts. In our hearts, we can be above the law. But in reality, we must answer to it.

If you generally tend to apply this secret rule to your life, look at how it is affecting you. Are you content with your internal loyalties, yet paying dearly for following your heart? If so, are the negatives outweighing the positives, or vice versa? Answering these additional questions will help you decide whether this rule is working in your life. Also consider that the secret rule behind answer A can get out of hand. Surely, for many of us, a dying mother calls for desperate measures. But do you *over-apply* the rule? Do you begin to rationalize shady or illegal behavior for less than lifesaving situations—a college education, a new home? Keep a careful eye out for self-deception. It is easy to convince ourselves that we can bend the rules because we are doing worthy deeds for loved ones. Yet this type of approach can turn into a slippery slope that leads us far from our deepest values. That, in turn, will create immense anxiety.

Choice B introduces a very different secret rule: *The law is supreme, even over the needs of my family.* If you chose answer B, you rely tremendously on the security of external laws. You value the order and justice that such laws offer, and you refuse to be a hypocrite by not observing them. Does that sound like you? If so, you are careful and honest with money. But ask yourself the following question: Does such a secret rule hurt more than it helps? Is there any circumstance in which you would disobey a law for the good of others? Would you steal a loaf of bread to feed your family? How far would you take this secret rule?

If you find that you've been applying this rule to extremes, not allowing any flexibility in your life—concerning finances or other issues—perhaps you want to work on being more flexible. Does your lifestyle demonstrate rigidity? Do you keep your life stored away in neat little boxes? If you have let financial codes or other imposed rules of behavior override your instincts and have found that you are racked with regret as a result, you might want to try thinking outside the box next time you need to be bold.

Finally, answer C reveals yet another secret rule: *My first financial responsibility is to myself. If I jeopardize my own self and get caught, I'll be no good to anyone.* I am not suggesting that you are selfish if you have selected answer C. You have foresight that calls you to look beyond the immediate desperation of financial need. In other words, you consider the possible consequences and choose the safest road. But also notice that your answer might be largely based on fear—for better or for worse.

Fear of potential outcomes plays a large role in how you conduct your life. Maybe that is what has kept you safe and has made you successful. In that case, this secret rule works for you. But maybe the secret rule that has kept you from making quick and passionate decisions has also ultimately left you disappointed in yourself. If so, consider forging another secret rule that is not built on fear for the self. Attachment to the "stable self" might be stopping you from fulfilling your true role in life. There is likely to be a time when you are challenged to break out of the normal routine and risk it all—financially or otherwise. Look to your life and see if you need to take more risks and avoid looking at your own security as the deciding factor.

4. As a government employee in the Department of Commerce, you are privy to a lot of information. You are content with your job—the work, the pay, and the security—and have never done anything to jeopardize it. But recently, a successful investor made you an offer that is hard to refuse. He wants some inside information, and you have access to what he needs. In exchange for the information, he would pay you the equivalent of your annual salary! Surely, you'd be violating your confidentiality agreement and putting your entire career at risk. Yet you are quite confident that you wouldn't get caught, and that the payment would double your earnings for the year. What will you do?

A. I'll pass him the information. I would be foolish to turn away from a great financial opportunity that poses no real harm to anyone.

B. I will not get involved in anything shady, especially not for extra money.

C. I will agree to trade the information but then use most of the payment to support my favorite charities.

In order to make additional money, would you do something that is ethically questionable? That is the fundamental question in the above scenario. You are asked to consider what risks you are willing to take for *extra* financial security. The secret rule underlying answer A says the following: *A wise person always takes advantage of a financial opportunity, even if it means doing something unethical.* If that's your rule, you have no qualms about being an opportunist. In fact, it's always a good thing. No harm, no regrets, right? But how far will you go in your pursuit of money? How close to the edge of "unlawful" will you get? What are your limits and ethical constraints? If you have no limits at all, you may be treading dangerous waters. You have quite an obsession with money, and that could cause you to devalue other areas of your life. Is it acceptable to threaten or scare someone for the benefit of a financial opportunity? How about lying to someone or deceiving people out of their money?

Furthermore, why are you so willing to risk security and contentment? What do you lack in your life—possessions, love, respect? Are you undervalued and therefore seeking to pay yourself your rightful due? How much do you need to satisfy your worth? The answers to these questions will decide whether or not "going for the gold" is always in your best interests. Try to set healthy boundaries that establish just how far you are likely to take this secret rule.

The secret rule behind choice B seems honest and straightforward: *Don't betray the trust of others to financially enrich yourself.* If you chose this response, you have a strong internal sense of right and wrong. Therefore, you are less vulnerable to temptations. But does this rule stem out of deep integrity, or is it more about not getting caught? And if you live by this rule, how has it served you thus far? The more you clarify your intentions, values, and resolve, the clearer your secret rule will become.

If true integrity is behind your choice of B, the rule works. For you, opportunity is far less important than dignity. But if fear is the primary motivation—fear of authority or punishment—then you still haven't gotten down to your *real* secret rule. You are covering up another rule that instructs you not to do anything that will make you vulnerable to anger and harsh judgement by others. In the latter case, realize that you could be boiling with anxiety. Fear never feels good. The decisions you make in the face of fear often end up creating regrets, anger, and the like. If this sounds familiar, try working through some of your fears and taking steps to change them into self-made, wholehearted decisions.

Do you feel better about making easy money when you are enriching not only yourself but others as well? If so, you subscribe to answer C's secret rule: *Unethical actions are justified if they are done mostly for the good of others.* You can tolerate an ethical breach if it enables you to help people. In the service of humanity, you are willing to bend your moral code. One thing this answer shows is flexibility. All of us must learn to be flexible in order to withstand society's many changes. If you chose C, you certainly are willing to rework your ethics and apply them to suit the situation. But only you can decide how much flexibility is the right amount. While it may be nice to share some of the cheer, ethically compromising yourself may make the cheer surprisingly poisonous. When can you no longer justify your actions for the greater good?

Look to your life in order to see if the rule behind C works. How much and how often have you been able to benefit others by being dishonest with someone else? If you are honest with yourself, you'll probably remember times when you were burned despite your good intentions.

Also, are you *really* taking the extra money in order to spread good fortune? Good acts are usually performed in a good, healthy spirit. A backdrop of deceit and disloyalty might not set the stage for good spirit.

5. Several years ago, you decided to start saving money for cosmetic surgery. Since that time, you have worked lots of overtime and many weekends. You have finally made your target amount. Your significant other now tells you that the surgery is a waste of money, that you don't need it, and that you should put the money into something both of you could share. Will you have the surgery anyway?

A. Yes, I am entitled to spend my money as I desire, whether it is on surgery or anything else.

B. No, it is selfish to spend money on my own desires.

C. No, I won't have the surgery. But I will be sure to spend part of my earned money on myself.

What rights do you have to the money you make? If you selected answer A, your secret rule shows confidence and resolve: *I am worthy and wise enough to spend what I earn.* You are to be commended for loving and trusting yourself. This choice demonstrates that you are in control of your life. You have chosen to exercise your right to follow your own life plan. If, in the past, you erred on the side of being too unassertive, you have been maturing and are making progress.

Answer A's secret rule is very healthy when applied with honesty and sense. However, it can be abused. The rule is challenging when it comes to finding the middle ground between your wants and the wants of those you love. Examine the difference between self-interest and selfishness. Where do you draw the line? Do you have any rules that promote sharing with others? Most likely, you do. But there are people who rely on a "Me first!" attitude as a means of survival, and that pattern is hard—but possible—to break.

Answer B highlights a secret rule that puts the self at a far second: *It is wrong for me to honor my needs over others.* Wow—you are tough on yourself! You probably feel guilt if you do something for yourself instead of the greater good. You are a selfless soul; the act of giving makes you feel content and complete. But is it always wrong to declare and satisfy your own needs in a responsible way? If your rule is always about giving and never receiving, maybe it's time to show yourself a little love. As long as it doesn't get out of hand, you can afford some luxuries and still lead a very giving, wholesome life.

If you chose B, also consider that you might be giving but resenting. Giving out of a sense of obligation, instead of true desire, can result in silent grudges and anxiety in your life. And must others approve of everything you do? Look into your need for approval as well.

The secret rule behind answer C seems to be built on compromise: *I am entitled to reap the benefits of my efforts, but I should also share that harvest with others. It's not right to take all for myself and give none to others.* This is a truly responsible rule and offers a compassionate way of life. But compromise often means giving up what you want most for something of lesser value. That can be very frustrating after a while. Is that the story of your life? Do you ever get the whole pie? When do you settle and when do you keep forging ahead for everything that you feel you deserve?

Remember that others are trying to learn to be selfless while you are learning to be more self-interested; do not deprive them of their lesson. Don't hesitate to give yourself a luxury or two if you've worked hard. Simply be careful not to get caught up in a cycle where luxuries and self-focusing become your main agenda. So this secret rule is great for a general approach to life, but it should be tempered when dealing with something you've really worked hard to get.

6. You have a stable job that allows you to pay the bills and build a nest egg. There is little left over for extras, such as a new car or a big vacation. But then again, one of the best things about your present situation is that you have plenty of time with your kids. Just this week, a headhunter called to tell you about two new job possibilities. One pays twice as much as your present position and is located in Africa. You would have to relocate to a newly developing country, and you would not be able to take the family for at least a year, but you could remain there as long as you wished. The available position is equally secure, very interesting, and in the same field. Moreover, you would live very well. The second offer is a job in a South American country near where the rebels are battling the government. It pays four times your present salary, is considered somewhat dangerous, but would be for one year only. You certainly wouldn't move your family to this area, but would definitely return home after that year. The position offers very generous disability or life insurance policies should you need them.

Upon your return, you would make twice the salary that you make now. What will you do?

A. I will remain at my present job.

B. I will take the job in Africa.

C. I will take the job in South America.

How much are you willing to sacrifice to have a more comfortable lifestyle in the long run? This question challenges you to set priorities in life—time with family; safety; more luxuries. It asks you to define your risk/reward ratio. If you are satisfied with modest means and plenty of time with loved ones, then extra risks seem foolish. Choice A applies to this perspective: *My family's time together is more important than money or career.* You believe that it is of higher value to stay close to home and have less money. That is a noble outlook on life. You are not charmed by excessive material perks. In fact, it seems as though you choose simplicity.

I suggest, however, that you confirm that the choice is based on a love of your present life, not on fear or complacency. Your rule says you are not a risk-taker by nature. You prefer routine and stability, even when opportunity comes knocking. Why? Sometimes we hide our lack of ambition and courage so well that we, ourselves, are fooled. Examine your motivations and make sure that your main goal is to be satisfied with a secure quality of life, not to avoid change.

The secret rule associated with answer B shows an invested interest in the future: *I am willing to make personal sacrifices for a better future.* Your rule says you are motivated, ambitious, courageous, and ready to make changes. Future possibilities are more persuasive than the "now." But if your family told you that they didn't need anything more and that what you were making was fine, would that change your decision? How do you decide where to draw the line between getting ahead and your family's need for you?

My suggestion is simply not to forget the importance of the "now." There is nothing wrong with investing in your future and making a few sacrifices. Yet keeping your eye on each moment is also important. The balance is delicate, but it is possible to find a happy middle ground and avoid later regrets. Make sure you are 100-percent confident in your decisions before doing something that shakes the most stable things in your life.

The secret rule behind answer C reveals that you are a risk-taker: *I am willing to take large risks to make big money.* Are you actually willing to risk life and limb for money and success? Why? Are you trying to make up for something you lack? Is there some part of you that is taking chances because life is too routine, not because you need the money? You have defined yourself as a big risk-taker. You have also placed money and adventure as top priorities. That's fine, if it makes you happy. But if you have applied this rule before, has it really left you feeling successful and happy? If you have not succeeded or, worse yet, if you have hurt yourself or others in the process, maybe life is telling you to take it easy.

Consider why you would accept short-term but life-threatening risk for affluence. There's nothing wrong with taking advantage of an opportunity, but many things are opportunities in life, including being safe and stable with your family. Examine how strongly you are guided by financial gain.

7. While taking money out of an automatic teller machine late one night, the machine breaks down and begins gifting you with twenty-dollar bills until there is two thousand dollars in front of you. The bank is closed and you are alone. The room is unusually dark. You wonder if a hidden camera could even pick up the situation. What will you do?

A. I will not keep the money. I will return it as promptly as possible.

B. I will keep the money. I feel it is okay to take it because the bank has billions.

C. I will keep the money if I desperately need it. Otherwise, I'll return it as soon as possible.

If tempted by an opportunity to receive money that is clearly not yours, would you keep the cash? When is it permissible? Is "need" a criterion? Is there any difference between taking money from a wealthy institution versus an individual? How much does getting caught figure into your rules? These are tough questions that might have crossed your mind as you selected an answer. The secret rule behind answer A says, *I don't keep money that doesn't belong to me.* You have a strong sense of justice and integrity. You don't tend to take the easy road for the sake of convenience, but rather stick to a well-developed moral code. But is there ever a time when dishonesty is permissible? What if you were hungry or ran out of gas and couldn't get home? And do you apply this rule to all situations, such as finding twenty dollars lying on the street? Could you take that? Why might that be easier?

Better than doing the right thing is doing the right thing for the right reasons. Do you secretly want the money, but are afraid you will get caught? If there was absolutely no way you could get caught, would that change anything? Is there a corollary rule—virtue is its own reward? Examine your thoughts on what does and does not belong to you. If they are conditional on fear of punishment instead of true honesty, you are still vulnerable, and fate will tempt you time and again.

The secret rule for answer B is quite clear: *I am entitled to take money that comes to me by accident and that no one claims.* You have decided that, if it is just lying there, it's yours. So if money falls off an armored car, you could rightfully take it? Why is it your right? How did you earn this right—by getting the short end of the stick too many times? What is the rationale here? And if the rich lose, is it okay because they have plenty? If you truly subscribe to this rule, realize that you have shifted your moral compass and that it no longer points to "honest."

Taking money that falls into your lap may be tempting, but that action subtly defines you as a "have not." You are telling yourself that you need or deserve more. Is that how you see yourself? Consider that a victim mentality is a constant source of self-sabotage and that you can never really achieve prosperity as long as you identify with it. Decide whether the overarching rule for answer B serves you or keeps you limited.

Answer C's secret rule implies that you make decisions on a case-by-case basis: *I can take what doesn't belong to me if there is an emergency.* Only you can decide how needy is needy. If you prayed for a miracle, maybe this is it. Few would begrudge you a meal, medicine, or a place to stay, but what about a car payment or a trip to visit your sweetheart? If you follow this rule, make some boundaries around it. Is it stealing when there is no "one" to steal from? What is an emergency? What would you expect from others in the same situation? Carefully define the rules under which you would not return something of value that you found.

Usually, but not always, there are just and straight ways to go about filling an emergency need. Taking from others—whether individuals or institutions—will leave the average good person feeling tense and guilty. Such fallout actually does as much damage, if not more, than the original deceitful act. So be clear on what situations actually excuse you from general ethical actions. It might sound fun to keep a wad of cash, but when you consider the aftermath, its fear and anxiety, you might decide that honesty is the best path.

8. You recently inherited half a million dollars from a long lost uncle. Prior to this stroke of luck, you maintained a steady job and made a nice living, but luxuries were few and far between. Now you can pay off all your debts, send Junior to the best university, and have money left over for fun and a great retirement. But your brother-in-law calls your attention to another possibility. He knows a man who is a genius in financial matters and says he can triple your money within a few years. Granted, it's a high-risk deal, but this man is very successful. In order to take part in this deal, you would have to fork over most of the money you just inherited. That means you wouldn't enjoy many immediate benefits. What will you do?

A. I will gladly risk most of the inheritance to make more money.

B. I will use the money I have now and enjoy my life.

C. I will put the money away where I can't touch it for a long time. I'll save it for a rainy day.

Is money an end, in and of itself? Is the object of life to accumulate as much money as you can? The secret rule linked with answer A suggests, *I can be satisfied only when I have made as much money as I possibly can.* You need more and more—as much as you can get. If this is your rule, you are in good company. Making the biggest profit and buying the biggest house, the biggest car—the biggest everything—is practically an American tradition. Such a secret rule is for the risk-taker—someone who likes to spin the wheel of fortune. You probably value possibility over security. This says that you are a gutsy person who is not afraid to lay it on the line. Just be sure you are willing to deal with the possibility of failure and bad luck, too. Try to match your strength with stability by considering both ends of the spectrum before launching into high-risk situations.

If you have just inherited a large sum, why do you need to risk most of it for more money? Is it money for money's sake? Will you feel better about yourself if you have three million dollars rather than one million? Remind yourself that it's just money. You might have a tendency to become slightly obsessive about getting more and more. Money can bring out very addictive behavior. Confirm your priorities before putting this secret rule into effect. Notice that you are putting the possibility of a lucrative future ahead of happiness and stability in the present. Are these the priorities that are most satisfying to you?

If you chose answer B, your secret rule shows that you are content with good fortune, not addicted to it: *If I receive a gift of money, I will enjoy it and not covet more.* Your secret rule shows that you know how to make the most of the moment. You like to live life. This is a healthy approach, as long as it's tempered with good sense. Evaluate your capacity to make good decisions in the face of easy money. If you tend to aimlessly and carelessly blow money, then place boundaries on the rule before going any further. That way, you will not have regrets. Maybe you want to consider spending some of your newfound money, and saving the other portion. Spontaneously spending all the money may cause you to feel foolish and ashamed.

Fevered spending releases pent-up frustrations and may be a good quick tonic in the short run. However, too much self-indulgence may cause you to lose the other life values, like hard work, that have served you so well. You are open to enjoying life—and that's wonderful. Just be careful to have a plan and not let money get the best of you.

Choice C points to yet another secret rule: *Long-term security is much more important than immediate pleasure.* In this rule, you acknowledge your respect for, as well as fear of, money. It is true that newfound wealth can change people and not necessarily for the better, but what is wrong with taking some pleasure from your money now? What will happen to you? Why can't you use some for what you need and put some away for later? If you chose answer C, you have a good head on your shoulders, and a healthy respect for what difficulties the future might bring. But you also live with a certain amount of fear that can debilitate you. Perhaps you want to consider allowing yourself to be a little freer. Try giving yourself just a few pleasures in the present, and see what that does to your life.

If you never feel secure with what you have, you have a poverty consciousness. By choosing C, you are saying that you cannot trust your own impulses when given some power and expanded choices. Is this how you live your life—afraid of your instincts, untrusting of your own desires? If you try, you can find a balance between intelligent saving and delightful indulgence.

9. Your best friend since childhood had an unexpected business boom. She made a huge amount of money over the past six months and decided to go on an extravagant four-month trip around the world. She invited you to come along—all expenses paid. It's a once-in-a-lifetime opportunity, but there's a catch. When you asked your employer if you could take a leave, he denied your request. You must decide between giving up your job and taking advantage of a great life experience, or putting financial security first. You've worked a long time to attain your current position and salary. What will you do?

A. I will quit my job in a New York minute, three shakes, a heartbeat.

B. I will forfeit the cruise and stay with the company.

C. I will claim that I am disabled in some way and have to take a leave of absence from work. Then I'll go on the trip.

While this question is similar to the previous one in its examination of whether you prioritize fun or foresight, it focuses more on the choice between a unique opportunity and an acceptable routine. The secret rule behind choice A clearly uncovers your priorities: *Pleasure and adventure are at least as important as, if not more important than, security.* If you are willing to quit your job, you are the adventurer. This is about a style of life. It is about enjoying life today and letting tomorrow take care of itself. Some might think it's foolish to give up a great job, but you want more than a big portfolio for your golden years. You are an independent thinker who is willing to think outside of the box.

If you are willing to face the consequences—if you will happily withstand a job search and a possibly less ideal job in the future—then you know yourself and what's important to you. You refuse to let tomorrow designate the actions of today. But keep in mind that it's best not to throw all caution to the wind. Make sure you rethink your decisions before making life-altering changes. There is a chance that you've been burned by your spontaneity. If that's the case, you might need to adjust your secret rule. It is possible to be too carefree. Do you need to grow up, stay in a job, and plant some roots?

Answer B shows that you value security over impulsive fun: *Long-term security is more important than short-term enjoyment.* You tend to be very practical and not prone to spontaneity. You are already an expert on delayed gratification. How long will it be delayed this time? Does your real adventure begin with retirement? Do you ever give in to your impulsive side? What if you yearned to see distant lands, but knew it might never happen unless you took this trip? Do you value security so much that other areas of your life have starved?

If your goal is to save and plan for the future, you are clearly showing mature and responsible qualities. But while it is important to be mature, there could be another side of life that you have missed. Have you let great opportunities pass you by because you were afraid to give up what you have, to get something better? While quitting your job may be too much change, consider taking advantage of some opportunities when they come along.

Choice C uncovers the following secret rule: *I am willing to be dishonest to have the best of both worlds.* On the surface, it says you are willing to be a bit shady in order to take advantage of an extravagant opportunity. You might even be able to rationalize that you are a great employee and are entitled to have it all. However, beware of this secret rule; it can lead you into disabling self-deception. You are trying to have everything at once; it's too greedy and will likely jeopardize your future.

It is very hard to make firm decisions in life, but it never feels good to shamelessly shy away from them. Work on your decision-making skills by restating your priorities and then sharing them with others. Why maintain a large-scale cover-up? Acknowledge that you are an intelligent person who is capable of making choices in life. Then choose one path. In the long run, you will suffer less and still preserve your integrity.

10. You have two wonderful children and a supportive partner, not to mention a stable job. Though you don't own a mansion or travel very often, you pay your bills on time and have savings for dire emergencies. Life is not desperate, but it could be much more comfortable. When lying in bed at night, reviewing the financial and familial events of the day, which of the following thoughts are you most likely to dwell upon?

A. Life stinks without that extra money. Mediocrity is unacceptable.

B. We're not rich, but we're content. That's enough for me.

C. I am personally satisfied with my life, but I need to earn more money for the kids.

When going to bed at night, we often think of what's closest to our hearts—our deepest worries and our greatest joys. If you are obsessing over money despite the fact that your life is good, you are fixating on the financial. In the privacy of your own thoughts, do you feel angry and resentful about what you don't have? If so, you chose answer A. It is built on the following secret rule: *Without more money, life is hard and unrewarding.* Ask yourself if you are too obsessed with money. Are you placing too much importance on a bank account? When going to sleep, remind yourself of the perks in life. Make an effort to be content in the moment. Life is much happier that way.

On the other hand, no one can rightly judge what amount of money you should be satisfied with. If you want and deserve more, by all means you should have it. But go after it in a healthy manner—with gusto and optimism, not decrying your hapless fate.

The secret rule behind answer B seems quite healthy: *I value my family and friends more than a large income.* It is hard to quarrel with a rule that honors human values over financial considerations. Your priorities are clear and you feel content with the "now"; that's the number-one sign of good decision-making. Furthermore, you are not provoked by our culture's fascination with always getting more. If this is your true secret rule, you are successful at much more than making ends meet.

To confirm your contentedness, however, examine the sincerity of this choice. Are you truly satisfied, or do you just settle into routine. Is there anything wrong with more savings or a bigger college fund? Are you afraid to rise above your social group, or do you feel discouraged about trying for more? Consider if your rule is really about contentment or if it's about settling for something less because you have limitation rules on how much energy to put into your work.

Answer C's secret rule involves a family perspective: *Children should have it better than their parents did.* There were once two schools of thought regarding how you should treat your children. One way said, "Let them do as their parents did and follow in the footsteps of their family." The other school valued the economic and social climb of the next generation and would sacrifice for it. If you chose C, you subscribe to the latter. Are you fully aware of the sacrificed time and contentment necessary to provide more *financially* for your children? What rules will you follow to determine when you have given all you can and not lost out on developing your own life?

If you have chosen this rule, make an effort to find balance. You have only a finite amount of time and energy, and you are entitled to explore your own desires and talents as well as be a financially successful family-person. Define your rules about giving to others without losing yourself in the process. You should be commended on your generosity and concern for others. But also remember that money isn't the only way to pass success along.

CONCLUSION

You have completed ten tough questions on money and life. Do you obsess about money? Do you feel as if you are failing yourself or your family because of what you don't have? Hopefully, this chapter has highlighted some financial perspectives that cause you anxiety and has helped you to come to some conclusions. The more you know yourself, the healthier your attitude and your decisions can be. Keep in mind that your secret rules should serve your best interests. If they do not, you will not make the most of your life. It's that simple.

2. Work and Career

IF THERE IS SOMETHING THAT HAS COME to define us more and more, it is what we do for a living. We may identify with a religion, a nation, or a political party, but how we earn our way in this life seems to be a primary way of expressing ourselves. Moreover, after the basics are met, the next issue for the worker is self-satisfaction. And beyond personal fulfillment and ample remuneration, many of us want a job that is socially responsible as well. The work experience is evermore an extension of your personal beliefs and much less about "making a living." Do you have any rules about what you need and want from a job? Are you sure you know them?

When we step back and look at our work life, we collect it all up and call it a career. Like charms on a bracelet, jobs are strung together into one grand jewel—a career. Those with special training or talent—be it with computers or a baseball—want some kind of forward progress in the professional sphere. Without this movement, even if all else is well, an individual may feel unfulfilled. Models invariably want to be supermodels and baseball players want to be legends. It's the human way. What are the rules that tell you when to stay in one place and when to take a risk in an entirely new direction? What is "enough" and "the best" for you?

Freud said, "Love who you're with and love what you do." That covers a good chunk of life. Your work is a significant part of your existence. Look at the following questions to see if there aren't some secret rules that keep you from loving what you do.

1. You have spent ten years with a large multinational corporation. You are very happy with your salary, your vested pension, and the progress you have been making as you climb the corporate ladder. And you have just been offered yet another promotion—but there's a catch. The corporation wants you to serve as top supervisor at one of its more remote locations. The

country to which you'd be relocated lacks the modern lifestyle and creature comforts to which you've become accustomed. Let's put it this way: The local delicacy is horsemeat sausages. The assignment would last at least one year and probably longer. On the other hand, the new position would give you higher company standing that would surely, in the long run, allow you advancement back in the United States. You discuss the option with your spouse, who reluctantly agrees to go if you so desire, mostly because you earn the higher salary in the family but also because your spouse values your climb to the top. Yet you know this move would mean leaving extended family and friends behind, not to mention the fact that your mate would have to make many personal sacrifices. The decision is up to you. What will you do?

A. I will take the overseas position for the sake of getting ahead, and my family and I will bear whatever inconveniences occur.

B. I will not take the overseas position. My personal life is too important to jeopardize.

C. I will take the overseas position, but I will quit if I don't like it.

How much are you willing to put up with to get ahead? How much inconvenience can you tolerate? That is determined, in large measure, by how important it is to be successful. The secret rule behind answer A prioritizes success: *Getting ahead may be the most important thing I do.* It certainly seems to imply that when push comes to shove, career is more important than your family. Is that true? You will, reluctantly, put your family through big changes so you can climb the corporate ladder. No judgment is implied here. Anyone who runs for high public office or takes a job of great responsibility has to make difficult tradeoffs to achieve their goals.

However, it is time to revisit the question of what you really want from life. Is it money or accomplishment or something else that drives you? How will you achieve satisfaction? Honestly, do you feel like a better person because of the money or achievement? While determination to succeed is an admirable quality, it can cause you to lose awareness of the needs of others—and even your own more profound needs. Be careful not to lose your personal life along the way or you will find no one with whom you can share your success.

The secret rule behind answer B is as follows: *No career move is more important than my family.* Is that because you don't care all that much about what success can bring or because you genuinely honor family closeness above all else? If you tend toward the latter, you are thoughtful of those you love. Happiness for you means joint happiness for your family. And chances are that you will be very satisfied because you make your choices out of love, not greed. For you, a personal life comes first. There's an old saying: "No one's gravestone reads, 'Here lies _____, who wished he spent more time at work.'"

Just to confirm that you are being 100-percent honest with yourself, review the motives behind your answer one more time. Are you truly acting out of concern for the best family life, or is there a little guilt for wanting to succeed in life? Many of us "know" that family and friends should come first. Most of us "feel" that home is where the heart is. However, as human beings, we are also driven by ambition and, perhaps, power. Are you shying away from that drive because it scares you? Are you afraid of risks? These questions will get you thinking about those unspoken motives that might also come into play.

Answer C's secret rule is the compromising answer: *I want to get ahead, but I am unwilling to sacrifice myself for the company to get there.* If you don't like your assignment, you feel justified in quitting. You are the kind of person who doesn't do any job that you don't really like. So what does career mean then? What about your obligation to your employer? Is there any? Oftentimes, careers demand time away from home and uncomfortable working conditions. There is nothing wrong with a dependable schedule and pleasant surroundings—have them if you must. But this rule might also highlight a lack of drive or determination to sacrifice what is needed to get to the top.

Choose life options that do not demand great sacrifice, and know that it may not be possible to have it all. Also be proud that you freely choose what you need most. Career doesn't dominate your life. You are confident that you can call the shots, and you will not be bullied by any corporate pressure.

2. You are a valued employee of a major oil company. As a result, you enjoy an enviable lifestyle and lots of job travel. In fact, you just received a new assignment. You are part of an oil search team that is being sent to the Amazon! The preliminary drilling necessary to carry out this assignment—not to mention the further disturbance of the forests if oil is found—is environmentally destructive. Environmental groups are already protesting this venture, and you find yourself in agreement with their views. What will you do?

A. I will accept this assignment. Placing professional duty over personal ethics is what job commitment is all about.

B. I will refuse the assignment and even accept termination, if necessary. My conscience is much more important than my job.

C. I will refuse the assignment, but if pressured with termination, ultimately I will accept the job.

This question asks you to determine if your ethics are more important than company loyalty and even your own financial security. What is your obligation to anyone or anything else in this world? If you are doing your job and playing by the rules, isn't that enough? How much are we supposed to sacrifice for the greater good of mankind? If you chose answer A, your secret rule prioritizes business obligations over humanitarian obligations: *My first obligation is to my company and not to my personal values.* The individual is smaller than the corporation. Well, loyalty to the company—like any loyalty—is something we all treasure. Who does not want a friend or employer to be loyal to them? But is loyalty a higher value than the health and safety of others or the environment? And does loyalty take away stress? We can be sure only of the answer to the latter question—no, loyalty will not diminish the stress you will feel as you betray your personal ethics and your world at large. Know that you must be comfortable with the ethics of your workplace or you will find that conflict and stress will make the job unbearable, internally if not externally.

While you are mulling over your rule to see if it needs changing in order to be consistent with your highest self, do realize that your answer shows that you are not blinded by idealism. Your security, and perhaps that of your family, is a priority for you. You demonstrate commitment and direction. These are good qualities that are evident through your choice.

Answer B expresses a secret rule that states, *I will not do a job that conflicts with my moral code; ethics come first.* This rule is about being true to your principles without regard to consequences. You are an idealist. Moreover, you trust that—if you follow your heart—things will work out in the end. Good for you! You know that you will suffer far greater consequences if you betray your own morals. In your eyes, the individual person and his world are more important than the corporate world. However, your path is not an easy one.

While it is important to have principles, be sure that your choices are not at the expense of loved ones who may not want that same thing. A likely consequence would be loss of income followed by difficult times. If you have a family, you are subjecting your loved ones to hard times as well. How much are you entitled to make others suffer for your principles? Would you default on your mortgage or risk repossession for your principles? These are important questions that will test how firm you are when it comes to putting principles first.

The third answer has a "halfway" secret rule: *I will stand on my principles until forced to change.* It is not easy being heroic. Taking the stand, in and of itself, is an act of courage. So you demonstrate personal conviction. However, in choosing to remain on the job if faced with termination, you acknowledge a reality that supersedes your beliefs. For you, the individual person and the corporation wield rather equal weight.

You have, however, defined your principles and begun the process of change. Sometimes when the reality of our idealism confronts our everyday life, idealism temporarily loses. If you have reluctantly chosen to work, feel good about what you have said and done. There will undoubtedly come another time to exercise your conscience. But also do some work on yourself. Define your rule about risking prosperity for principle, and you will be ready when the time is right.

3. You and your best friend are struggling actors. You attended acting school together and share a long history. Furthermore, you always trade career tips and information on auditions. Today, you received word on an audition for a part that both of you would be suitable for. If you could get the part, it would be a very big break. The fewer the actors that show up, the better your chances are. Your friend is very talented and would certainly be a strong competitor. Will you tell your friend about the audition?

A. I will tell my friend about the audition. It's only fair.

B. I will not tell my friend about the audition. I need to protect my own interests.

C. I will mention the audition at the last minute. Hopefully, my friend won't be able to make it, and our friendship will be preserved.

This question is about integrity. In short, are friends expendable at some point? Can your friend also be your rival and someone to be eliminated? The secret rule behind answer A prioritizes friendship: *Friendship is more valuable than personal success.* Wow, that's some statement! Let's face it, you risk losing advancement because of your rule. How would you feel if your friend got the part? Could you be proud of another's success even at the expense of your own? You better be prepared to be proud, for the alternative may be ugly. Yet, you will be a winner either way because, in your heart, you will know you've done what your inner voice tells you to do. It would be better to lose the part honestly than win it with deception.

It is hard to imagine how, in the long run, your rule will not serve you very well. You might get a little angry with yourself for being so "good" sometimes. You might get frustrated when you feel that you are the only surviving person who has such strong loyalties! However, if you are being very honest with yourself, you will not regret putting your friend before yourself. You are expressing some of the highest qualities of humanity and will never lose that great feeling of being strongly dedicated to someone.

Is there anything wrong with taking advantage of an opportunity when it knocks? Do you have to tell everyone it's knocking? Are you not entitled to get a "leg up," especially when fate takes a hand? Sure you are—according to answer B! The secret rule behind the second choice is clear: *Career is more important than friendship.* Sounds awful, doesn't it? But at least you are being honest and realistic. You have chosen to take care of your own needs and have clearly established your priorities. Because of this clarity, you might not suffer any guilt and resentment in the future.

Yet, has this been an effective strategy so far? Is this your usual approach to life? If you got the part, would you stand proud of taking care of yourself, or would you feel ashamed of being sneaky? Only you can decide what is of greater value—career or friendship. Be prepared, though, to have less loyal and more superficial relationships if you follow the secret rule behind answer B. You cannot have what you cannot give. If you don't want that kind of a life, work to change your secret rule.

The secret rule for answer C states, *I am basically honest, but sometimes success demands a little deception.* You want it all; you desire to be the good guy and still get a leg up on the competition. You naturally want the best for yourself and don't want anyone to be hurt in the process. So you keep a foot in both worlds. If you quickly chose this option, you have probably played both ends against the middle before. How is it working out? Do you trust your friends to be square with you? If this is a life pattern, you may have a history of awkward moments and a reputation for not playing straight with people.

Do you yearn to be a more decisive person when it comes to career gain? Choose a value, make it your rule, and stick with it. The middle ground can only work for a while. One day, you will not be able to play both sides and will most surely lose one or both of the things you value most. So if your choice was answer C, reevaluate your priorities and attempt to come up with a firmer secret rule.

4. You are a big-time financial entrepreneur. Some people believe you are a financial genius! You have made millions already and are now on the verge of the biggest deal of your life. It will take place over the next two weeks. You have invested a lot of time and money in the making of this deal. Unfortunately, a recent physical examination, occasioned by chest pains, revealed that you have serious coronary artery disease. The doctor tells you that you are at risk for a heart attack at any time, and instructs you to stop working at once! You need to have bypass surgery as soon as possible. If you quit, someone will take over and you will not reap all of the benefits of the deal. You will have to share your baby! Then again, you'd still have millions in the bank. What will you do?

A. I will stop work immediately and get the surgery. There is more to life than work.

B. I'm not quitting this deal until it is done. Forget the surgery for now. Nothing is going to keep me from doing what I enjoy most.

C. I don't quit anything. So I will finish this last deal and then spend more time on my health.

Are you obsessed with your career? Does it define who you are? Superficially, this question is about choosing health concerns over work or vice versa, but it is really more about how work is integrated into your life. Is career a part of life, or is it all of life? If you selected answer A, your secret rule is as follows: *I am a person first and a professional second.* You believe that your health is more important than getting the deal done. In the long run, this secret rule should serve you well. You define yourself in a number of ways and see your life for all it is worth.

In theory, answer A seems like a healthy choice. However, expect to suffer some consequences when your priorities shift. Sometimes it does not feel okay to end something that has been a source of pride and satisfaction. You will have to do a lot of readjusting if a health crisis (or other crisis) occurs. So back your priorities up with ideas for activities that can fulfill you in the absence of work. Work is about making or producing something. It's a good idea to be further prepared for a sudden change by having other hobbies and interests in life. Then you will be ready for anything that may come.

Can you see life not as something to do but rather as something to experience or appreciate? It is most common for men in our society to feel that they have no purpose to their lives without work. Do you judge yourself by what you produce or accomplish and find that without work, life holds little interest? Apparently so, if you chose answer B. The secret rule behind this choice clearly identifies career as the purpose of life: *Without work, life has no meaning; I am a professional first and a person second.* If work has been your reason for being during all your adult life, it's hard to find something to replace it. If this is your issue, think what it is that work provides that cannot be replaced by something else.

Sometimes we are creatures of habit, and that is all we know until we consciously choose to break the habit. Your secret rule says that outside of work, life is dull and there is little to interest you. Your choice speaks to a lack of love or willingness to appreciate what you have in the personal arena. Review what the meaning of your life is now and how it can be enriched before it is too late. The same qualities that make you a success can make you resistant to advice. Can you see how you are limiting yourself to one dimension when you place all of your value in your profession?

Answer C's secret rule states, *I must complete what I start to feel good about myself.* Wanting to finish what you start is a mark of character. No one can fault you for lack of integrity. But why must you risk your own life in order to feel good about yourself? Is it your pride that demands your taking great risks for a job? If you chose this rule, you are proud of your accomplishments, but you also constantly need to prove yourself to feel worthy. You have more work to do before you are comfortable with yourself. You have to learn more about yourself so that your self-value is not hinged on a deal.

Why not take your collected successes and call it a day—or a career? The question at hand is whether or not your last hurrah is worth dying for. Is quitting now the same as failing? Consider what makes you feel good about yourself and decide if you still require one more deal. Perhaps you will find that there's more to life than money and prestige. Perhaps you can channel that undying motivation into healing and developing another area of your life.

5. Both you and your spouse hold good jobs, have high career goals, and build much of your self-esteem on professional success. Recently, you had your first and only child—a girl. Your daughter suffers from a rare genetic disorder resulting in multiple disabilities. The doctors have explained that if either you or your spouse is willing to stay at home and work with the child on a daily basis, the development of her language and motor skills will be better than they would if she were placed in a special-care facility. You can certainly afford the finest care, but you can also afford to be a full-time parent. What will you do?

A. I will stay at home and personally care for my child.

B. I prefer to enroll my child at a special-care facility so that my spouse and I can continue our careers.

C. I will suggest that my spouse stay at home with our child, since my spouse is better at parenting.

The question is simple. What do you see as your primary role—your role as professional or your role as parent? Do you choose your child or your career? Now, be honest! The question also asks whether you or your spouse may be best suited to care for a difficult child—who wants or needs to be the caregiver rather than who "must" work. There is loss and gain in any choice you make. If you selected answer A, your secret rule is as follows: *My most important life role is that of a parent; it supersedes my career.* How did you decide that? Is it love or guilt that motivates you? Do you, in any way, believe that your spouse's career is more important than your own? Does your spouse "owe" you anything because of your choice? The challenging part is answering these subtle questions. For most of us, there will be a mix of obligation and devotion. And there is no reason, of course, why a switch or change could not be made later on.

If you quickly chose this rule, you recognize the needs of others and are willing to take action. It is something to be proud of and, in most cases, will be balanced by the intangible rewards you receive. If you are always doing for others, however, and never choose for yourself, you may be too deferential and may feel cheated as the years roll on. Here's the crux of the issue: If you chose answer A, you *are* choosing for yourself as well as for your child. Everyone wins. You truly desire to put parenting first. Quite differently, if you would define your answer as "choosing for my child," be sure that you are able to get your needs met and values expressed in other aspects of your life. You are at risk of experiencing anger and resentment later in life.

Answer B's secret rule clearly places career as your defining role in life: *Above all, I am a career person—even over my role as parent.* It takes courage to check this answer off because no one wants to verbally admit, "My career is more important than my child." But if that's your style, then so be it. You will live a happier and healthier life if you really listen to yourself and continue to develop your career. There is great diversity among the human race in terms of being loving and parental.

Don't be even a little defensive if you chose this response. You certainly may be as loving as anyone else but find the task of full-time parenting of a special-needs child too difficult and consuming. Therapists' offices are filled with individuals whose parents would have served them better by letting someone else raise them. There is no right or wrong way to be. However, make sure that you are completely comfortable with your choice before moving on. You don't want to taint your later life by ignoring inner calls now. Simply confirm that you are listening to your highest self.

The secret rule for answer C offers the following conclusion: *I'm not best suited for full-time parenting responsibilities, but I believe in keeping those responsibilities within the family.* That's perfectly fine, as long as your spouse is content with the situation as well. Yet there's one note of caution that must be offered. In all honesty, what is your main motivation? Are you simply scared to care for this child? Do you just want to keep your fantastic career? Or do you truly believe that your spouse is the better person for the job when it comes to raising a special-needs child? That's where the deeper self-evaluation kicks in. In order for this rule to truly work in your life, it must come out of a true belief that your spouse will do a better job. Otherwise you will feel guilty or disappointed in yourself.

You don't need a degree in sociology to guess that most of the women will be at home and the men will be working outside. If you are a woman and would prefer that your hubby stay home, you are expressing yourself in a way that was practically impossible just a few decades ago. Your secret rule communicates that you need to fulfill yourself in more ways than parenting, so be true to yourself. If you are starting to feel guilty, don't. Honor the fact that your secret rule demands something nontraditional because if you don't, you will feel resentful and display your feelings in a way that won't be healthy for anyone concerned.

6. You have received three job offers. All positions pay the same salary and are available in the same city. One opportunity is in the corporate world of finance. It offers lots of possibilities for advancement, but it is also inherently insecure—people get hired and fired all the time. The second opportunity involves working for the government in a safe, secure, and not overly taxing environment. The third option is working for a refugee relief organization that is not affiliated with the government. It is likely to include some travel. It comes down to your personal preferences. Which job offer will you accept?

A. I will take the corporate position. I like to take chances.

B. I will choose the civil service position. I like predictable security.

C. I will work with the refugee relief organization. I need meaning.

The question asks you to determine why you work. Besides just paying the bills and surviving, what—if any—greater purpose does your work serve? Your choices are the sum total of what you learned growing up and what is intrinsic to your nature. Choice A involves a secret rule that says, *I thrive on high risk and high reward.* It's a jungle out there and if you are a tiger, the corporate world is where you belong. These days, working for a corporation provides little of the security of old. The whole rise and fall of the "dot.com" culture gives testament to that. Your rule says you enjoy risk and expect to be rewarded.

What kind of job are you in now? Are you fulfilled? Of course there are other kinds of work (outside of corporate life) that include great risks and great rewards, such as careers in the arts and self-employment. These alternatives, too, carry the basic insecurity of whether or not the work will be there tomorrow and how big each paycheck will be. So you could consider those options as well. Regardless, you have searched yourself enough to know that you enjoy the feeling of a fast-paced, risky career. If you are bored with sameness and security, it is time to break out and express the real you. You probably find a little stress stimulating instead of scary. If so, you have chosen a rule that lets you work more to your liking. But this rule is clearly not for everyone. If you have lived too long this way and it has made you anxious, perhaps a more stable life is in order.

Answer B's secret rule is for those of us who like to feel safe: *I like routine and security, so I choose a low-risk lifestyle and accept low rewards as a consequence.* There is something very comforting about knowing that your job will be there as long as desired. There is a lot more to life than work. Maybe you get your thrills in other areas, such as fun with the family or exciting travel. As for the monetary rewards, you have made a decision that you simply need enough—not more and more. Do these statements describe you? Are you happy with them? If so—if you are uncomfortable with uncertainty and like to plan your future very precisely—this rule serves you well and you are in the right place.

The job would not be finished if you didn't ask yourself a few more probing questions, however. Confirm that you chose the stability out of personal choice, not fear. Examine your motivations. Are you happy as well as safe, or only the latter? Taking this thought process a few steps further will help you decide whether or not this secret rule truly works for you.

The secret rule for answer C reveals the multifaceted meaning you find in career: *I prefer to use my job as a means to help others and have less concern with compensation.* Your joy is found in helping others, not in making the big deal for profit. You worry less about security and more about personal satisfaction. If this description fits, you must follow a career path that allows you ethical and humanitarian satisfaction. It is very important to pursue this desire. Otherwise, you will suffer from feeling that you didn't fulfill your life's role, and that is one of the worst ways to live.

Have you continually done what others think is best and ignored your own yearnings? Tomorrow morning, when you wake up for work, ask yourself, "Why am I doing this today?" If you cannot find a solid answer, it is likely that you need to adjust your professional lifestyle in order to give your life more meaning. On the other hand, you might be fulfilling the part of yourself that strives toward the greater good, yet also feel frustrated and resentful that the "me" is being sacrificed. If that's the case, this is not the secret rule for you. You need to reevaluate.

7. The company at which you have worked for the past seven years has several managerial positions opening up. Because you have been a loyal and respected employee, your superior offers you a promotion and gives you the opportunity to choose from three different jobs. The first is in the sales department. It involves long hours and a lot of contact with clients. While the position is very stressful, it offers the highest salary and the fastest pace. The second option is in the accounting department, where you would work with figures all day. It is the most stable of the available positions and involves little stress. The salary is reasonable—not as high as the other positions, but some advancement would come with seniority. Moreover, your workday would not be characterized by a frenzied pace. Finally, there is a position in the creative department, working with graphics and design. This would involve a moderate stress level and pace, as well as a considerable salary. You could use your artistic abilities and work with other creative minds all day, in addition to having the potential to move up very quickly. Which job will you choose?

A. I will choose the sales position.

B. I will choose the accounting position.

C. I will choose the creative position.

What kind of work gives you the most enjoyment? Whether determined by genetics or by the stars, every person has one area in which she can most naturally express herself and succeed. Answer A's secret rule declares the following: *I feel most fulfilled when in a fast-paced, high-paying position.* You don't mind stress; in fact, you thrive on it. You simply desire to be where there are numerous challenges and high stakes. Most likely, you would be labeled as a type-A personality. You give your all to your job, and you have sizable expectations concerning what you will get in return.

Does your present work experience allow you to enjoy the speed of the professional world? If not, you might consider talking to your colleagues about your job position—what it lacks and what can be changed. There is nothing more frustrating than having energy and motivation but not being able to use them. Yet it is important to keep in mind that pressure and stress can *initially* be motivating but *ultimately* be very unhealthy. If your secret rule chronically results in burnout, consider consciously curbing it. You could practice setting goals and then enjoying the fruits of your labors, instead of setting goals and then re-setting them at higher marks.

If you chose answer B, your secret rule reveals a passion for numbers and routine: *I feel safe and satisfied with a low-stress job that revolves around facts and figures.* You have a gift for working with numbers, and you like the fact that you can calculate firm answers in a relatively quiet environment. You are motivated by a craving for stability rather than a drive to make top dollar. Routine appeals to you, and you are not tempted by a competitive edge. As long as you know the drill and can produce the set answers, you can face work with a smile.

There is something to be said for a job that is manageable and secure. In today's world, too many people allow their careers to become their families and their lives. The obsession with money and climbing the professional ladder has proven unhealthy for many. Your approach allows you to enjoy what you do without being consumed by it. If your present job does not enable you to benefit from such stability and responsibilities, consider making a change in your professional life. There are many fields that would allow you to work with figures, from bookkeeping to accounting to statistics. Just be sure that your secret rule will not leave you with long-term regrets. Sometimes security feels best, but our hearts and minds call us to push the envelope. Confirm that your decision to play it safe and steady is compatible with the vision that you have for your future.

You crave creative license if you selected answer C. Your secret rule states, *I will be fulfilled only if I can share my innovative ideas, producing work that is both attractive and lucrative.* You have confidence in your ideas and pride in your skills. That's why you have selected a job category that provides both artistic assignments and a very decent salary scale. You don't mind pressure if it stems from creative endeavor.

Creative people are given their gifts for a reason; they are meant to share their talents with the world. If at all possible, allow yourself to express your creative side on a professional level. Unfortunately, many such fields—painting, drawing, and writing, for instance—are not reliable in terms of income. However, there are plenty of success stories, too. If you do not presently have a job that engages your innate abilities, consider starting a search for a more satisfying position. If, however, you are lucky enough to already work in a creative environment, and you have found contentment there, your secret rule has served you well.

8. You have been developing a special medical device for your company over the past several years. It is finally finished and about to be marketed. While at a meeting with the big boss and your immediate supervisor, your supervisor takes the lion's share of the credit. A few hours later, you find out that he is getting a big bonus. Your supervisor tells you not to worry, that you will be promoted very soon. When you happen to meet the big boss in the hall and he waxes on about how much your supervisor has done, while saying little about your accomplishments and contributions, what will you say?

A. "I did the work! I was cheated! I demand recognition!" (But you say it politely, of course.)

B. "The most important thing is that this product is made available to the public and will help so many people."

C. "Yes, I have a great supervisor who treats me well."

This question looks at a couple of different aspects of your personality, one of which is whether or not you have any political instincts. Do you know how or care to play the corporate game? The other aspect has to do with how much you need to be recognized for what you do. If you do some very special piece of work, such as inventing a very helpful medical device, is that satisfaction enough, or must everyone know? Must you be specifically praised as well? There is no right answer in general, but there is a true answer for you. If you chose answer A, you generally subscribe to the following secret rule: *I will not allow others to take credit for my accomplishments; how others see me is very important.* Is that true, even at the expense of your career? The rule says that you are strong, assertive, and unwilling to compromise; you despise being used. If you have such strong convictions, you should certainly do something about it. It's better to speak up, lest you be consumed by anger. That anger would move from your mind to your body and, in the end, you would suffer in many ways. So do be sure to voice your concerns.

Now, to play the devil's advocate, who cares if everybody knows what you did? Would you upset your boss and sidetrack your career just for the principle of it all? If quality accomplishment gives you personal satisfaction, why is it so important that others recognize you? Isn't a job well done its own reward? Earlier in your life, did someone refuse to acknowledge you, making you feel like second best? Check your motivations and find out if you are creating unnecessary stress for yourself.

Sometimes it is better to let things go. While entitled to fair recognition, examine the rule on its importance above all else. Don't let your pride usurp other important values.

A job well done is more satisfying than recognition; how others see me is not so important. That's the secret rule behind answer B. If you chose B, you enjoy the process of work rather than the rewards. If that is true, you do not need "hooray's" to feel fulfilled at work. While this rule sounds great in theory, examine yourself to see whether this would work in real life. Perhaps you are immune to the need for large-scale affirmation. If that's the case, this rule works wonderfully for you. But does it really not matter if someone steals your ideas or takes credit for your efforts?

Maybe you are just practical and afraid to rock the boat. In such a case, resentment and anger will eventually build up. If you are uncertain about owning your accomplishments, consider whether you are being a little too self-effacing in life. Review the rule about being proud of your accomplishments and claiming your rightful due.

The secret rule behind answer C is not so pretty: *I must do what it takes to keep my job, even if that means letting myself get used.* You have a chance to set the record straight and you pretend that everything is just fine. Is this the way you operate in other areas of your life, as well? When is diplomacy a cover-up for fear of saying what you mean and being who you are? There is no foolproof way of telling when discretion is the better part of valor, and when to scream foul. But if you avoid necessary confrontations routinely, you are cheating yourself out of much more than a company bonus.

This rule highlights a possible pattern of protecting and pleasing to your own detriment. It is time to reevaluate the rules about being loyal to yourself versus being loyal to another. Very few people could follow this rule without having serious consequences, such as self-loathing for being weak. Work on giving yourself some credit and some options.

9. You are invited to a coworker's house for a Sunday barbecue. You observe your host lifting a heavy log in his backyard. He grimaces and grabs his back. A few minutes later, you make it a point to ask how he's doing. He waves his hand and says, "I'm just fine." The following Monday, while at work, you see the same coworker lift a box, cry out, and fall to the ground. He claims, "I hurt myself lifting the box!" The supervisor comes to the scene. Your coworker explains that he has just hurt his back and that

you are a witness. The injured man plans to file a workers' compensation claim and pursue a paid leave of absence. You are asked to fill out a report on the incident. What will you report?

A. I will confirm that my coworker's claims are accurate. I won't mention what I witnessed during the barbecue.

B. I will report exactly what I saw at work *and* at the barbecue.

C. I will deny that I saw anything, asserting that my back was turned until I heard the box drop to the floor.

To whom, if anyone, do you owe loyalty at the workplace? If you are unaffected by the outcome, where does your moral compass lead you? Is it your business at all what goes on between another worker and the management? Answer A is built on the following secret rule: *My loyalty is with my coworker and not the company.* Unless you work entirely for yourself, you have a boss. Whether at the New York Stock Exchange or a mom-and-pop grocery, you have coworkers and you have superiors. Is support of your coworker simply an "either us or them" deal? Do you care at all if he fudged a little on how he got injured? Is it okay to support a little dishonesty because "they"—you know, the big guys—always take advantage of you? Is that how you divide the world—us and them? These are not easy questions, but they hit on the motivation behind answer A. Your perception of work involves bonding with the common man against the big guy.

Maybe you have not been burned by this rule. Perhaps it works fine for you. You function best when you can define yourself in regard to others. However, there is also a chance that this rule doesn't work for you. If you feel some resentment against your coworker, if you feel some shame associated with your report, then you are only doing damage to yourself. You are on a slippery path of compromising your ethics for group loyalty. Moreover, you are bound to feel unhappy with yourself if this type of action is continuous. Evaluate your self-respect and ask yourself whether or not it's okay to be used in order to keep a friend.

The rule behind answer B places company first: *My loyalty is to the company over another individual.* If you chose this answer because you value honesty above all, then this rule works for you. But there's another possibility. Did you side with management because it is the morally right thing to do or because they can offer you more? Did you select this choice out of fear that you could damage your status at work? By rank or inclination, are you basically doing whatever you need to do to get ahead? Maybe you even find yourself feeling angry at being used, and therefore want to get back at your coworker!

If your decision was based on fear or anger, reevaluate your inclinations. Perhaps another secret rule would work better for you. Any decision based on a negative motivation is likely to have negative results. On the other hand, if you just want to be honest, make sure that risking your relationship with your coworker is worth it. We cannot argue that honesty is not the best policy, but be sure that you want to expose your coworker to such an embarrassing point and be prepared to take a hit for championing honesty. Are you ready to endure all of that? If you are, then go ahead with your convictions.

Answer C's secret rule plays it safe: *If it's not my problem, I don't get involved.* If you chose this as your secret rule, you like to stay out of trouble and avoid conflict. It's a compromising and comfortable answer. Is that true for this work situation only, or is this a pattern for you? Do you usually avoid having to choose one side or the other? Do you dislike being the "bad guy" so much that you will lie or deny rather than tell what you really know? Are your coworkers entitled to your unconditional support?

While at times it certainly makes life easier not to get involved, just like an orchestra or athletic team, a crew at work is an interdependent group whose fate often depends on its individual members. Consider whether your rule has helped you more than hurt you over the years. Do you feel like a sell-out? Perhaps getting more involved—on either end of the spectrum—would make your life richer or more meaningful. This secret rule is likely to get you by at times and keep you out of trouble, but it also might allow you to become a watered-down version of who you are. Are you really okay with playing blind?

10. Due to a recent company merger, a new manager has been assigned to your office. That individual has begun to verbally harass you on a daily basis about the quality of your work. Before the new supervisor arrived, you were a respected and productive employee, but now you are constantly being belittled and berated. You have spoken directly to this manager, gone to human resources, and even attempted to explain the situation to the company president. But you have received no support. As the months have gone on, the stress has taken its toll. You can't sleep well, have lost weight, and suffer from terrible headaches. You are now seeing a therapist, as well as taking antidepressants and tranquilizers in order to cope. What will you do?

A. I will quit. I don't deserve to be abused.

B. I will file a lawsuit and fight for my job for as long as necessary.

C. I will stay at my job as long as I can and try to tough it out.

You have an established, satisfactory job, and someone comes along and ruins a good thing. Do you fight with all you've got or do you just give in? At what point do you take your health into consideration? Does the financial consideration of leaving your job take precedence? How do you best help yourself? Answer A's secret rule states that helping yourself means knowing when to walk away: *My health and pride are more important than my job.* One of the most important lessons to learn is how you wish to be treated by the world. To a large extent, the way you are treated, whether on the job or anywhere else, is dependent on how you view yourself. This answer shows that you see the inherent value in yourself. Self-care is more important than job security. Just be sure that you don't view walking away, in some way, as being defeated.

By quitting, are you giving your new manager exactly what she wants? Do you boil inside with anger? Are you just letting the same thoughtless person perpetuate the same indignities against someone else? Do you have any obligation to your fellow workers? While respecting yourself is a sign of good self-esteem, is there any rule that not only helps you but may help others (and justice) as well? Consider all the options before deciding to clear yourself from the conflict, in order to be sure you make the healthiest secret rule possible.

Answer B's secret rule says, *I will fight for what is mine and am not afraid to do it.* You would rather fight than quit. This secret rule highlights your tenacity and courage. You refuse to walk away from conflict; in fact, you'll jump right into it when given the choice. You have a strong sense of purpose, justice, and self-worth. That's wonderful! Yet as always, let's look at all angles.

How far will you go with this secret rule? Will you fight on, even if you feel physically worse? Is it the job itself or the principle you are fighting for? If you are already feeling the signs of severe stress, might it not be wiser to leave the whole mess and let someone else deal with the jerk?

Are you trying to teach this person a lesson? Where do your obligations to justice and your coworkers end and the obligation to yourself begin? Consider the rule about the importance of any one job in relation to your health. Decide how tough it's supposed to be to make a living.

The secret rule behind answer C suggests that you don't put your physical and mental needs first: *I need a job to take care of myself and my family, so I will push myself to the limit in order to avoid serious change.* You need this job. You're tough; you can take a little garbage from some bozo. You have a lot of obligations, and a little stress isn't going to get you down. Hey, everybody has some stress. That's the way the world is, right? A person has to make sacrifices for the good of others. Right? But where is the endpoint? We're not talking about a little conflict; we're talking about therapy and medication! Will you wait for the day you can't get out of bed anymore?

If your secret rule tells you to take the abuse, you are terribly insecure about your talents, worth, and abilities. It is clear that you are under-valuing yourself both as a worker and as a human being. Trust yourself to find a better opportunity. You do not have to voluntarily choose suffering in this lifetime. And yes, everything is a choice. Staying at such a job is a choice, not a necessity. Allow yourself some options and work on changing this destructive secret rule.

CONCLUSION

Work reflects and affects many of our core values. What is important to you, after all? How much money do you need to be happy? How important is prestige or recognition to your career choice? How important is the feeling of satisfaction derived from helping others? An integral part of health and happiness comes from feeling satisfied and emotionally rewarded from your work. Do you feel rewarded? Is there a secret rule that keeps you from doing what you really enjoy and feel called to do? Hopefully, this chapter has shed some light on options and attitudes that will help you make the healthiest professional decisions.

3. Gender Roles

Life was simpler for everyone in the 1950s, when I was growing up. In those days, everyone seemed to have very set roles: mothers stayed at home and fathers worked. My mother could work if she desired, but it was expected that my father would make enough to care for our needs. It was in those olden days that women expected they would not have to work and that their husbands would always take care of them. And men assumed that the women would be fulfilled in their numerous domestic tasks, despite the lack of glory, change, or recognition.

Fast-forward a generation and only the most naïve of trust-fund babies would believe that you don't have to fend for yourself in this life—be ye man or woman. Most of us have had to change our beliefs about what men and women are supposed to do. That has not been easy. If you change the rules in the middle of the game, you can expect some of the players to cry foul and resist. The game, of course, is the unstated but generally accepted way that men are supposed to treat women and vice versa. The game has rules, and the players have *secret* rules on dating, marriage, parenting, work, and civil liberties.

Your sexual identity is part of your skin. You can move to a different country, change your religion, or speak another language, but your sexual identity stays with you. Gender identity is at the innermost core of the self. Ask a man if he would rather have PMS or his legs cut off and you will get the picture! Now it turns out that sexual identity does not determine social roles. It certainly seemed that way for thousands of years! Due to the longtime connection between sex and society, it is taking longer than some would like for gender equality to completely take hold in society. Yet that's the wave of the future. The secret rules that limit the self must be uncovered in order to achieve maximum personal development in today's culture. The following questions and answers will help you identify your secret rules on gender.

1.♦ Your new infant is born with both sets of genitals—the baby is a hermaphrodite. The doctors inform you that one set can be removed through surgery and that you can actually choose the sex of your child. Your spouse asks you to make the decision. Which sex do you decide upon?

A. I choose to have a son.

B. I choose to have a daughter.

C. It doesn't make any difference; I will flip a coin.

In your vision of life, what does the "ideal child" look like? Does a particular gender immediately come to mind? If you quickly chose a gender, you probably assign rather fixed traits and activities to each sex. In addition, you have certain notions about your own abilities to interact with those qualities. By selecting answer A, you identify a secret rule that confirms the following: *I desire to closely associate myself with male energy.* Maybe you are a man and want to share the excitement and adventure of your youth—playing ball, flipping skateboards, steering toy cars into piles—with your own child. Or perhaps you are woman who wants to explore the masculine side of life. Maybe you are tired of Barbie dolls and want a remote control car!

Choosing to have a boy might also highlight an attraction to the dominance that is commonly linked with maleness. A natural and striking power is associated with testosterone, and you might want to create and access that power by bearing a male. Or you might feel that a male offers you the opportunity to continue your family name, even though many women are deciding to maintain their maiden names in this day and age. There are countless reasons why it would be wonderful to have a male child. While you are thinking about them, you might also consider the exceptional qualities that come with the female gender. Appreciating the power of both sexes will make your world a very exciting place to live. Also keep in mind that today's girls have many opportunities to engage in traditionally male activities, from excelling at competitive high school sports to making aggressive career moves. So some of the qualities that you associate with the male are now quite typical for both genders.

The secret rule behind answer B states, *I desire to closely associate myself with female energy.* Regardless of your gender, perhaps you are drawn to the soft and nurturing qualities that females are known to possess. Maybe you enjoy doing "girl things," such as playing with dolls and make-up, skipping rope, and baking cookies. You might even think that girls are less trouble, or be attracted to the greater calm they supposedly possess during the early years of life.

If you are a female, this might be a chance to relive your life with even more feminine power and sensitivity. If you are a male, this could be your opportunity to know the other gender in a profound and love-centered way. Whatever your personal reasons are, you are sure that female energy will fill you with positive experiences. Certainly explore the numerous reasons why a female child could be the best thing that ever happened to you. But also consider the positive qualities of the male sphere. Maybe you never dwell on the benefits of male energy, either because malehood is unfamiliar or because you feel you already know it well. By acknowledging that *both* genders can be powerful, you will fill your life with even more excitement and appreciation.

Answer C's secret rule confesses, *I do not feel the need to associate myself more closely with masculine or feminine energy, but rather feel equally comfortable with both.* What could be more egalitarian than that! If you have a boy, you will delight in everything that maleness offers. If you have a girl, you will celebrate each feminine quality. Most likely, you are open-minded and positive, willing to embrace the familiar and tackle the unfamiliar with equal gusto. Your approach to this question underscores an optimistic approach to life that should serve you very well.

Of course, there is also the possibility that you are afraid to decide between the genders. Does this highlight a pattern in your life—avoiding hard choices and hoping that, magically, things will come out okay? Some of us feel uncomfortable expressing preferences and making decisions that will alter the course of many lives. If you truly don't have a preference between the male and the female, that's fine. But if your decision is rooted in fear and passivity, your secret rule could prevent you from fully living your life.

2. You are a woman on a first date with a man your own age. While sitting in a dance club and enjoying each other's conversation, another man approaches and asks you to dance. You are not interested and pleasantly refuse. It is quite obvious that your date is irritated by the advance and would not have been so polite. Fifteen minutes later, that same man returns and, once more, asks you to dance. Again, you decline. Your date tells him not to bother you anymore, words are exchanged, and in a matter of seconds, your date has knocked the man unconscious. Did your date do the right thing?

A. Yes, my date had every right to assert his presence and defend me.

B. No, I can fight my own battles.

C. While the intention was good, there is no justification for being violent toward someone.

What are your secret rules about a man who will fight for a woman he cares for? Whether it seems noble or primitive will undoubtedly tell you much about where you have come from and where you are likely to go. The man, of course, fights for himself as well as the woman; he is re acting to his perceived threat of displacement. In this day and age, though, does a woman really need protection? And from whom—another suitor? Answer A's secret rule accepts stereotypical male protection: *Aggressive behavior is normal and natural in heterosexual encounters.* Was there no other way? How much is proving oneself and marking one's territory a worthy part of heterosexual dynamics? If you selected answer A, you still like to lodge yourself in traditional male/female roles. You feel secure with the brute male and passive female stereotypes.

Confirm that you truly can maintain the lifestyle you imply in your answer. If you feel that aggressive behavior is acceptable in heterosexual encounters, you'll have to carry through in other situations too. What happens when you receive phone calls from a friend of the other sex? Will aggressive reactions be acceptable then? What about situations with opposite-gender coworkers? Should the male step in? With this rule, you have implied that the female needs or wants a male to back her up. You are not quite ready for the equality in relationships that you might complain you don't get. You will be more ready for give and take when love is not quite so much of a competitive sport.

Choice B is structured around a secret rule that asserts the following: *A woman can manage her heterosexual relationships without the need for aggressive male behavior.* It says that a woman can handle a male companion or suitor without the need to use force as backup. It says that the woman expects— or, better yet, demands—respect from a man. This respect includes giving her power and space to manage the attention that she receives.

Being assertive is a necessary trait in the modern world. The more self-reliant we can be, the better off we are. There are exceptions, as in all generalizations, but aggression should be a rare event rather than the cultural norm. If you have chosen this as your secret rule, you are a little closer to obtaining equality and happiness in your relationships.

The secret rule behind answer C claims, *I understand the old male pattern of aggression in heterosexual relationships, but I no longer want to be a part of it.* You are finally starting to realize that the macho attitude of "one man besting another" is something you want to leave behind. Yet you don't get heated up about today's changing gender dynamics. What is the measure of a man? Is it how much of a wallop he packs? Is a man's sense of worth determined by how much or how little he needs to defend his "territory"? Is a woman unable to stand up for herself, say "No thank you, Mister," and really mean it? Your secret rule says that you believe so and are in transition to accepting a more assertive female position in society.

If you chose answer C, you are really starting to apply new gender rules to your life, but you are still very sensitive toward old roles. You are moving at your own pace, and that is fine. Instead of looking at this question as a gender issue, you opted for a cultural statement on violence, and that's a start. But don't shy away from making stronger statements and demands on gender roles today. It's your life and your world—don't be afraid to assert your opinion on what a woman wants and needs.

3. You have entered middle age and have noticed a waning sex drive. Moreover, you don't enjoy sex when you have it. Your latest physical exam did not reveal any biological problems, so your doctor suggests that you speak to a sex counselor about your concerns. Clearly, the counselor should be trustworthy, understanding, and insightful. Who do you think would do a better job—a man or a woman?

A. I think a woman would be more helpful.

B. I think a man would be more helpful.

C. Gender would not affect my decision, but rather how comfortable I am with the counselor's credentials.

Who will best understand you in your most vulnerable moments? Often, when we want to understand ourselves, we look to a same-sex person because we figure that he or she can relate. We find the opposite sex useful when we need feedback on or understanding of the mysteries and maneuvers of our counterparts. But we might also have cultural notions of women as better listeners and of men as more realistic problem-solvers. What's behind your perspectives? If you chose answer A, you have a secret rule that confirms woman as the listener, nurturer, and helper: *A woman will be sensitive to my sexual problems and counsel me back to a healthy place.* If you are a woman, you probably seek the security of sisterhood when it comes to sexual concerns. You find comfort and company through another woman's words. Maybe you feel less embarrassed about admitting certain shortcomings, using particular vocabulary, even crying a few tears. If you are a man, you may be drawn to the patience and listening capacity of a woman. You may also feel that she can enlighten you with a different-gender perspective.

You need to feel safe with your counselor, and if a woman will naturally provide you with a more protected feeling, then follow your secret rule. But try to base your decision on positive motivation. In other words, choose a woman because you like the sensitive atmosphere she provides, not because you are frightened of or intimidated by a male counselor. Rationally, a trained counselor of either sex could help. If you find yourself absolutely shunning the idea of a male counselor, you are limiting your sphere of help. It is difficult to go through life lacking trust in one of the genders.

The secret rule behind answer B says, *I trust a man as a healer and helper when it comes to sexual dysfunction.* Maybe it's the strength and certainty of the male character that draws you to this decision. If you are a woman, you are a modern thinker! You have shed the stereotypes of men as poor listeners and insensitive souls. In fact, you are determined to make progress, and you feel that a man's perspective will open your eyes to various possibilities. If you are a man, you feel secure in an atmosphere of brotherhood. You want to talk to someone who can confirm your feelings and understand your deepest insecurities.

By all means, select a male counselor if that will give you the comfort and qualities that you need to start healing. It is vitally important that you choose a counselor with whom you can be honest and open, without fearing judgment or embarrassment. But also realize that there are effective counselors of both genders who could provide help. A good counselor will see you, first and foremost, as a hurting human being, not as a typical member of a particular gender. That counselor will work with you on a neutral and objective level. You might be pleasantly surprised to find healing with a female counselor as well.

Answer C's secret rule is for those of us who look for rational function: *When discussing the sexual dynamics of my relationship, I am comfortable with either sex and am simply drawn to information.* You are not looking for someone to relate to you on a social level or to pass along any "insider" secrets. You just want solid, fix-it advice from a well-trained individual. You probably don't suffer much from insecurities and gender stereotypes. With your rational and confident approach, you are poised to start making therapeutic progress.

But dig a little more deeply into your answer. Are you being totally truthful with yourself? Answer C sounds like the politically correct choice. But when it comes down to unlocking bedroom details and revealing your innermost thoughts on age and body image, you might feel differently. Question yourself to confirm that you are not simply shying away from a very real issue. It is not easy to reveal the intimate details of our sex lives in a professional atmosphere. You might benefit from seriously considering what type of counselor could provide you with a comfortable emotional space in case those emotions do take over at some point.

4. You are on the board of a large corporation that produces men's health products. The company has very few women in top management. A high-ranking position just opened up, and you are asked to vote for a candidate to fill that position. The choice is between two people of equal skill, seniority, and reputation. However, one candidate is a man and the other is a woman. You don't know either of them personally. For whom will you vote?

A. I will vote for the woman. It's only right to have equal numbers of men and women in top positions.

B. I will vote for the man. The company revolves around men's products, so a man would be the better choice.

C. I will request that the candidates take a test for further assessment. Based on the results of their performance, I will make a decision.

This question has to do with perceived fairness and corporate wisdom. All things being equal, should a woman be given preference in a situation where she is in the minority? Yet your opinion might be swayed by what the job entails. Aren't there jobs that a man can do better because he understands the male psyche, regardless of how many degrees and fine qualities a woman has? The secret rule behind answer A reveals something profound about your concept of gender dynamics: *I must take an active part in increasing women's roles in the professional arena, regardless of how male-oriented a job is.* Fairness demands that equally qualified women should get equal job opportunities and a "leg up" where possible. And if the man were just a tad better qualified, should it still be given to the woman on a fairness basis anyway?

If you were choosing your team to compete with another team and wanted the absolute best person for your team, would you still choose the woman? Are there such things as products or services that women don't understand as well as men, or is this just an old-fashioned belief that went out with the Hula-Hoop? If you have chosen this rule, you feel strongly that a woman can never be less qualified than a man just because she is a woman. You are promoting the cause of gender equality. While pressing forward with your secret rule, let yourself still be open to any possible exceptions or circumstances that have not yet crossed your path. Beware of being overly loyal to the cause, essentially practicing reverse discrimination.

Answer B's secret rule shows that you still believe in male and female spheres: *Men know men better than women know men, and business must recognize this reality.* You do not see a problem with adjusting gender issues to particular situations. You don't make sweeping efforts to bring gender equality to this culture. One of the universal laws—as basic as the law of gravity—is that men know and understand themselves better than women can. Is there any truth at all to that statement? Apparently you believe so and adjust your gender dynamics to suit the fact that certain male and female spheres should be allowed to remain that way.

If you chose answer B only because this situation is very specific to men's products, not because you disregard the importance of women representatives in the workplace, you live pretty close to an ideal of equality. If, however, you conceive of numerous places where this rule applies, you might still be caught in old-style beliefs and maintain more rigid roles than would be most beneficial in today's world.

Finally, the secret rule behind answer C reveals, *I accept that men and women can work equally well on any product for either sex, and neither should be given preference due to gender; merit counts above all else.* In other words, no position should be awarded to a woman solely to serve the need to be politically correct. Likewise, a woman may do any job with any product—even so-called "male products"—equally as well. If you have endorsed this choice, you are in effect saying that men and women equally understand each other's needs, from a business sense anyway; they are, in concept, identically qualified. The most skilled person should get the job.

Your choice of answers certainly shows that you make rational, fair efforts to treat the genders equally. Simply avoid equalizing so much that you wipe out the differences that make this world so dynamic. What is so wrong about recognizing that a man might do a particular job better and a female might do another job better? Is it so offensive to give gender roles that much credit? In your perspective, men and women are good at understanding each other in business. But where do the wheels fall off this wagon when it comes to the rest of life? Even with all of the attempts to be fair to women, especially in the business world, does there remain some immutable or inscrutable barrier that keep men and women apart? Try not to ignore the fact that we do have differences that sometimes make it seem as though the genders are from two different planets.

5. You serve in the military and are presently in combat. Your safety depends on the courage and skill of your superiors. An error in judgment could be fatal to one or more members of your squad. Your direct superior, who is a woman, commands a specific course of action. One of your team members—a man who is a highly experienced fighter—disagrees and refuses to comply. Whom do you follow?

A. I trust my superior and I will obey her commands.

B. I don't have confidence in my commanding officer; I feel better going with the man's opinion.

C. I have a tendency to trust the man's opinion, but to avoid court-martial, I will do what I am told.

This question asks you to decide with whom to place your trust: a female superior or an experienced male. (Note that the question assumes that the female superior is also highly experienced, as she is in a place of authority.) So you are left with choosing whether or not to trust your female leader in a traditionally male role. Answer A is developed around a secret rule that says, *I unconditionally accept the rule and command of a female superior.* The implication here is that you respect her and understand that gender is no barrier to leadership. In our day, it is difficult for some women and men to accept the new order of things. With rare exceptions, those who grew up before the 1960s and 1970s find it hard to believe that women have the interest or temperament for combat. Yet you, regardless of your age, do trust that a female can perform well in a combat situation. You have blasted through stereotypes and look to women as equal leaders, even in previously male-dominated spheres.

By choosing this secret rule, you also demonstrate the likelihood that you would accept women in other leadership roles, such as those of business and government. If you are open-minded enough to trust women on the battlefield, you probably do not have a problem with women in the boardroom. Because of your trust in the rationality and talents of both genders, you are likely to establish good dynamics in the world today. You do not struggle with male-female competition and probably have a very healthy approach to your coworkers.

Answer B's secret rule involves slow progress with gender dynamics: *I don't yet accept women in many risky leadership positions.* Your choice shows that you would trust the experienced man over a superior officer. What if the situation was reversed? What if a highly experienced woman disagreed with a man in authority? Would that make a difference? Do you believe women should be in combat at all? Your choice of answers shows a distrust in female authority when it comes to high-tension, traditionally male-oriented roles. You struggle with stereotypes that, in today's world, are antiquated.

Has this struggle affected you, professionally and personally? How well have you done with superiors on the job? If you quickly chose to follow the man, you may be struggling with women in authority at *many* levels. Consider whether your perception of women in combat situations would be the exception or the rule. How well has this attitude worked for you? It is important to trust women in authority as the numbers increase. If you are realizing that you carry resentment against or lack of confidence in female superiors, you have found something to truly work on over the next couple of years. This is a self-defeating outlook to have in our modern world of equal opportunity.

Answer C takes a middle ground: *I reluctantly but faithfully do what I am told by female superiors.* This implies that you will take your risks out of respect for authority, whether that authority is projected from a male or female source. You are trying to see the genders as equally competent; you are trying to do the right thing—either for justice's sake or out of fear.

You do have some hesitation, which means that you are not completely confident in a female leader. That's okay—the transition can be a difficult one, and at least you are trying.

Examine your motivation behind choosing answer C one more time. Did you choose C largely out of fear of punishment or because you are revising your gender stereotypes slowly? In order to check whether or not you truly are aiming to see men and women equally, ask yourself if there are any other high-tension situations in which you would have no problem following a woman's orders. If you still find yourself suspicious of female leaders in risky situations, look at how that attitude has furthered or hindered your career and what kinds of relationships you have with other women. You have more work to do before you can healthily function in today's world of gender equality.

6. You have registered your child for kindergarten, and you just received a packet with all the pertinent information. Reading through the papers, you notice that the school employs three kindergarten teachers—two women and one man. Your child has been placed in the man's class. You hadn't expected a male teacher, simply because women have traditionally filled the job. But then again, there has been a recent increase in the number of male elementary school teachers. Do you feel comfortable with the placement, or do you consider switching your child into another teacher's class?

A. I have absolutely no reservations about the male kindergarten teacher.

B. I will try to switch my child into one of the women's classes.

C. A male kindergarten teacher is fine for a son, but I will switch a daughter into a woman's classroom.

How much do you want traditional gender roles to remain as they were? Are there jobs that are primarily female and should stay that way? If you chose answer A, your secret rule has been updated to fit our modern culture: *Men can be just as competent as women in professions that involve childcare and other stereotypically female roles.* When typewriters first came out, they were used exclusively by men as they were said to be too difficult and complicated for women! Then slowly, over time, that idea was completely reversed to the point at which now, with rare exceptions, we assume that an office secretary will be female. Do you place any limitations on what jobs are "normal" for men? Is there anything that is too feminine or demeaning for a man to do?

By choosing this rule, you endorse the idea that there is no right sex for kindergarten teachers. The rule also implies that there is no "bad" role model for your child. If you are true to your rule, you will also allow your child to make maximum use of his or her potential and individuality. Congratulations on a very progressive choice.

The secret rule behind answer B highlights your comfort with society's twentieth-century traditions: *I feel that certain jobs should remain entirely female—especially those involving children.* By extension, then, there are probably jobs that should be the exclusive province of men. What exactly is it that bothers you about a man in the role of kindergarten teacher? Do you actually think that a man cannot be trusted with children somehow? If you immediately chose this rule without a second thought, you are still struggling with the gender changes that are going on in our culture. Your criterion for "acceptable" is what is familiar. If this is your secret rule, you may be making judgments and creating conflicts that are hurting people around you.

If you want better relationships, and if you want your progeny to grow healthily in a modern world, it may be time to evolve your thinking and look at different rules for yourself. The old barriers of gender roles in the professional world are being successfully challenged every day. You will be caught in a time warp, and catch those you love in it, too, if you hold too tightly to the old, familiar roles of women as elementary school teachers and retail associates, men as cops and firemen, and other stereotypes.

Answer C's secret rule implies a lack of trust or confidence in role-modeling when it comes to men and girls: *Male teachers are appropriate for young kindergarten boys, but they would not serve as appropriate role models or caretakers for any daughter of mine.* How would a male teacher be better for a boy? What do you find desirable about a male teacher? Discipline? Camaraderie? If this is your secret rule, you seem to feel that early role models are important to the development of a boy and that seeing a male in this position is a positive step. That's a healthy perspective for today's world! Look further at whether your concerns for your son are some way of healing your own wounds that remain unresolved. But there is more to the answer.

You do not find a male teacher acceptable for your daughter. This implies one of two things: you don't trust men around girls, in the sense of being gentle or soft-spoken enough to make your daughter feel comfortable, or you do not have confidence in a man's ability to positively influence a young female. You still have problems with crossing the gender barrier; you believe that men have *their* sphere and women have *their* sphere. In today's world, that type of thinking is not too constructive. Men and women share college dorm floors; men and women share offices; men and women share role models. Why decide to put your daughter at a disadvantage by fostering an "all-female" parental world for her? She will have to deal with male authority figures at some point, and the sooner she begins, the more natural it will seem.

7. There has been an upsurge of interest in women's wrestling. The media portrays female wrestlers as athletic, aggressive, attractive, and usually very financially successful professionals. Your eighteen-year-old daughter, a recent high-school graduate, now tells you that her dream is to become a female wrestling star. She wants you to pay the tuition for her training, and you can easily afford it. Will you provide the money and support her dream?

A. Yes, I will pay for my daughter's training and support her all the way.

B. No, I oppose her career choice as unsuitable for our family and will discourage her in any way possible.

C. I agree with my daughter's right to choose her own path, but I don't feel I am obligated to pay for something that I find personally offensive.

How much have you accepted and even approved of aggressive female behavior? Women's wrestling is big business and these women often become as admired as rock stars. For some, wrestling is controversial enough; many fathers wouldn't advocate this profession for their sons. How do you respond to the new career choices open to women? The secret rule behind answer A is as follows: *I support women's participation in nontraditional professions—even ones that involve physical aggression.* If you are willing to let your daughter take part, then you certainly support all women who wish to take advantage of new opportunities, regardless of the physical and emotional challenges involved.

If you chose this rule, you are indeed a most accepting and loving parent. Your choice suggests that you are likewise minimally judgmental of others. In order to get to know yourself better, try to think of something that you wouldn't readily accept when it comes to your child. While it is certainly democratic to accept your children without judgment, are you not also obligated to show some discernment of what is or is not ethical, just, or even tasteful? Are there any professions that you would at least caution her about?

The secret rule of answer B displays your concept that there are acceptable and unacceptable behaviors for women: *I do not feel that women should partake in all the same activities as men and I have the right to expect my daughter to remain somewhat traditional.* There are, of course, all kinds of reasons why you might not support your daughter as a lady wrestler. The fair question is whether you would hold your son to the same standards. If you would encourage your son but discourage your daughter, then you must explore your double standard. What are the limitations you place upon a woman versus a man? Does it have to do with the aggression involved in wrestling, or does it have to do with a perceived social embarrassment for your family? Are your motivations selfless or selfish?

Think about your life. Is this attitude an isolated incident, or is it more commonly the way you approach gender roles? If you are opposed to your daughter's wrestling because it is violent or aggressive, consider racecar driving or being a soldier. Your rule admits that you are retaining control of acceptable female limits. Whether this represents wisdom or tyranny will depend on your overall support of your child's creative endeavors.

Answer C's secret rule reveals the following: *I honor my daughter's right to self-expression, but I don't need to agree with it or support it.* You accept your daughter's right to wrestle, but you refuse to encourage her or fund her. If you accept her right to choose, why do you not support it? Do you want her to fail? Is this a character test of her real desires?

If you have chosen this rule, you are able to separate what you feel is right from what you impose on others. You have a very mature perspective on parenting, and you also have developed enough of a "selfhood" to voice your opinions. Just confirm that you want to make your daughter feel "unsupported" by withholding financial help. Are you sending a mixed message when you say, "Hey, go ahead and follow your dreams, but I'll only back you up on the ones I like"? If you subscribe to answer C, check your consistency—the solidity of the messages you send—when it comes to gender dynamics. Meanwhile, however, congratulate yourself on being an honest and strong person who will not be pushed into supporting something for the sake of acceptance.

8. Your sister is a highly successful businesswoman. Over the past year, she has fallen in love with a man who barely earns a tenth of what she makes. But that doesn't seem to matter to your sister. She describes her boyfriend as a generous and caring man. He thoroughly enjoys his job as a probation officer, working with troubled youths and making a difference in the community. This man seems to make your sister very happy. In fact, she wants to marry him. You have not met him yet, so you can't possibly have much to hold against this boyfriend. How do you feel about the fact that his income is dramatically lower than hers?

A. I think my sister is going down a doomed path by choosing a man who makes less than she does.

B. I support my sister's choice of mate and do not foresee problems for her.

C. I distrust and tend not to respect a man who makes much less than his wife, but I will not voice my opinion to my sister because it's her life.

This question studies power and gender roles. It is often believed that money means power in a relationship. It is the "golden" rule: He who has the gold rules. By tradition, men make more money; women are not considered the breadwinners. Of course, now women have self-made fortunes, and they can likewise choose men for reasons much more romantic than their prosperity. Yet answer A's secret rule shows that you are comfortable with the old parameters: *Relationships work out better when the man makes more and the woman makes less.* That has been the predominant thinking for a long time. Is that because it is emasculating for the man to earn less money? Do all—or even most—men need to make more money than their partners to feel good about themselves? Are you frightened that a man might do or say something if he feels inferior?

If you chose answer A, you still tend to feel that the man should earn more than the woman. In the final analysis, can you accept and find joy in your sister's choice? Perhaps it is time you realize that women are just as competitive and just as successful as men in the professional arena. It is not odd that a woman makes an equivalent or even better salary than her spouse. While that takes some getting used to, as long as the woman is comfortable with that, why can't you be?

In choice B, the secret rule states that salaries will not make or break the relationship: *If people love each other, it doesn't make any difference who earns more.* Healthy heterosexual love relationships include a man who does not resent his wife for making more money and a woman who is not afraid to be the best that she can be. In other words, you believe that a man should feel exactly the same about himself and his wife even if she makes ten times more than he does. Is your secret rule based on your beliefs about how the world ought to be, or on what you have seen with your own eyes?

If you have chosen this rule, you have accepted that at least some people can be mature enough to value an individual for his character rather than his net worth. This is the ideal approach—refusing to let salary figures dominate where love and emotion should. However, there are many people who have not yet caught up to your progressive gender stance. Do not be surprised to find that a lot of men still want to bring home the big money and a lot of women feel more secure when their husbands are the breadwinners. It is very difficult to break patterns that have been part of our culture over hundreds of years. Yet, the culture is changing and your secret rule is integral to making the changes happen.

Answer C's secret rule asserts, *I can't trust or respect a man who would be with a woman who makes much more money than he does, yet I keep my feelings to myself.* As a sibling, you have difficulty trusting that a man will not try to take advantage of your "naïve" sister. Everybody knows that no self-respecting man would let a woman essentially support him! Therefore, his motives must be suspect. Does that sound familiar? But aren't you essentially saying that a man without money can't possibly love a woman regardless of her financial status? Do you *really* believe that? The position sounds kind of absurd when you put it that way, right? If you have chosen this rule, you must fear for yourself as well as your sister. Do you, yourself, wish to be supported by wealthier male figures? Besides looking for crafty gigolos, do you often find yourself distrustful of others of lower financial status? Your basic distrust will more often lead you to misjudge others than give protection to the ones you love. Your belief that a self-made woman requires protection from an insincere ne'er-do-well is a quaint relic from another age.

However, there is a very important second part to your answer: You are keeping your suspicions to yourself. That means that at least you are starting to work on controlling your prejudices. You are not teaching others to distrust men who end up with wealthier women. In and of itself, your choice of answer C shows that you respect others' personal decisions and do not feel the need to stamp your gender notions into their minds. You are heading in the right direction!

9. You serve on the Athletics Board of a public high school. Recently, there has been much interest concerning coed sports: Should female athletes be allowed to play on traditionally male teams? A new female student has tried out for an all-male sports team and has proven herself quite capable. You have the chance to vote on the politics and fairness of the situation. Do you think she should be allowed to join the team?

A. Yes, capable female athletes should be allowed to play any sport—even a full contact sport—with capable male athletes.

B. No, males and females should not compete on the same team in sports.

C. Coed teams are fine for non-contact sports, but if this concerns a contact sport, the girl should not be allowed to join the team.

This question is not about athletic prowess as much as what is most fair to all parties concerned. Does treating someone equally necessarily mean fairness? Answer A's secret rule reveals how strongly you feel about equalizing the sexes: *Women should be given the opportunity to compete with men on the physical level just as they do on the intellectual level.* Do you feel it diminishes women to have to play on teams with other women? If the boys strenuously objected, would you force them to accept a female athlete? Would it be fair to displace one of the boys on the team and give his place to a female athlete? What if a man wasn't good enough for a male team but could make the female team? Think about these questions to confirm that this is truly your secret rule. Basically, you are arguing that single-sex teams should be a thing of the past.

Can we ever be too equal? If you have chosen answer A, you believe that few, if any, limitations should be placed on a gender. Just check whether or not you are being consistent. Sometimes, the rule works for a few women or for a few situations, but cannot be applied across the board. Examine why you are so eager to mix both genders into all activities. Are you resentful about former limits placed on women? Must we blur the lines so much that we don't let men and women have their own spaces at all?

In choice B, the secret rule argues that *males and females should be allowed to maintain single-sex clubs in some areas.* You feel it is better for even the best of female athletes to stay on their own teams. Is this for safety reasons? Is it fair to keep a top female athlete from expressing her full potential if she can do so on a mostly male team? Your choice says that some kind of inequity or harm would come from allowing a girl to participate on a boy's team. Would the boys lose self-esteem if they had to play with a girl who was better at their own sport than they are? Must their egos be protected? Is this your primary concern?

Your choice of answer B shows that you are not terribly threatened by a world that maintains some gender barriers. When it comes to sports, at least, you don't have a problem saying, "There's a place for girls and a place for boys." You respect that females do share certain bonding practices and similar physical dynamics that make all-girl teams more appropriate. Your relaxed attitude about these specific gender rules is probably beneficial to you because it means less fighting and upset. Yet make sure that you would maintain this attitude if your daughter were dying to get onto the men's basketball team for a scholarship. If you can honestly say you would still believe in single-sex teams, then you've found your secret rule.

The secret rule upon which answer C is built states, *I accept women as equal competitors, but there are some limitations.* Here you have compromised and accepted that girls can compete effectively and should be allowed to form coed teams with boys—with restrictions. Do you object to the idea of girls in contact sports, or would some change in equipment make any difference? Do you understand why some females want to play rough? Shouldn't everyone be entitled to stretch her abilities to the limit?

If you chose this rule, you have some objections to women playing rough. You continue to hold onto an older view of what girls are capable of doing. They are already soldiers and police officers. While it is not easy to change old belief patterns, try to see that women are doing more than ever, and that the differences between men and women are getting fewer and fewer.

10. Your best friend, who is a woman, excitedly tells you about the great business deal she just made. You are very happy for her—until she explains how she won the client. Your friend wore a sexy outfit, flirted mercilessly, and agreed to hold meetings over dinners. When you challenge her for using her feminine wiles instead of her professional skills, your friend claims that she has every right: "The guys are always making deals on the golf course and in the men's sauna. They use their brotherhood. Why can't I use my wiles?" Does she have a point?

A. Yes, a woman can and should use whatever she can to compete in a man's world.

B. No, it is wrong and degrading for a woman to use her sex appeal to make a deal.

C. A woman may be flirtatious and act sexy, but if she actually has sex with a client, she is hardly more than a common prostitute.

What conduct is right or appropriate for women as they compete with men in the business world? Do men have some advantage in business over women because they can do certain things together? Should not a woman then be able to use whatever she can to make the deal in her way? By what rule should she remain entirely "professional," while her male competitors drink and go to strip clubs together? Answer A's secret rule demands a woman's right to do what it takes: *A woman has the right to do whatever she pleases—as long at it's legal—to compete in the professional world.* In other words, all is fair in love, war, and business. The courts have long acknowledged that men's clubs have a distinct advantage, and have forced previously men's-only clubs to accept female members. But are there any limits at all? Should a woman dance with a client? How about a kiss? How about sex? Is there a line beyond which she should not go?

While deciding where the limits might be, you will do well to remember that a deal is still just a deal. A woman still must face herself in the morning. Is the victory as sweet when a woman has gained it by sexually charming someone? Then again, we all use some degree of charm. People charm each other all the time in the boardroom, with big smiles, nice clothes, and pleasant talk that essentially says, "I have it together and I am going to take care of you." You must decide where a professional should draw the line.

Answer B is built on the following secret rule: *A woman should be genderless in the professional world.* Women should not accentuate their sexual allure for career purposes. In an ideal world where merit and character would count most, there wouldn't be a need to wear sexy clothes. But is business ultimately—maybe unfortunately—about the whole package? Can you deny that women and men use their sexual identity all the time, unconsciously? Maybe we can't just turn it off. Maybe sexual power is so deeply engrained in some of us that we cannot help but use it during the times when we are the center of attention.

If you chose answer B, you feel strongly that any kind of sexual tension in a business situation is clearly inappropriate. If that is so, you are hopefully judging others fully and completely on the content of their character and the quality of their product or service. If you are not, then you are being at the very least a bit hypocritical, don't you think?

Answer C is the compromising choice: *A woman may use her natural appeal but should not provide physical favors to gain business.* So the line is clearly drawn, or is it? Is any kind of touch allowed? What are you really saying with this rule? It is okay to tease, as long as it stops right there. Any flirting is okay because it's just a game. There are no feelings hurt or diseases spread. Then playfulness has a place in high-stakes business.

If you chose this rule, you are in some sense trying to be practical or accept the obvious already in play. What is your advice, then, to a woman who feels that she needs to compete but who is not sure how far she needs to go to get the job done? In the end, what are you willing to say or do to sell a few more widgets? Your decision to compromise may seem realistic, but to avoid future problems, you might want to make some hard and fast rules about what is acceptable in the business place.

CONCLUSION

For some men, washing the dishes or diapering the baby is a big deal. Depending on how old you are and how you were raised, the gender changes of the past century can be positive, negative, or both. Two hundred years ago, women were chattel. One hundred years ago, women worked very little in the urban world, played very few sports, and were trying to establish the right to vote. Fifty years ago, women were largely homemakers. There was great resistance to every incremental change, just as now. We struggle, as a society, to balance gender equality with comfort and appropriateness. The secret rules that you and your friends possess are forming our customs right now. The more rules people have in common, the more traditions and laws are established. But before critiquing society's decisions, we must try very diligently to critique our own. Do your secret rules regarding "man" things and "woman" things serve your best interests?

4. Power and Control

Do you get a rush from "pulling rank"? Do you enjoy feeling in control of a situation? Or maybe you don't like to call the shots; maybe you would rather let someone else take control. Then there's the possibility that you have struck a happy medium, assuming power in some places and relinquishing control in others. Whatever the case, understanding your need for—or fear of—power and control is extremely important. It is ultimately what makes you choose a certain lifestyle, succeed or fail in particular situations, and get or lose what you want in life.

There is no denying that power and control can feel like drugs. If you are naturally aggressive and motivated, power might feel too good. You can get things done easily, and even get others to do them for you! But all of a sudden, you might find yourself exploiting your power, be it professional or personal. Isn't it important to recognize such a trait, so that you can avoid needlessly harming yourself and others?

Of course, it can also be frightening to hold the reins of power. If you tend to be timid and lack self-confidence, using power and taking control can actually feel horrible! You might suffer from anxiety and ultimately decide that being a big player is not worth the stress. Once you recognize the secret rules that keep you from being everything you can be, maybe you will conquer some of this timidity and fear. After all, being scared and doubting your capabilities is no way to live. Try the following hypothetical situations that study power and control. You might learn something very valuable about yourself and ultimately be motivated to change your entire approach.

1. You are the single parent of a twenty-year-old son who wants to marry someone of whom you disapprove. Ordinarily, your son would do anything for you, but he won't break up with this woman. As far as you are con-

cerned, your child is being headstrong and not listening to reason. You absolutely want to stop the wedding. You've even threatened not to attend. That hasn't swayed him. At this point, it seems that the only option left is to threaten to take your errant child out of the will. What will you do?

A. I will remove my son from my will if he does not obey me.

B. I will threaten to remove my son from my will, but I would never actually do it.

C. I would never threaten my son or resort to such manipulation in any way.

How much do you try to control a loved one when you feel that person is making a terrible mistake? In order to be a good parent or a good friend, how far will you go to influence or manipulate your loved ones to save them from themselves? Answer A's secret rule claims that you have a natural right to steer the behavior of your children, even if they are now adults: *I have a right to control the behavior of my children, and I will use all my power to do so.* You believe that a parent's job is to prevent a disaster, even if that means rejection and disapproval instead of compassion and acceptance. If you chose this secret rule, you obviously have no qualms about strongly asserting your opinion, and you take it to the point of intimidation.

It is important to look at your feelings of entitlement. You feel entitled to intervene, but some might call it interference when your child is actually an adult. If this is the rarest of events and you feel that strongly about the circumstance, it may well mean that you are being a good parent and making a very hard choice. If, however, this is a common pattern of attempting to influence and manipulate those around you, you must consider that you are trying to hold onto others who otherwise wish to be out of your sphere of influence. Many of those around you might not be there out of love or free will, but because of intimidation. Ask yourself if these are the kinds of relationship dynamics that you really desire. Controlling the choices of your children may be only one manifestation of this attitude; it is not unlikely that this tendency spreads to your relationships with other people too. Examine your means of communication and think about alternatives. By all means, it is best to tell your loved ones exactly how you feel. But also consider drawing a line and practicing compassionate acceptance at a certain point.

Answer B's secret rule reveals that your control tactics involve putting on a good show: *I am entitled to threaten others to gain influence, but I do not feel justified in actually taking action against them.* You are willing to make a threat in hopes of making your point. Yet you then tend to feel guilty about carrying through with that threat. You are ultimately bluffing. Do you want to play such games with a person you love? What will happen if your son does marry this "wrong woman"? How will it affect your life? Why is he not a free agent to do as he wishes? If you chose this secret rule, you are hoping to scare your son into doing what you want.

You obviously feel desperate enough to test your child's loyalty. If he relents and gives up the woman of his choice, what have you proven? Does he really love you or does he just want the security of your money? Do you suppose that you have increased or decreased the trust and love between you? Consider that you may gain his compliance but lose his respect. If fear tactics are a pattern of life, let's face it—you are a bully. It is time to start studying your relationships. Life is about learning from, not controlling, others. You will probably lead a much happier life with more fulfilling relationships if you change your approach.

Answer C reveals that you do not desire to control another: *I have no need to threaten or manipulate others in attempts to get them to do what I desire.* If you chose this secret rule, it is clear you recognize the right of even young adults to make their own choices—perhaps bad choices—if that is what they elect. Sometimes the hardest thing about helping someone you love is not helping at all. If your relatives and friends know that you can accept their behaviors, flawed as they may be, you probably have good relationships that are true and lasting.

By not reacting in a controlling manner, you are likely to establish a healthy trust and confidence with your loved ones. Don't lose this diplomatic trait. It will serve you well, not only with your family, but also with others. Just do one quick check: Do you have no need to manipulate others because they always do what you want anyway, or because you recognize you may lose more than you gain by overtly trying to control them? Confirm that you have let your loved ones develop a healthy sense of their own decision-making skills and that they are not simply making the same exact choices you would make, as though you programmed them long ago.

2. You have a loving, responsible spouse. Lately, however, your mate has been less communicative, while spending more time on the Internet and refusing to explain why. In fact, your spouse simply states, "An adult can do what an adult wishes." You have heard about a new software package that can track a person's e-mails and website visits. Considering the hurt and confusion you are experiencing, will you use this software to investigate what your spouse has been doing?

A. I will use the software to check my spouse's communications indefinitely and secretly. It's my right.

B. I will use the software just to do a brief check. If nothing is amiss, I'll stop prying and respect my spouse's privacy.

C. I will never invade my mate's privacy under any circumstances.

Does it seem fair or reasonable to use a powerful technology at the expense of your partner's privacy? How much are you willing to use the power and control available to you to protect your own vital interest— your marriage? Is it more important to know what is going on or to suffer a bit of anxiety yet maintain the integrity of the relationship? The secret rule for answer A uncovers your belief in full knowledge at all costs: *It is my right to use any power necessary to discover if a loved one is doing anything to jeopardize the relationship.* Are you justifying your snooping with thoughts such as, "Wouldn't it be better to know with whom my spouse is communicating before real problems begin? What is the harm of just checking to see that nothing is amiss, like a checkup at the dentist? If there are no cavities, the peace of mind was well worth it. But if decay is beginning, it's best to nip it in the bud." Probably so. You feel justified in prying into the communications of your mate. If you chose this secret rule, you feel your right to know your spouse's doings supersedes a right to privacy. Obviously, you wouldn't mind if someone checked up on you. Would you?

Cybersnooping is relatively new. How do you feel about checking up on calls or opening your mate's mail? Is there a limit; is there a rule? If you can justify continuous prying into your spouse's private communications, you already have a fundamental lack of trust. Clearly you feel threatened by something or someone. If this lack of trust is a repetitive life pattern, it is something you must clearly reexamine or you will find that there is no one with whom you will ever feel safe or secure. Your tendency to investigate things in devious ways could come back to harm you. What if your partner finds out? Moreover, are you prepared for what you might find? To avoid further problems, consider approaching your concerns in a different way—one that doesn't assume you have the right to delve into someone else's privacy. Try to loosen that notion of control and get your spouse to open up to you on a different level.

Answer B leads to a secret rule that supports exceptions and temporary fixes: *Under special circumstances, I may invade the privacy of my loved one.* In other words, if you feel threatened, you feel justified in using the power and technology available to allay your fears. And once you feel everything is okay, then you are going to stop immediately. And do what, exactly? Throw away the software and never ever check again, or just use it when suspicion rears its ugly head at a later time? If you chose this secret rule, you have rationalized a break in the trust that you have with each other. You have told yourself that you don't really want to spy or know everything your mate says, that you are really a good person acting under extraordinary circumstances. Is that what you really feel?

What constitutes a "little" violation in privacy anyway? And could you really control yourself beyond just a quick check? If this is your secret rule, be wary of self-deception. It is tempting to think you can control any desire to misuse this power, but can you? Consider that your relationships might be clouded with deception and mistrust. Beware of trying to remedy difficult situations through attempts to secretly control your loved ones.

Answer C shows that you uphold honor and respect, even in the face of fear and available power: *There is no justification, whatsoever, for invading my loved one's privacy.* You see signs of change in your mate's behavior. You have a chance to find out something that could be extremely important to your marriage, but you won't. In the end, your integrity will be rewarded and you will be trusted and respected in turn.

In return for your respect, however, you expect honesty. If you are rebuffed in your up-front attempts to find out what is wrong, what will you do then? Will you remain passive and respectful, or will you find another way to uncover the truth? The temptation to reassure ourselves is often very strong. There are so many uncertainties in life. Who can blame a person for wanting to know that something is certain and secure? Your ability to resist the power offered by technology shows that you trust your mate and have a healthy respect for privacy. Privacy is about letting someone have a special place to put his thoughts and feelings. That's probably what you want for someone you love and for yourself.

3. For the past five years, you have been a doorman at a swanky New York City apartment building. You know all of the residents by now; you have a good sense of their personalities and family situations. One man has been particularly demeaning of your role as doorman. He is consistently nasty and negative—not to mention the fact that he never gives you a tip during the holidays, unlike the other tenants. Recently, while this man's wife was on vacation, you saw him in the company of an unfamiliar young woman. He was acting suspicious, avoiding eye contact and rushing past you. You are tempted to tell his wife upon her return—perhaps just to get him in trouble. Will you do it?

A. I will threaten to expose him and see what he does. I want him to hurt a little.

B. I will tell his wife. He needs to be punished.

C. I will not use this power position to hurt anyone involved, even though my feelings are hurt.

Each of us is often in a position where we know information or secrets that would be embarrassing, if not outright damning, to another individual. A personal code of ethics generally prevents the average person from hurting even a relative stranger for no reason. In some ways, we are all a bit beholden to one another. But what if someone who is beholden to you abuses you or makes you feel like less of a person? Does there come a time and place to even the score—to use your little bit of knowledge or power to get back at that person? Is it childish or fair play? If you chose answer A, you do not really believe in harming another with your advantage, but you like the power and will play with it: *I am willing to use my power to scare or threaten someone who has hurt me.* You have a chance to make this man squirm. Of course, it could come back at you. He could try to get you fired for some infraction, real or not. You could also blackmail him for anything from a bottle of whiskey to monthly payments. There are many possibilities available to you.

Remember that wise old saying: "It's all fun and games until somebody gets hurt." Think about the outcome of this power play. What is it you really want from him—reparations for past harm? Do you want him to feel weak or scared? How about an apology? Isn't that what you really want? You have been given an opportunity to get back at him, but not to right some wrong. You can be as mean-spirited as the man who hurt you, or you can find a way to use your situation to smooth some ruffled feathers and not become the type of person that you dislike so much.

Do you believe in "an eye for an eye"? If so, you chose answer B and have the following secret rule: *I am entitled to revenge and to exact punishment on those who hurt me.* You are prepared to create conflict that could have disastrous consequences. Are the consequences commensurate with the harm he inflicted on you? If you chose this secret rule, you are prepared to use your power directly to hurt someone. Do you often feel taken advantage of? Sometimes our anger and desire to right various wrongs can lead us to overreact to a situation with unfortunate consequences. Your secret rule reveals anger and impulsiveness. Be careful.

Consider now whether this secret rule has helped you advance your life and get what you want. This needs to be addressed. Do you like the person you are? Does it feel good to make a mean person suffer? If so, for how long? And don't forget that when you hurt one person, you are probably hurting a whole score of others, too. Is this the way you want to be? Examine your life and see if there isn't a healthier, more direct way to get those who hurt you to apologize.

Answer C's secret rule highlights not the control you seek over others, but the healthy control you have over your own anger: *I won't use my power to intentionally threaten or hurt someone.* Your answer is certainly admirable. You have conquered the human tendency to hit back when hurt. Most likely, you act carefully and have few regrets afterwards.

While you are thinking about reactions, study your motivation. In other words, does your answer represent nobility of spirit or fear of being aggressive? Is it okay for this man to continue abusing you? Do you usually allow people to pick on you? Hopefully, your answer simply represents a solid maturity; you do not need to play dirty. But consider that you might also just be frightened. If you would really like to rat on this guy but are afraid of what would happen to you, then your avoidance might be very wise but also very unsatisfying. You might be angry inside and end up channeling your anger in other unhealthy ways. Examine *why* you won't hurt that obnoxious man, in order to find out more about yourself.

4. You are a high-ranking military officer who has gotten to know your subordinates quite well. In fact, when off duty, your division enjoys a lot of socializing and camaraderie. If the truth be told, you have had your eye on a particular subordinate's significant other for quite some time. You are not involved with anyone. Moreover, you have heard that the subordinate's relationship is on the rocks. Maybe that's why the object of your affection has been anxious to talk with you and has been returning your flirtatious glances! It is within your power to transfer your subordinate to a distant location for six months. That might accelerate a breakup, and would at least give you a better shot at that special someone. Will you order a transfer?

A. I will not order a transfer. It is an abuse of my authority to interfere with the lives of my subordinates.

B. I will transfer the subordinate only if I think the subordinate is bad for the person I desire and doesn't deserve someone so special.

C. I will transfer the subordinate if I feel I love or could love my subordinate's significant other and we have a real shot at a good relationship.

The question is as old as the Bible. In fact, there's a Bible story in which a king covets Bathsheba and sends her husband to be killed in battle. The willingness and ability to use one's power to take sexual advantage represents one of the oldest ethical dilemmas. Answer A's secret rule reveals that you have great self-control when it comes to the relationship between work and love: *I will not use my position of power to advance my romantic life.* One cannot quarrel with your principle. Due to the high standards that are evident in your answer, you are probably equally responsible concerning other opportunities for personal gain.

The question then becomes one of motives. Do you make your responsible choices because you fear being found out? Or, quite differently, do you avoid directly harming a relationship because you respect others' quest for love? Hopefully, you make your decisions out of a healthy respect for others. You fully understand your power, yet fully choose not to abuse it as well. If you have reached that point, you deserve a promotion!

Answer B is really a justification for taking advantage of power opportunities. Its secret rule is as follows: *I will use my professional power for personal gain only if I can see that others will benefit as well.* This answer affords a compromise of standards. Are you capable of making judgments about what is best for other adults? This may be the ultimate rationalization. You are using your position to potentially destroy a relationship. Is that a fair and wise use of your power?

The only way one learns how to use power is to have power. And the only way to determine whether or not you have been using your power righteously is to look at how many lives you have helped and how many you have hurt. If you have exploited your power, you are likely to find that your actions returned to cause you or others grief in the end. Beware of kidding yourself with "pretend compassion." Usually, taking advantage of a power situation does not leave us feeling good at the end of the day.

Answer C's secret rule asserts that taking advantage of power is fine when affection is involved: *Love is so important that I may use any power to obtain it.* Poets and singers have sung the praises of the wonder and beauty of love. Spirituality focuses on how the world needs love, and if we can love and be loved, then everything will be all right. You never hear anyone say, "Don't use your power to get love. Love should come in a different way." When love is involved, everything else seems to take a back seat. If you chose this secret rule, you too believe that love trumps all other considerations.

Is that really what you believe, or are you justifying your actions? Realize that you are taking advantage of your professional power for personal reasons. That is significant. Do you draw a line? Can you lie about another to protect your love? Can you physically harm or intimidate another to foster your love? At some point, then, there must be certain rules that govern your willingness to get or maintain love. Look carefully at your secret rules to see if you have not mistaken love for desire, control, or dominance. If "love" makes you use your power to do or say harmful things to others, maybe you have ultimately missed the point of what love really means. Try winning love without taking advantage of your power position. I bet it will feel even better!

5. You are a highly placed administrator at an organ transplant center. Therefore, you have access to all lists and records. Over the past six months, your young nephew has experienced liver failure, and he now needs a transplant in order to survive. Your brother—the child's father—has begged you to use your "insider" position to adjust the transplant waiting list and move your nephew to the top. None of your colleagues knows your brother's family, so they are not likely to be suspicious of changes made to the list. On one hand, it's not fair to disregard the other families who have been waiting for a long time. But on the other hand, perhaps you are in this very position for a reason—to help your loved one. What will you do?

A. I will not hesitate to help my nephew by placing him at the very top of the list.

B. I will not move my nephew to the top of the list, and I will tell my brother that it was impossible to do anything of the sort.

C. I could justify moving my nephew up a notch or two to satisfy myself and my family.

How much are you willing to use your available power to save the life of someone you love over the life of a stranger? Imagine that you have the power and that no one would be the wiser if you used it. The secret rule behind answer A says, *It is acceptable to use my professional power to help my family, even at the expense of others.* You live by the adage, "Blood is thicker than water." You choose love of family and responsibility to your kin over fairness and integrity. No one can judge whether you would be right or wrong for doing so. You must live according to your own sense of justice.

To confirm that this rule functions well in your life, examine how your conscience would handle the decision. How well could you live with yourself, knowing that you have violated one of the principles of your job, let alone risked the life of another person whose family members feel equally as desperate as your family does? If this secret rule works, you will be fine with using your power to manipulate circumstances for loved ones. You will not suffer guilt, regret, or self-hatred after you fix the list. However, if the rule doesn't work, your sense of internal peace and contentment will be shaken and you will find yourself going over and over your past actions. If that's the case, the rule is in danger of causing you great grief and obsession later in life. Consider making efforts to change it.

Answer B's secret rule claims, *It is not right to use my power to benefit a family member over a stranger.* The list stays as it is, despite your brother's pleas. You have chosen integrity over family needs. And in order to calm your brother's possible wrath, you intend to make an excuse: "I couldn't help it." Your choice reveals a very principled and fair personality when it comes to professionalism. But your white lie—made to calm your brother—shows that you are not 100-percent confident in your decision. Are you likely to beat yourself up in the future, especially if your little nephew doesn't make it?

Is it selfish to help the ones you love? Should you fight your nature to put your family first? If your principles ostracize you from those you love, are they worth it? These questions are asked for the purpose of confirming your choice. You can expect some discomfort either way. But if you find yourself severely torn apart inside after sticking to the rule, then you should reevaluate your rule.

Answer C's secret rule says, *I would cautiously use my power to help a loved one because I would feel too guilty not doing anything.* You have attempted to find the middle ground. You give something to the family and only somewhat violate your oath of fairness. It seems like a reasonable compromise. Is this your usual style—giving a little something to everyone? Maybe in business or politics, such compromises can work, but this is potentially about life and death. Should you apply the same rule? Your desire to find compromise is generally a valuable trait. You are probably an excellent arbitrator. But when it comes to using your power to affect many lives, you are dealing with heavy consequences. If you stick with your answer, know that you will have to tell some lies and do some funny business at some point. A "halfway strategy" will not be as easy as it may seem at first. The demands of the power/love connection are different from those of business and pleasure. Confirm that your secret rule is well suited to the occasion.

Notice that your answer points to the issue of guilt. Your main motivation is that you would feel *guilty* if you didn't manipulate the list in some way. You are likely to suffer less in the long-term if you base your actions on careful thought and true conviction, instead of being bullied by guilt. Your answer may come from a temporary place of fear instead of a permanent place of principles. Once the crisis is over, will you be content with your decision?

6. You have finally become a supervisor at work and now handle a lot more responsibility than before. That is why you are anxious to get the plans for a special presentation completed by this afternoon, but you need a file from your assistant's desk in order to finish. Unfortunately, your assistant is out to lunch and will not be back for an hour. Since you are deter-mined to make progress right away, you decide to get the file from her desk drawer. Upon opening the drawer, you find a bag of marijuana sitting right on top of the papers! What will you do?

A. I will confiscate the marijuana and, when my employee returns, call her into my office, deliver a stern lecture, and fire her.

B. I will leave the marijuana where it is, but when my employee returns, I will give her a stern lecture and tell her to remove the substance from the premises immediately. I will not fire her, but I will give her a firm warning.

C. I will leave the marijuana where it is and simply pretend I didn't see a thing. I'll never mention it to my employee.

Although being in a power position has its perks, there are also many responsibilities involved. Sometimes we are put in the uncomfortable position of calling someone down for misbehavior or a misdemeanor. Some of us will not hesitate to take full command and follow the letter of the law. Some of us will show leniency, while others will shrink from rep-rimanding another person. If you selected answer A, you have no prob-lem exercising your power to its fullest degree. Your secret rule states, *When in a power position, I must take total charge and make aggressive decisions so that I can maintain order.* You take both the law and your job very seri-ously. For you, having power means establishing rules and sticking to them, no matter what. Your answer reveals a certain amount of inflexibil-ity—which is neither good nor bad, for only you can be the judge of how it works in your life. It also shows a respect for justice and the proactive desire to avoid future complications.

Your secret rule allows you to be a strong and efficient leader. It makes you very capable of holding power positions in the professional arena. And chances are that you apply this secret rule to other areas as well, taking a no-nonsense approach to dealing with family and friends. How has this rule functioned in your life? Are you content with the type of relationships that you have at work and at home? Do you feel that you lack forgiveness and often suffer from regret much later? Or has your rule allowed you to keep things simple and surround yourself with those who never inappropriately challenge you? At its worst, choosing answer A highlights an obsessive thirst for power that could isolate you and hurt others unnecessarily. However, at its best, this answer highlights that you know who you are and what you need in order to function in a healthy and successful way.

Answer B's secret rule includes a built-in forgiveness policy: *When in a power position, I should weigh my options and opt for leniency in order to give all parties a fair chance.* In our scenario, you know that the marijuana is illegal and that this employee could cause big problems for the company. But your nature leads you to bend the rules. You have no problem establishing yourself as an authority, but you also shape rules to suit the situation. Answering the following question will let you know whether your secret rule works well in your life: Does this middle ground allow you to feel good about yourself and your ability to work with others, or do you secretly feel resentful, frustrated, or wronged?

By choosing answer B, you reveal that you are not consumed with a thirst for power and control. You are comfortable with being in authority—as shown by your stern lecture and reasonable demands—but are not terribly concerned with following the letter of the law. Knowing this about yourself, you should choose positions that safely allow leniency. If you are in a high-power position where every move counts, your tendency to compromise could get you and those who depend on you in a lot of trouble. But in the right atmosphere, you will prove to be a compassionate leader who often brings out the best in those around you.

If you chose answer C, you do not feel comfortable with power and control. Your secret rule says, *When in a power position, I should avoid conflict by remaining neutral and unassuming, despite rules and regulations.* The truth is that you are easily intimidated and do not enjoy being in power positions. The responsibilities and need for aggression at times makes you feel uncomfortable. Given the scenario above, you probably would feel embarrassed about opening your employee's desk without permission, and would place the guilt on yourself and choose to avoid confrontation. If you didn't realize it before, you now know that you will do better in positions that do not require you to take the lead and be stern.

For you, power and control are not enticing or meaningful. You have no natural thirst for power, nor do you have any draw toward authority positions. If you have found yourself in such positions, you probably experienced a lot of stress and discomfort. This rule is most likely rooted in your personality and would be difficult to change. However, if you are angry at yourself for being fearful and timid, you can take measures to become more assertive. From seminars to self-help books, there is advice out there for those of us who tend to shy away from leadership.

7. You are a photographer who is just starting out. A friend of yours has gotten you a big assignment—a wedding. You initially offered to do the job at a very low price because you just wanted a chance to show how good you are. Yet when you get to the wedding site, you realize that the father of the bride is fabulously wealthy and that you could have charged ten times what you originally requested. The wedding will start in a few hours, and although they might be able to get someone on short notice, the wedding party will be in a vulnerable position if you decide to alter the photography fee. You have them over a barrel and are thinking about upping your price. What will you do?

A. I will not change my price because I agreed to it and that is only fair.

B. I will take advantage of the situation and get as much as I can. I have them just where I want them.

C. I realize I underbid and will make up some story to get at least a little bit more money.

Power comes in many forms. One of the ways to be powerful is to be needed very badly. When in that position, you can set the terms of your service. In such a position, you can also exploit others. If you chose answer A, your secret rule points to the responsible use of power: *It is not right to use positions of power to take advantage of others.* You could easily get more money from this wealthy man, and he might not even mind. For all you know, he might still think it's a bargain. He might even think you are a fool for charging so little. But there is also the chance that he might decide to keep you from ever working in this town again.

Your selection of answer A shows you realize that having power doesn't mean that it is always wise, let alone honest or moral, to use it. You might even realize that the real power will come from the work you do and the reputation you build. You have recognized that trust is a form of power, and that when you are trusted, you will gain even greater opportunities and power in the end. Your secret rule is safe, and as long as you don't beat yourself up for weeks afterwards, it should function very healthily in your life.

Answer B's secret rule says, *I am entitled to use my power to my personal advantage, even if it means taking advantage of others.* You have decided to exploit the opportunity afforded you by being the crucial person at the right time. And you will milk it for all it's worth. There is the possibility that you will anger some important people at the start of your career, however. Try to think two steps ahead. You are vulnerable to the temptations that come with power, and that can harm you in the end.

Moreover, what is your deepest motivation for changing the price? Is it about the money or the chance to feel like the little guy who finally evens the score? Just a short while ago, you were perfectly content with the original earnings. What changed so much between then and now? There is nothing wrong with being a good businessperson and getting what you think you are worth. It is called having self-worth. If, in the past, you encountered a similar situation and exploited it, consider if it worked out as you hoped. Did you gain more respect or friendship because of your shrewd use of power? If this is your first such situation, follow where your actions take you and see how well this secret rule works for you.

The secret rule for answer C is a compromise position: *When opportunity knocks and a little power comes my way, it would be foolish not to get something from it.* You are not crazed with power, but you like to get a little extra benefit from it. So you'll make something up, such as a little lie about the price of film suddenly going up or a fictional assistant who needs to be paid. You find yourself somewhere between feeling a little guilty you are reneging on your agreement and feeling that anybody would do the same thing in your position.

You are fundamentally an honest person just trying to use your power position to gain a little more. But where are your boundaries? Where is the line where you tell yourself that something doesn't seem right? Deciding to squeeze out a few more dollars—even from a billionaire—is a choice, and maybe it's not a big deal. But this secret rule will lead you into other quandaries that will have more severe consequences. How far will you let your secret rule take you across your own boundaries of honesty? That is what you need to know.

8. As personnel director of a large corporation, you have a great deal of latitude regarding who gets hired. Recently, an old friend who hasn't been doing much with his life since high school asked you to get him a job.

Your friend is not the most responsible person—or at least hasn't been in the past. While he is not *unqualified*, he is certainly one of the least qualified candidates applying for a position. If you bring your friend aboard, the department will be deprived of someone more capable. But then again, you wonder if you should give this guy a break. What will you do?

A. I will help an old friend by hiring him. That is what friends are for.

B. I will not hire him. It would be a stupid waste of my power.

C. I will definitely help him by getting him a smaller position in my company, but I cannot hire him for a significant position.

How much will you use your power to help a friend? Power is often about making things happen as you direct. Moreover, it feels good to use your power to help family and friends. Yet the careless exercise of power also makes you vulnerable. You carry responsibility for any mishaps that result from your decisions. So this is a tough question. If you selected answer A, your secret rule ultimately tells you that your power should benefit your personal loyalties, not necessarily your professional integrity: *I should use my power to help a friend, even if I'm not creating an optimal situation.* Part of your concept of power involves the responsibility to provide for your personal connections. And you enjoy being such a provider. That is generous, but consider whether you are truly benefiting yourself and those you love.

Your heart is in a good place; you truly desire to help a friend. Now, are you willing to face all the consequences of putting someone where he might not belong? You could burn yourself *and* your friend if things turn out poorly. Think about tempering your secret rule so that your loyalties are balanced with the practical application of power.

The secret rule for answer B reveals the following: *My power needs to be directed towards my personal success and is not to be frittered away on "favors."* You don't want to waste what you have. You recognize that power should not be foolishly spent on those who might weaken you or make you vulnerable. After all, you will ultimately be responsible for the failures of your old buddy, and that may harm you. Not choosing the best person for the job might also weaken your power.

While on the face of it, your reasoning is quite logical, choosing this rule also suggests that you might tend towards a close-minded—perhaps even selfish—attitude. The wording of answer B reveals that your concern is not largely for the company or for your friend, who might eventually be very embarrassed. It is for yourself. Would you ever use your power to help someone else and not expect anything in return? In other words, can you use your power to help someone who is less fortunate just because it is a nice thing to do? If you are secure and content with your rule, then by all means keep it. But if you find yourself uncomfortable with its focus on self-preservation above all other considerations, you can make efforts to reshape it.

Answer C's secret rule fosters a responsible use of power when it comes to personal connections: *A great benefit of power is being able to help personal connections, but not to the point of putting myself or others at risk.* You might help your friend if he is reasonably qualified, albeit not the best. You are ready to use your power to do a kind act. But you make efforts to assess the risk/reward ratio before you put yourself on the line. And you actively seek a compromise so that all benefit.

You believe you can find a balanced approach to having and using power. You recognize that power in a vacuum—without a chance to exert your will when you want to—is of little value. Just promoting yourself without being able to do something simple such as helping a friend is not desirable to you either. You have a knack for looking at the bigger picture, and that means you are able to wield power wisely, without losing yourself or those for whom you are responsible in the process.

9. You have been diagnosed with a terminal illness and told that there are no treatment options except for a very toxic experimental drug therapy. Success with this treatment is considered a long shot. You don't want to suffer, and you don't want to have your family watch you suffer. Furthermore, you don't want to spend your last days practically comatose; you want to enjoy whatever time is left. In your final days, you wish to be in maximum control of your life. What will you do to ensure that maximum control?

A. I will end my life before there is too much suffering and I am too incapacitated to do so.

B. I will accept my death, and will live as long as I can while taking a minimal amount of pain medicine.

C. I don't accept "terminal" and will use whatever treatments I can to fight death to the last minute.

Terminal illness is an extreme situation, and this question is not meant to look at it lightly. It is meant to highlight how desperate you are to control your own existence. Here is your opportunity to think about how much you will take control of your death in a situation of severe and painful illness. What is the secret rule that governs how you will attempt to control your death? If you chose answer A, you desire absolute control over your life and your experiences: *I own my life and have the right to end it at the moment of my choosing.* This rule highlights a pattern in your life: You like to call all the shots—clearly and loudly. What is your main motivation—fear? Someone who wants to call every shot and make quick decisions usually is consumed by fear. Has this pattern gotten you into trouble? Have you ever tried another approach? If you have always required and demanded self-control, you may enjoy letting go a little more. Sometimes it is a surprisingly fulfilling experience to let life unfold on its own.

On the other hand, if you read this question and have only now decided this is your last chance to control something in your life, perhaps you have come to realize that you want to be more aggressive in life. It is never too late to take greater control of your circumstances. Do not wait until a terminal illness hits to think about this. Imagine that you are just as fearless as in this hypothetical situation, but you are not dying. Now, how much more can you control your life? There is nothing left to be afraid of anymore. You're back in control. But concentrate on finding positive ways of control—not quick fixes.

Answer B's secret rule says, *I do not need to control everything concerning my death, and I will accept help to maintain comfort.* If there is anything that individuals fear more than death, it is suffering. With the final acceptance of mortality, there is a spectrum of tolerance concerning whatever unpleasantness remains in those final days. You wish to live as much of your life as possible and to maintain some control by remaining somewhat alert. Yet you have no problem surrendering a certain amount of control to nature and to medication. This seems to be a healthy compromise. You will allow the experience to unfold, which shows that you are not compulsive about control.

Interestingly, your control comes from not trying to fully control what is happening. Is this your general approach to life—to go with it and take it as it comes? It is a courageous stand and an honest way to live. But the misuse of this rule would be to allow yourself, while alive and well, to unnecessarily suffer through emotional and physical pain when help is available. That may secretly involve too much pride. Strive to find the balance that your answer suggests.

The secret rule for answer C highlights an optimistic approach to control: *I can control when my own life and death will occur if I believe enough in my own power.* If you want to have a miracle, you must believe. That may be a spiritual belief or a belief in new and alternative treatments for what were previously viewed as terminal conditions. But when is belief a form of denial and an obsession with control? After all, at some point, we are all terminal. If you chose this secret rule, you have not yet accepted your mortality, and you insist on controlling it. That does not mean that you should not try anything and everything available. It means that the reality of finality hasn't quite sunk in yet.

It is a common occurrence to hear of someone surviving well beyond his or her doctor's prediction. If we all passively accepted our supposed fate, many would succumb who surely could have overcome their afflictions. The area of concern in this chapter is control, though. What does your answer say about your need to control every aspect of life? Wisely used, your secret rule gives you perseverance and toughness. But foolishly applied, your secret rule could bring you tremendous anxiety and unrealistic expectations. Think of the pattern that this question highlights. Do you expect too much control from yourself? Are you ever willing to let nature take its course after putting up reasonable resistance?

10. You are the coach of a very promising athlete. Your protégé is definitely on the road to becoming a world contender, if not a world champion, in his sport. But you notice that he has become distracted over the past few weeks. You have seen too many athletes ruin their chances by getting caught up in romance issues and family problems. While this player is under your training, you are in a position to control how much outside contact he maintains. In effect, you could keep letters, emails, and phone calls from him. These communications might be very supportive, even uplifting, but they could also be quite upsetting and distracting. If you give this athlete the choice, he is likely to request his mail and calls, making you feel obligated to allow him such contact. If you just take the initiative and control all communication until after the championship game of the season, you might help this athlete's entire career—as well as, of course, your own! Think fame, endorsements, and big money. What will you do?

A. I will explain that I could control his outside contact for his own good and then let him decide what protocol is best.

B. I will certainly ask his opinion on the matter, but will ultimately do what I feel is best.

C. I will not ask him at all. I will tell him that I'm the coach, I know what is best, and he had better do what I say.

This question is about the morality of using power to control others' lives—for their benefit and for yours. Ostensibly, your intentions are to do something good for the person involved. Can you rightfully suspend an individual's liberties for his own good? Then there's the element of your own ego and pleasure. Answer A is built on a secret rule that says, *I do not have the right to control another person's personal life, even if it means that neither of us benefit.* You will let a young, possibly emotional and immature person call his own shots. You feel it is more important that his rights be respected; you value an individual and his free will more than any amount of success. You feel that helping someone against his will is fundamentally wrong, and that making money or advancing his career does not mitigate the wrong being done.

Your choice of answer A shows that you are not a very controlling person. You must also believe that individuals are supposed to make their own mistakes and you do not need to protect anyone from himself. Are there any circumstances in which you might feel justified in maintaining some kind of control? Suppose the athlete's father died hours before the big match. Would you still tell him, even though a couple of hours difference might make the greatest difference in how he performs?

The secret rule behind answer B argues, *I value others' opinions, but if I am in a position of control, I ultimately call the shots.* You are not scared of controlling things; in fact, you probably like it. You feel you know best. On one hand, you are in a power position for a reason, and perhaps your authority will help all involved. But being controlling can also backfire. For example, you might be rejected by your protégé if he finds out you did not respect his wishes. If he tells you that he wants to get everything sent to him and you lie, does success justify your decision?

You are willing to risk a lot to help someone. Do you often feel the need to control loved ones or friends to prevent them from making life mistakes? Your heart may be in the right place, but you may not be able to shield anyone from life's harsh realities for any length of time. Making one's own mistakes is part of growing up and maturing. Make sure that your good intentions do not ultimately interfere with the natural growth process that we all must experience.

Answer C underscores an obsession with control: *I feel justified in exercising whatever control is necessary to ensure success.* If you chose this secret rule, you desire dominance and absolute authority. Has this control benefited your coworkers, protégés, and friends? You are probably headstrong and, at times, overbearing. Do you intimidate others? Are they afraid to tell you how they feel?

While your steamroller approach may have benefited some, you may have hurt many others, perhaps unwittingly, as you strove for success. Are you content with such a way of life? If not, you can rework your secret rule, making great efforts to see situations from many perspectives—not just your own.

CONCLUSION

What have you decided about your perspective on power and control? Did you learn anything new about yourself? Hopefully, this chapter has highlighted both destructive and constructive patterns in your life. If you realized that you tend to be a little heavy-handed when it comes to being in charge, making a concerted effort to share power is definitely an option. And if you found out that you have not been giving yourself a share of the say, perhaps you can consciously and slowly work on asserting yourself. There are always opportunities, big and small, to adopt a healthier perspective. Remember, the best goal is to strike a balance. When it comes to power and control, respecting yourself and others is a healthy goal and the ultimate ideal.

5. Health

A votre santé . . . salud . . . l'chaim . . . to your health! We habitually toast to our health because, in truth, what could be more important? Beyond money, even beyond love, is life. So what will you do to stay alive and preferably healthy? After all, you must endeavor not only to survive but also to be reasonably mobile and energetic.

There is a wide variation in what people will do to maintain health. I have a colleague who is a strict vegan and finds that lifestyle most healthful. He lives on a fraction of what most of us take in. His water is purified, and he never eats pasta, rice, cake, ice cream, sushi, or anything fun! Would you do that to save your life? How disciplined or motivated are you to survive? Would you run two, five, or even ten miles a day? Your secret rules regarding the maintenance of your physical structure are most important to discover. What is your obligation to yourself to know the latest treatments that could be of value to you? Acupuncture, homeopathy, and chiropractic have had a great following lately. Have you heard of them? What is your secret rule on using these types of therapies?

And then there is mental health. Most people don't realize how powerfully our emotions affect our bodies. There are many things we can do beyond diet and exercise to improve general health. How many do you know about? How many are you doing? Training in meditation and stress management techniques is widely available. Have you explored any of those paths? How do you remain calm and centered in a crazy world? You will find your answers to some of these questions by reading and answering the health-related questions below. Don't be surprised if you grow motivated to change a few of your secret rules and pursue a healthier approach to life!

1. You are fifty years old, married, and have two adolescent children. Recently, you were diagnosed with a rare form of cancer. Your doctors

believe there are no treatments for your condition. They can offer only pain management. So they advise you to make the best of the six months to a year that you have left. Yet upon doing your own research, you hear about an alternative treatment performed by certain Swiss physicians. It offers some hope for a remission or cure, although there certainly is no guarantee. This new option is very expensive. Your insurance won't cover the treatment and the cost would deplete your savings account. You'd even have to sell your home in order to pay for it. Moreover, you would have to move to Switzerland for several months, and you cannot afford to take your family with you. Your spouse would have to continue working and the family would be financially stressed. If the treatment were not successful, they would receive a modest payment from your life insurance—$50,000. While that money would help, it would not restore their former lifestyle. You must decide whether the possibility of this treatment's success is worth your family's present security. What will you do?

A. I won't waste the money on unproven treatments; I'll simply accept my fate.

B. I will try any treatment and spend any money—anytime, anywhere—to save my life.

C. I will go to Switzerland *only* if my family gives me total approval.

Some of us feel more strongly than others when it comes to prolonging life. Is it worth risking everything for a chance at recovery, given the sacrifices required? If you selected answer A, your accompanying secret rule states the following: *My health is not more important than the security and safety of my family.* You accept your fate and will not risk your family's security on the slight chance that you might enhance your health and gain extra time. There are things worse than dying, and one of them might be the feeling that you have left your spouse and children to suffer because of your own fear of death. If you chose this secret rule, your health concerns do not take priority over your family life. You see your health needs as one of several priorities.

This answer also points out that you have begun to accept your death. This is a big part of your perception of health. For you, health is not just physical. It involves healthy decision-making for everyone involved. It involves a healthy spiritual outlook on this life. This choice indicates a deep sense of love and, more than that, a sense of fairness. If you live this way already, you have a deeply ingrained sense of family community that will bring you peace in times of need.

The secret rule serving as the foundation for answer B shows that you heavily prioritize your own health: *My life is more important than the economic and physical comforts of my family.* This does not imply that you are selfish; perhaps you feel that without you, your family members would be miserable. Maybe you are scared for them. But while granting that everyone should and naturally does have a desire and will to survive when faced with death, we all have limits. We may not, for example, steal a life jacket from a weakened person, causing her death to save our own lives. Of course, others might draw the line at cannibalism. The problem with having this secret rule is that it might also imply a generalized narcissism.

With a world centered on yourself, you might find it hard to discover or meet the emotional needs of others. Consider whether or not this pattern has brought you the closeness in relationships that you desire. Moreover, your secret rule might promote a tremendous fear of illness and death. Consider that you might need to work on the acceptance of illness and death as part of the natural cycle. Also know that you can start changing your fears by reading books and attending seminars on spirituality, acceptance, and awareness.

Answer C's secret rule attempts to take a middle road: *I am willing to compromise my health status according to my family's opinion and needs.* Compromise is often a good thing in life, but for this particular question, it may not be so good. Are you just passing the buck to avoid making a decision yourself? Are you asking too much from family members? Are you confident that, in the end, they will do what they can to reestablish your health? The military tradition often encourages its members to avoid leaving one of their own behind on the battlefield, even if saving them would cost others their lives. Family loyalties aren't much different.

While it is intelligent and caring to solicit your family's feelings about your health options, it is not fair to actually ask your loved ones to make that decision. How can a child vote against his parent's chance to live? Therefore, it is an illusion that this answer provides a democratic and considerate approach. Your answer suggests that you are scared to be the primary agent in your own health issues and that you might rely too much on others to take the responsibility out of your own hands.

2. Your family enjoys longevity. None of your older relatives has suffered from heart disease. Yet your doctor recently found that you are at high risk for a heart attack. She attributes the risk to poor lifestyle habits and instructs you to lose weight, clean up your diet, and exercise regularly. She also urges you to get a less stressful job. You, however, feel fine. Except for slowing down a bit with age, you feel as though you have nothing to complain about. So you have a little tummy—who cares? Your job pays well and, most of all, you really like it. How many of the doctor's orders will you follow?

A. I don't *feel* ill, so I am not going to follow any of her instructions.

B. I will make all of the necessary changes to improve my health.

C. I am committed to changing my eating habits and altering my sedentary lifestyle, but I will not leave my job.

Your physician recommends that you change your whole lifestyle so you can live longer. How far does your secret rule allow you to take this advice? The secret rule corresponding with answer A is quite clear: *I judge my health on how I feel, not on a lab report or on what a so-called "average" person should do.* You feel fine and that is the main criterion in determining how you live your life. If this is your secret rule, you are self-reliant and have never put too much stock in others' advice. You rely on your feelings and instincts to guide you, even when it comes to health problems. But is your self-reliance turning into self-defiance? Are you defying your physical body because you don't want to admit that you are as vulnerable and fragile as everyone else is?

You find it hard to believe that the rules of life should apply to you. You are an individualist. You believe in following your instincts. But if you honor these instincts, you must also be willing to face what could be some chinks in your armor. It may serve you well to live intensely and freely for as long as you can. But you may have to pay a price for that, and it could be as high as your life. Your present approach is undoubtedly high-risk. Consider listening to yourself *and* others, and making an intelligent decision from there. Also consider listening with more than your head; listen with your body and your deepest self. If we just listen with our heads, we can jumble things up with anger, stubbornness, and arrogance. The downside of the individualist is an unwillingness to listen to and learn from others—sometimes more qualified others.

Answer B's secret rule says, *I trust a physician's orders completely and I will follow all advice so I can live as long as possible.* Your doctor's recommendations have just turned your life upside down. You now have to make significant changes. Are you willing to base all of this on a professional's opinion and not your own instincts? Aren't you going to miss all the things you used to do? If you chose this secret rule, you are very open to others' advice, and that can be healthy. You are willing to follow orders, and seem not to be obsessed with controlling every aspect of your life. You show some real flexibility in your personality. Flexibility is probably one of the key traits to maintaining good health.

This secret rule would seem to serve you well, except for one small detail. Give yourself the right to question advice and contribute to your own health regimen. Do not be afraid to take part in your own healthcare and to consider your own instincts as well. Remember that making such significant changes can result in boredom and lack of purpose, which can also shorten one's life. It is important to become proactive. Search for ways to stimulate your life and give yourself something to look forward to. That is as essential to good health as "taking it easy." You will be missing the work you really enjoy. If you can replace the work with something equally stimulating, then you will succeed in making major health transitions.

The secret rule behind answer C is a halfway response to the advice of your health practitioner: *I realize I have to take care of my body, but I refuse to give up everything I really love; I will take some of my doctor's suggestions, but not all of them.* You recognize that you have not cared for yourself by today's standards. You accept this, but are also determined to continue your work and feelings of productivity. You know your own mind and are strong-willed. To acknowledge that big changes are required and yet stand firm on your need to do what gives you pleasure represents a good balance of giving and receiving. That's one way to look at it.

Here's another. Strong-minded people are prone to self-deception, and your greatest weakness could be that you denied or ignored real warning signs because you were afraid to give up your work. Is your ego wrapped up too tightly in your profession? Do you equate "career" with "life"? If you can manage work by reducing the stress load and making significant changes, maybe you do not have to stop completely. But if your job is truly hard on your body, you really ought to consider the advice of someone who knows and cares about your health.

3. You have always been unhappy with your physical appearance and have finally decided to get reconstructive surgery. A new look is sure to boost your confidence, and might even increase your chances of finding someone special. But your doctors inform you that, due to your diabetes and a congenital bleeding disorder, the surgery is much riskier than usual. Friends and relatives, while understanding your desires, have advised you not to go ahead with the surgery. They say you look just fine. Considering the possibility of complications, will you go for it?

A. No. Appearance is not *that* important.

B. Yes. I need to feel attractive to feel happy.

C. Yes. If I die or become ill, it was God's will and my destiny.

On one level, this question is about vanity over health. On another level, it is also about health status as a matter of destiny—chance, luck, fate, karma. If you chose answer A, you hold a secret rule that honors life over looks: *My health is much more important than my looks, so I won't place it in jeopardy.* Obviously, you take a conservative approach to life and health. In some sense, you feel vulnerable to forces around you. You don't consider yourself lucky and, in fact, probably think you are already getting more than your fair share of bad luck. But because of your prudent outlook, you will most likely be safe and, barring tragedy, your health will remain good. Yet here's an important question: Are you happy enough? It is understandable not to take this risk, but do you ever take any risks at all in order to get that extra kick out of life?

If you follow answer A's secret rule to its fullest conclusion, you might feel frustrated with life. This was your big chance to finally get what you really wanted and now, once again, something is going wrong. Certainly, you should avoid taking risks that don't seem worthwhile. But, at the same time, you should try to find other ways to make up for what you cannot have. Maybe you can buy yourself some great clothes, go for an expensive spa weekend, or purchase a pair of trendy glasses. Find other ways to treat yourself instead of just abandoning all effort.

Answer B's secret rule shows a definite firmness once you set a goal for yourself: *I am willing to take certain health risks to look my best.* In a nutshell, your cosmetic woes are so severe that you are willing to put your health at risk in order to overcome them. If you chose this secret rule, you are a risk-taker. Maybe it hasn't always been true, but you've somehow learned that a no-risk approach to life hasn't given you what you want. It may appear to be about vanity, but your secret rule also involves finally feeling great about yourself. It's your life and your call. Just confirm that your priorities are where you want them to be.

Continuing with answer B's secret rule, someplace inside your head you either feel you are not destined for complications or, quite frankly, it doesn't matter much. Only you can decide how important the surgery is. Only you know what it feels like to live in your present body. Your conviction is admirable. But realize there are also middle roads that might suit you well. Perhaps you can channel your conviction into other approaches. Maybe you can take the risk of treating yourself in other ways. Maybe you can take the risk of loving yourself for exactly what you are right now.

The secret rule behind answer C states, *My appearance is worth reasonable risk, and whatever results from my efforts to improve it are simply fated.* You are a fatalist. You want this surgery and feel that if it is your destiny to be more attractive, life will work out just great. Whether you call it God's will, fate, or destiny, you have lived long enough to see that there is illogic and unfairness in the world. The only sense you can make of it is that each event is not random but, indeed, part of a greater plan.

This secret rule may provide you with the courage to go ahead. It's not just good doctors and vitamins that keep you strong. You see yourself as part of a larger design and if you are optimistic, you also believe that the plan will let you stay alive, look more attractive than ever, and enjoy the happiest days of your life. But also realize that this answer implies that a greater force is in control—not you. Do you tend to chalk up all events and their results to fate? Can you draw a healthy line between fate and personal responsibility? After all, you could say that fate decided to give you the original face and body in the first place.

4. You are the captain of your college sports team. Your efforts and talents have truly gotten the team where it is today. Moreover, your teammates desperately need you to win the championship. It is your senior year, and perhaps your only chance to win a big tournament and become a national champion. But in the last game, you seriously injured your knee. The medical team says there is a strong possibility that if you run on it or are hit by another player, you could permanently injure your knee and suffer chronic pain. The coach and the trainer know the extent of your injury. They

believe that with medications and special taping, they can get you through the game without permanent injury. You are not sure whether they have your best interests at heart, however. A college championship would boost their careers too and put the school on the map. Ultimately, it is your decision. If you don't play, your teammates will be disappointed at the very least. You love those guys and don't want to let them down. What will you do?

A. I will play, for my sake and the team's sake.

B. I will not play, despite the recommendations of my coach and trainer.

C. I will play only if the team is losing toward the end of the game and there is a chance to turn things around.

How important is it to be a champion? How much of your health will you risk for your team? Behind answer A, there is a secret rule that reveals the strength of your conviction and commitment: *I am willing to risk full health for a possible victory that may happen only once in my lifetime.* You look at victory as a priority, and you are willing to risk your health in the face of a challenge.

If this rule has worked well for you in the past, stick with it. But has it served you well? Be sure that you consider the big picture before jumping to a decision out of momentum or excitement. Doesn't it matter if you are permanently injured and forced to live in chronic pain? For you, going all out is what gives life meaning; you abandon all sense of risk or consequence to realize your original goals. Again, there is nothing wrong with this lifestyle; just make sure that it serves you best. You will be faced with such health challenges at some point in your life, if you have not been already. It could even happen when you are much older and have the chance to climb a tree with your grandchild. If the glory of the moment and the resulting memories are enough reward, then go for it. But if you tend to get angry with yourself and carry regret, this secret rule might be harming you.

Answer B's secret rule prioritizes the whole picture instead of the moment: *My long-term health is not worth risking for any single event.* You accept the wise advice of those who have nothing personally to gain from your actions. You tend to weigh the prize against the loss. Here, you have decided that it is not worth risking pain and debility for a cheer and a trophy you can't even take home. You may disappoint others, but you are entitled to save yourself.

If you chose answer B, you are a practical person. You are not prone to excessive risk or excess in general. That is a sign of neither weakness nor lack of devotion to your teammates. A few minutes of glory will not replace years of pain. If you forced yourself to play against your better judgment, or because you were shamed or goaded into it, and then got hurt, you would feel angry and bitter for a long time to come. The championship victory would be bittersweet. You can only take great risks with an open heart, for you rely not simply on padding and medicinals but on a deep sense of self to get yourself through an ordeal.

Answer C stems from the following secret rule: *My health comes first, but I will take chances with it if that is the absolute last resort available.* You are planning to sit it out. You have decided that it is too risky to play, but you feel a bit guilty that your team may lose because of you. So if necessary, you will play the end of the game. If you chose this secret rule, you tend to be indecisive, hoping that decisions will be made for you.

There is no right answer to this question. But you chose an answer that plays a middle ground so that you do not have to make a firm decision. This is probably a pattern in your life. You often hedge your bet, hoping that events will decide themselves or that extreme situations will sway you at a key moment. Exploring your true nature and priorities, making a firm decision that suits you from the start, is as important as being the hero.

5. This has been a terrible day at work. You lost clients, fought with the boss, and had your best assistant quit in order to accept another job. Then, on the way home, someone cut you off and forced you onto the shoulder of the highway, nearly causing a serious accident. When you finally get home, you are very upset and tense. How do you release your unpleasant feelings?

A. I expel them somehow, either through physical activity or by sharing with friends and family.

B. I bury my feelings in food, drink, or other substances.

C. I withdraw into myself for a while.

How do you handle stress? All of us have ways to manage disappointment, conflict, frustration, and loss. There are many approaches, and the one you have been using may not be the most calming and healing.

Some strategies are more effective than others. Answer A is the result of a secret rule that allows you to express your upset: *I can release unpleasant feelings by expressing them in movement, noise, and words—without any shame.* You expel your stress by throwing it back into the world. You don't like to keep things pent up. Exercise can help you sweat it out; talking with others lets you verbally release it. These are healthy outlets. You have already found that they work.

If you chose answer A, you have learned to care for yourself and honor yourself through proper stress management. Whether it involves a friend or the treadmill, you understand the secret to stress management and will stay at your peak most of the time. The frustrations and irritations of life cannot be avoided and you seem to know this. You are far ahead of so many others who allow stress to take over.

The secret rule behind answer B points to a quick but unhealthy remedy: *I am entitled to a quick fix; if I'm anxious, I'll distract myself with substances that make things bearable.* Actually, you are entitled to something much healthier and more reliable than a quick fix. You have told yourself that the least you deserve is something to eat or drink to make it all feel better. You have found that temporary physical fulfillment gets you through life's ugly stuff. Comfort food, calming drinks, and perhaps even other substances certainly can bring your mind into another world, but not for very long. You are caught in a dangerous cycle.

For most of us, there is nothing wrong with a drink after work or some chips and dip to feel comfy inside. The problem is that it calms and soothes but never relieves what is really going on. These solutions are much like painkillers. They mask the problem, and briefly at that. If the underlying pain is never addressed, the problems go deeper and the cover-up eventually must be more powerful to do the same job. Consider that this secret rule should be modified or expanded to allow for a discharge of the underlying unpleasantness. Keep the comfort, but use it more sparingly, or only when you have already faced the worst of it and are truly ready for a reward.

Answer C is born from a secret rule that prioritizes silence and aloneness: *I expect myself to carry my stress alone and in silence; by waiting it out, the stress will subside.* Wow! You expect a lot from yourself! Sometimes letting time pass and being on your own *can* give you the needed space to let the stress drain away. But don't be so sure that this is always the best choice. Has this rule really worked for you? Have you tried talking to someone who knows how to listen? Have you let yourself throw your stress into a jog or onto the piano keys? Try a more active alternative and see if the stress drains more quickly.

I am not suggesting that rehashing old business makes things better or that flinging yourself onto an exercise machine will solve all of your anxiety. But sometimes "retreat" means avoidance or even denial. When alone, do you force yourself to devise new methods of management or do you just let stress stew? The danger in retreat is that you might never face or try to fix what is really going on. It might even be a way to bury the problem deeper, which is definitely not helpful. Moreover, retreat might be a sign that you see yourself as too fragile or beaten to fight your stress in a more active manner. Look to your life so far, and decide whether or not this rule has done more harm than good.

6. Lately, you have been experiencing increased fatigue, headaches, and even a few strange spots on your skin—definitely not normal. You are still able to perform your daily activities, but life is getting more difficult. You find yourself struggling through what used to feel like a normal day. What will you do?

A. I will wait for the spots, headaches, and fatigue to go away. I am probably fine.

B. I will go to a doctor right away. This could be serious.

C. I will use alternative therapy and get a little extra rest. I can help myself if I believe I can. To rule out a serious problem, or as a last resort, I may consult a physician.

This question has to do with how you handle a possible health challenge. Most illnesses are self-limiting—statistically. If you wait long enough, most things will go away on their own. But we all know that every problem doesn't go away on its own, and that immediate action is sometimes required. On occasion you are literally in a fight for your life. So what do you do when you feel or see your body changing? If answer A is your choice, you put a lot of hope and faith in the body's natural resilience: *I'm not interested in medical attention unless I am severely ill and literally cannot function.* In the past and maybe for most of your life, you have probably been faced with medical problems that were ultimately resolved on their own. You continue to count on the law of averages or some such mythical law. But besides sheer confidence in your fate, this rule could be rooted in fear or laziness.

Getting ill to you means that you are vulnerable and ultimately mortal. You don't like mortal; mortal means death. If you are in the middle-age years, this is a way of avoiding the realities of aging as well. If you don't see a doctor when symptoms start to get serious, you are eventually bound to pass the point of no return—a place from which you cannot be cured. If you tell yourself that treatment is too expensive, that doctors are in it for the money, or that only complainers or weak-willed individuals need doctors, you are in deep denial. There is a balance that you must find between running to the doctor for the smallest complaint and avoiding something serious. If you fail to adjust your secret rule to a more moderate point of view, it could lead to a fatal error.

Answer B's secret rule reveals your faith in the medical community and your acceptance of help: *When faced with symptoms, I need solid reassurance from a medical professional that I am okay.* Generally, this approach does little harm and potentially much good. If you chose this secret rule, you accept that serious illness is possible and that you are not invincible. You also accept the reality of your changing body and understand that we are mortal beings who generally get sick before we die.

The downside of going to the doctor for every single health complication is that you live in constant fear of bad news and become reliant on a professional's word. You may find that you expect catastrophe from the mildest of symptoms. When symptoms are not so severe, do you ever try to change your lifestyle first? For example, if you are chronically fatigued, have you actually tried getting more rest and better nutrition? Do you make everything a medical issue when, in fact, it may be social? Self-help is often an option. Do you ever use it? Consider how much you really expect a doctor to do. If every symptom is perceived as being serious or life threatening, then you have other issues which you are failing to address.

Answer C's secret rule asserts, *I use medical doctors as a last resort and rely almost entirely on myself for healing.* You are self-determined. You like to use natural methods before seeking medical attention. If you chose this secret rule, then you place a large responsibility on yourself to diagnose and treat your medical problems. It can be a heavy burden. Are you adequately knowledgeable? You also are likely to be a bit skeptical about

Western medicine and have come to rely on alternative or holistic methods. While these can be very helpful, they are often best used for chronic conditions that were already diagnosed. If you feel that Western medicine has virtually no place in your life, then you are missing out on some of the great advances of the civilized world and placing an inordinate responsibility on yourself, which may not be wise. It is intelligent to be involved with your own treatments and aware of all treatment options, but only good can come out of at least listening to professional advice.

We all have a blind spot to our own health. That's why doctors are advised not to treat themselves and their families. And most individuals have some denial about a serious or life-threatening illness. If you think that everything is stress-related or that all problems can be solved with a self-help book, your zeal may land you in dire circumstances. A more moderate approach and less antipathy toward modern medicine may give you the greatest health and longest life.

7. A good friend invites you to a party at a very luxurious home. You do not know the hosts personally, but you are aware that they enjoy high economic and social status. You might make some great business contacts over the course of the evening, so you are more than excited to go. After being at the party for a while, the guests begin to pull out various recreational drugs. You are very surprised and also feel a bit awkward. After all, you experimented a little when you were young but have not been around drugs for a long time. You are offered everything imaginable, and certain guests are pressuring you to "join in the fun." You are aware that this drug use is illegal and can harm your health. Other guests argue that they use drugs responsibly and continue to feel great. Furthermore, they claim that every adult has a right to regulate his or her own tastes and desires. One guest poses the following question: Suppose eating beef was declared illegal because it was presumed generally unhealthy and morally wrong. Would you blindly accept that restriction? After thinking about their comments, which of the following statements most closely defines the rule you live by?

A. If the government says something is bad for us, there's a reason. We should obey the government and not use what it prohibits.

B. Every adult has the right to consume whatever he desires—without interference from anyone.

C. Doctors and specialized health professionals know what is best for us. We should follow that advice.

Who makes your health decisions—you? The government? The health-care community? Choice A's secret rule looks to a centralized authority figure: *I trust the government to tell me how to manage my health.* So if something is illegal, you won't use it. You feel that the government knows what is best for you and has your best interests at heart. You probably also suspect that many people cannot be trusted to manage their own health concerns and that they must be protected from themselves. You are concerned that people will hurt themselves without proper controls. But where should the restrictions end? Should the government tell people what they should read or see?

While your beliefs about what is best for the citizenry are certainly heartfelt, you lack confidence in yourself and others. You see people, in general, as prone to self-destruction when it comes to health and habits. On the positive side, you have respect for and faith in your government. But be aware of blind acceptance when it comes to your health. If the law is the only reason for not making your own health and substance decisions, you are stopping short of full awareness. Part of you lacks confidence in yourself to make health and lifestyle choices; you cannot trust your own judgment, so you point to Uncle Sam to legitimize your fears and feelings. Why can't you trust yourself? In the final analysis, who owns your body—you or the state?

The secret rule behind answer B reveals your belief in self-made health decisions: *I have the right to do whatever I desire with my body so, ultimately, I make the decisions concerning what I consume.* You are saying that there should be no set rules governing what a person does to or for himself. If you follow this secret rule, you clearly feel that you are the master of your own fate—regarding health and other areas of life—probably as long as no one else is harmed. This nice sentiment, however, must be contrasted with the reality that although many individuals claim to be able to handle one or another substance, legal or otherwise, they cannot. It is a known fact that many people cannot quit drinking, taking drugs, or smoking cigarettes without some real support and aid. You believe in a sense of absolute freedom, but do you really believe that everyone is healthy enough to make good decisions? Do you have a problem even with limited legal control such as the establishment of a drinking age?

If you are truly in control of yourself, your secret rule will function well in your life. But if you feel that you can trust everyone to behave sensibly, you will undoubtedly experience some losses and pain for your principle. Sometimes it is not such a bad idea to have regulations enforced by the law or the medical community. Your distrust of authority is certainly understandable regarding certain issues, but it may lead to unhealthy idealism concerning some substances.

The secret rule behind answer C is as follows: *I trust health professionals and experts to provide sensible advice about what is and is not healthy.* You don't want the government to make the rules, but you are willing to trust presumably impartial scientists to decide what is best for you and the rest of the citizenry. If you chose this secret rule, you have faith in the health community. By choosing this rule, you have tried to find the middle ground between absolute freedom and intrusive government regulations and laws. You are willing to listen and to take some advice—that of health professionals—which shows a healthy attitude. Yet at the same time, confirm that you are making your own decisions as well.

No one has certain knowledge of the best way to go about ensuring safety while appreciating freedom. Yet answer C presents the most measured and balanced approach of those offered above. It seems that you listen to both sides of an issue and present the most reasonable answer. Your measured approach to difficult problems should be sought out as a valuable resource, and one would hope that this trait is active in all aspects of your life.

8. At forty-something years of age, you have been diagnosed with a serious illness. You are married and have a young child. In fact, you have every reason to live. While you are trying to believe that your will can pull you through this sickness, your spouse has become very negative, growing angry with you and, in effect, blaming you for getting ill and messing up your family's life plans. You have put great faith in some new holistic methods, but your mate only ridicules you for trying alternative treatments. Your mate also expects you to continue working despite extreme fatigue and weakness, and you have begun to feel that you are somehow failing the family. With all that is going on, you are becoming depressed. You see a psychiatrist who, after several sessions, advises you to separate from your spouse for the duration of your treatment. He says that you have a good shot at getting well, but not in such a difficult environment. What will you do?

A. I will separate from my spouse, if only on a trial basis, in order to save myself.

B. I could never leave my spouse—not even to get well.

C. If I continue to worsen over time, despite my best efforts to get well, I will reluctantly consider a separation.

How much of the established order are you willing to disrupt in order to pursue your own health? Does an individual really need the support of others to get well, or is it only an added bonus? And if the support is lacking from the person closest to your heart, is it wise or even fair to leave in order to save yourself? This question has been presented to me on several occasions; it is very much a real issue and one that receives very little attention. Many people assume that, in times of crisis, the life partner routinely stands shoulder to shoulder to fight the illness. But that is not always true. What would you do if you needed all the energy and luck to fight a serious illness but your partner was working against your healing? If you chose answer A, your secret rule places your recovery first: *Above all else I must survive, even if it means leaving my life partner to do so.* You realize that your partner is making you worse. Now you gotta do what you gotta do.

If you follow this secret rule, you are a strong, self-respecting person. You have mobilized your energies and truly intend to get well. This may be a new behavior for you, but crises often bring out the deepest parts of ourselves when we least expect it. Somehow you have realized that getting well is more important than maintaining your home life, if it comes to that. After all, your mate is not really fulfilling the promise of unconditional love. You recognize that there is a relationship between support and health. Overcoming a serious illness often depends on positive thinking and an unbending determination to do whatever is required. Having done what is required, one would expect your prognosis to improve dramatically.

Answer B's secret rule does not allow you to break from your marriage commitment: *My primary relationship is the most important part of my life and supersedes any concerns about how it affects my physical health.* You'd make a great soldier, political confidant, and spouse because you value relationships and commitments over any personal needs. It is an admirable trait in its place. Is there no room for exceptions, though? Are you not entitled to save yourself? The passion of your devotion is certainly noble, but it causes you to disrespect and devalue yourself. Is that noble?

Moreover, do appearances or convention play a role in your decision? Review the times when you put loyalty above personal needs. Did you feel good about the outcome? While your fidelity is to be commended, consider whether you allow yourself any flexibility for exceptional circumstances. Sometimes it is the bending willow that survives the storm while the solid oak is toppled despite its deep roots. It is not selfish to tend to your own needs in times of distress, particularly when your partner is not supporting you at all.

Choice C attempts to etch out a blurry secret rule: *I would consider leaving my relationship for my health only in the most extreme of circumstances.* Either from loyalty or disbelief, you choose to wait until there is no doubt whatsoever that your spouse is negatively affecting your health. There is a spark of self-preservation hidden within your undying devotion. If this secret rule functions in your life, you have traditionally honored the needs of others over your own needs. You have usually expected that your needs would be the last to be met. If leaving is an option, what do you fear most about it? How will you know when it's time to go? Do you understand the concept of getting your own needs met?

As an individual reluctant to stand up for yourself, even when you are in the direst of circumstances, choosing the life-saving option may begin a whole new era of self-expression and assertion of your equality. Sometimes it is scary to do the right thing. When we do it anyway, we call it courage.

9. You are a health counselor assigned to a sixty-year-old patient who refuses to continue on a life-saving treatment called dialysis. In addition to failing kidney function, this patient suffers from severe diabetes that has resulted in significant loss of vision, the amputation of one leg, and chronic pain. Furthermore, his one son lives very far away. Local nieces and nephews don't seem to care. So he has decided not to prolong his life with complicated treatments. After hearing his story, what will you recommend?

A. The patient should be allowed to cease treatment immediately.

B. The man should be considered suicidal and forced to continue treatment.

C. The patient should be strongly encouraged to take the treatments— even shamed into taking them, if necessary—but he should not be forced against his will.

When it comes to situations in which health is very poor, who is to decide when a life is still worth living? Are we each entitled to make that choice, or should a professional decide for us? Is it important to live just to be alive, or is life valuable only in the context of health and something to live for? The secret rule for answer A gives the suffering human being the power to decide on the termination of life: *Individuals without mental impairment should be allowed to decide when life is no longer worth living.* You believe that—with the exception of a truly suicidal individual with impaired judgment—a person owns the right to stay or go as he chooses. At least that's true when health is fading and the future is bleak and painful. If you chose this secret rule, you relate health and vigor to the purpose of life. You want to live only if your health is good enough to allow you to physically and mentally enjoy each day. You are self-directed and also more afraid of suffering than death.

If there was some way to reduce the discomforts to a very minimum while everything else remained the same, would you still feel it wasn't worthwhile to stay around? What do you need to make life worth living? Would a new romance, an intriguing challenge, or someone who needed you badly be enough to keep you going? Your answer implies that you do not trust nature and would prefer to decide when life is no longer worth living. Consider how this secret rule shapes your attitude toward ill people in general. Do you see any inherent value in those who are sick and lonely?

The secret rule underlying answer B sees the decision to terminate one's own treatment as suicide: *It is suicidal and sick to want to die before nature takes us and this option must be prevented at all costs.* You feel that life is precious, so precious that no one—no matter what—should be allowed to prematurely end it. According to your beliefs, life must be lived no matter how you actually feel. Should everyone be forced to take treatments? After all, isn't it unnatural to treat illnesses in the first place, to some degree?

While your view of life as something to cherish and preserve under all circumstances is a noble ideal, are there ever times when letting life slip away might be the right thing to do? Is there no pain so great or suffering so intense that it becomes more merciful, more loving, to let that individual go? While your care for this individual is unquestioned, consider whether there is any flexibility in your rule that allows you to find exceptions when another's suffering is unbearable and no hope for a better future exists.

The secret rule that serves as the foundation for answer C tries to offer a compromise: *Life is so precious that all pressure and influence should be brought to bear before allowing anyone to terminate a life-prolonging treatment.* You believe that despite his great suffering and lack of hope, this individual should be wheedled, cajoled, manipulated—whatever it takes—to make him realize how important his life is. You won't literally force him, however, to take these treatments. If you follow this secret rule, you believe that choosing life is always best, yet you also know that you cannot ultimately demand that another human being stay alive. While your motivation seems to come from a place of love and caring, you nevertheless want to control the person under discussion—as you undoubtedly desire to control others. Since you ultimately will let him determine his own fate, why make him feel bad about the choice he must make?

When people in your life are making difficult choices that you don't agree with, you might consider letting them decide, and supporting them either way. Perhaps you could try unconditionally supporting that person in the most difficult hour. This question is an extreme hypothetical, but it underscores a pattern that you might follow over and over again. Are you prone to stick your moral sense into other people's decisions? If so, do you involve yourself with openness and love, or do you assert your beliefs with self-righteousness? If you are unhappy with the answers to these questions, you are not benefiting from your secret rule.

10. You are an assistant campaign manager for a senator who is running for reelection. While working late one night, you come across some papers that you hadn't seen before. The papers document secret donations made to the senator's campaign. They are from one of the largest chemical companies in the world. There are memos regarding the dumping of toxic chemicals into a local water supply, as well as the company's desperate need to avoid getting caught. You realize that the company is asking for protection against investigators. Upon doing your own investigating over the next couple of days, you discover that, in fact, there has been an increase in cancer and birth defects in the very location at which this company has been dumping. What will you do with this significant information?

A. I won't do anything. It's really not my business, and it's not *my* health.

B. I'll go to the senator and explain what I've found. It is up to him to do the right thing. Once I say something, I'm free from responsibility.

I'll take matters into my own hands and make sure that the right people know what is going on. Too many people's lives are at stake to do otherwise.

How much are we responsible for the health of others? If we become aware of a health threat to others, are we morally or ethically compelled to take action? Answer A's secret rule maintains a "hands-off" policy: *It is not my business or obligation to involve myself in public health issues.* This rule upholds that old saying, "I am not my brother's keeper." If you chose answer A, you don't feel connected to the community of strangers around you. You are living your own honest, hard-working life, and have neither the inclination nor the inspiration to save the world. Health is a personal and individual matter to you.

Why would it be your task to blow the whistle anyway? True, there is no law or custom that insists you get involved in others' business. However, there are consequences for nonaction. For starters, if you suffer from any sense of guilt or regret, your secret rule is not functioning optimally in your life. Second, studies on health show that the more connections we have to other individuals and groups, the healthier and happier we are. It is good for our heart and our immune system to be involved and feel like we are doing our part to save the world. Whether the issue is about public health or not, to improve your personal health, looking out for others may be just what the doctor ordered.

The secret rule associated with answer B argues, *I can help my community's health best by informing a person in authority of any questionable situation, and letting him handle it.* You have made the commitment to get involved with the health of your neighbors, but only to a limited degree. You have discharged your obligation by informing your boss, in this case, and now your conscience is clear. If you chose this secret rule, you have begun to recognize that you are not a single individual in a faceless crowd, but part of a greater whole. You believe that we are all subject to the same health concerns and all responsible for one another's well-being. It is an excellent first step, but is it enough?

What if the information becomes buried and nothing becomes of it? How much do you owe your neighbors? It is now a question of the good of the one versus that of the many. Take time to reexamine your secret rule. If you have done all that feels right, commend yourself for your efforts and hope that somebody will do the right thing. If you are bothered by your limited actions, though, maybe you want to try a more aggressive rule with more involvement.

If you chose answer C, your secret rule is as follows: *When an opportunity presents itself to help the health of my community, I must take responsibility and get fully involved.* You are willing to take on a great task and at no small risk to yourself. You are the rare humanitarian who sets an example for others. Your rule is courageous on many levels. It requires a lot of energy, risk, and determination. Your approach is not for everyone. Many will not even understand why you would take on such a task. Most people are so used to passing the buck that your behavior will seem foolish or unnecessarily risky. It may even cause conflict with your friends and family, as they may oppose your actions.

Your conviction is very noble. It is because of you and people like you that our world changes and improves. But for your own benefit, ask yourself whether this rule highlights a pattern of trying to do too much by yourself. Being responsible doesn't necessarily mean being *solely* responsible. So consider exploring your limits and asking for help when you need it.

CONCLUSION

From a professional perspective, part of today's healthcare approach is seeing the individual not as a passive patient, but as a self-directed advocate for self-improvement. For example, the patient is now expected to take active steps concerning the reduction of cholesterol and blood pressure. When I work with people on their health-related lifestyles, I always begin our discussion with this question: Are you willing to do or say anything necessary to get well? The discovery of their secret rules regarding what they would and would not do has been most enlightening and healing for a number of my patients. I hope that you have been honest with yourself throughout this chapter, and have come to an enlightenment of your own. Review your rules and mark the ones you desire to change. Your renewed journey to health can begin today!

6. Personal Expression

What does your soul yearn for? Do you have a hidden passion? If there is anything really new in this New Age, it is not ancient healing remedies from the Far East, a belief in angels and spirits, or even technological breakthroughs. It is our self-interest. It is the new belief that we are entitled to enjoy ourselves and express ourselves to our hearts' content.

If you look back at history, whether someone was a slave in Babylonia, a citizen of ancient Rome, or an Irish peasant living under English rule, a person rarely got the chance to truly express herself. Straying from expected traditions and striking out independently was limited to the very courageous. If you weren't having any fun toiling to an early grave to eke out a living, there wouldn't be much sympathy; after all, life was about survival. But now it is different. You can make your own destiny. Do your secret rules allow for this new way of thinking? If they tell you not to rock the boat—not to embarrass or disappoint anyone—maybe you have been missing something.

Is there anything you wish to see, feel, hear—experience in any way—but dare not dream about pursuing? Are you stuck in a life circumstance in which you feel you must conform to your family, your friends, your religion, or your culture? Personal expression is also about how you express yourself emotionally. Do you hold back your feelings of love or anger because it just doesn't seem right to let them out? Do you say what you mean and mean what you say? When are you being selfish and when are you just expressing yourself? Are there any lines or boundaries that you are not supposed to cross? Look at your secret rules about when, if, and how you achieve personal expression. You might truly understand yourself for the first time!

1. Every week you have the same fight with your spouse. It comes time for the weekend and you want to do your thing—golfing, going to the

movies, . . . whatever. You have worked a long hard week; the weekends are the only time to indulge your passion. But you are told that there are too many chores to complete. "You have to be responsible," your spouse scolds. "There is so much to be done around the house." This weekend, will you oblige your mate or insist upon your leisure time?

A. I will oblige my spouse and forgo my interests to keep the peace.

B. Leisure comes first because life is short. I will do what I desire and get to the chores when and if I can.

C. I resent having to do chores, but my spouse is kind of right. So I will do a little something I enjoy first and then finish the chores.

How well do you assert your needs and express your wants? Is it ever really *your* time, or are you forever meeting everyone else's needs? The secret rule behind answer A ranks your personal interests beneath household responsibilities: *My relationships and practical responsibilities are more important than my interests.* You know what you like, but you know it will create problems for you, so you forgo your leisure. Are you angry, resentful, or depressed by this total sacrifice? Is peace in the house always more important than what you value?

If you chose this secret rule, you are in a common dilemma. There seem to be more things to do than time available to do them. What you are saying is that a good part of you must be submerged to the greater relationship, the greater good. Consider whether this compromise will make you happy in the long run. Your present secret rule keeps you from your fullest humanity. You do not have to kick and scream, but try articulating your needs. Respect yourself enough to seek a compromise between everyday responsibilities and some personal freedom. Your relationships are likely to get healthier when you are kind to yourself.

Behind answer B is a secret rule that doesn't deny the self: *My leisure comes first; compromising for my primary relationship and household duty comes second.* You have decided to honor your personal expression and let the relationship take second place. You recognize that personal expression, whether it is simple fun or something of greater import, is best for your well-being. But what limitations, if any, do you impose on yourself?

If you have chosen answer B, you are self-interested. If that works for you, so be it. The question then becomes, when do you become selfish?

Confirm that you are truly happy letting your desires and needs for expression override the needs of others. Sometimes we have to go along to get along. If you find that you feel a little selfish and guilty, you can work on attaining personal expression without being inconsiderate and self-centered. There's a balance somewhere.

If you chose answer C, your secret rule reveals a healthy understanding of personal expression: *Realistically, I can't do everything I desire, but I will try to express myself as much as I can.* You have mastered the art of compromise; you tend to both the good of others and the good of yourself. This choice sounds mature, thoughtful, and very logical. Is there any downside to this approach?

There is a snag in the plan only if you do not *really* apply the rule. Are you truly able to insist on your time, no matter how much has to be done? Can you be easily shamed or manipulated into changing your mind? Hold onto your natural sense of balance and stick to it, even when it seems that the chore list is seven miles long!

2. You enjoy racing cars for a living—the speed, the adrenaline rush. In fact, you never feel more like yourself than when you are on the racetrack. But, frightened after seeing you through two serious crashes, your family has asked you to stop. Except for some arthritis, you feel fine and should have several years left before you lose your competitive edge. Then you could easily find work in a related area and make a good living. Will you quit?

A. It is my life and I must determine how to live it. So I'm keeping the career that most excites me.

B. I will give up my passion for car racing so that my family feels more secure.

C. I will compromise by cutting back on my racing, but I will not stop altogether.

Do your relatives and friends discourage the pursuit of your self-expression? Imagine that you have a great feeling of aliveness by doing something that is fun, dangerous, and lucrative at the same time. A great tightrope artist once said, "The only time I feel alive is on the high wire, all the rest is waiting." Should you give up something so self-enhancing? Answer A's secret rule refuses to let the excitement diminish: *I will pursue the passion of my life regardless of what others think or feel.* Your peak experience takes precedence over relationships and even health concerns. You are lucky, indeed, to have something that gives you such pleasure and satisfaction.

It may well be that others cannot understand your passion or don't have any equivalent in their life. And there is certainly no right or wrong answer when it comes to compromising your happiness. Just consider what you might, in fact, be giving up by offering no compromise. Our passions give us the most pleasure, but often cause us the most pain as well. Be sure that yours is worth the risks involved, and that this one form of personal expression is not excluding other forms, such as family fun.

Answer B's secret rule asserts, *I will give up my passion because the security of my loved ones is my greatest purpose in life.* You have placed others above your passionate self-interest. When you are forced to truly decide, your *greatest* passion is your family, not your racecar driving (or its equivalent). However, that doesn't mean that you have to choose only one form of expression.

When we make important life decisions due to pressure from others, it can lead to hidden resentments that can surface at a later date. In order to avoid regrets, look for a compromise. Perhaps you could selectively choose safer tracks and make efforts to take higher safety precautions. If you desperately crave that one activity, you should not have to completely abandon it. There must be a way to find some fulfillment in this special area of your life.

The secret rule behind answer C reveals, *I can curb, but not eliminate, passionate self-expressions in my life.* You see that there is some cause to compromise. Perhaps it is your love for family and the fact that you cannot truly be happy if they are not happy. So you have tried to compromise, and this is a healthy approach. You have a winning attitude about finding a balance when it comes to the loves of your life.

In choosing this rule, you make it evident that you are still connected or addicted to the peak experience that others may never understand. But you are willing to reduce your involvement for the good of your loved ones. You think clearly about others and yourself. You are on a great track!

3. Your mother is still very critical of you, even though you are over forty, have your own family, and maintain a successful business. Somehow, in her eyes, you are never good enough. She continues to compare you with your twin who, by Mom's standards, is "doing better and making the family proud." Sometimes the comments get unbearable. Today, your mother has come into your house and begun to criticize your furnishings and décor. She chides, "Your twin's tastes are so much more sophisticated! You really got the short end of the stick!" What, if anything, will you say?

A. I don't want to hurt Mom's feelings or start a fight. Therefore, I won't say anything about how I feel.

B. I will tell Mom that she's gone too far. If she cannot stop her critical ways immediately, I will end all contact with her.

C. I will try to express my anger and pain in a calm manner. Perhaps, if I am honest and open, my mother will realize how hurtful she is.

Personal expression involves communicating your deepest feelings, even when it hurts. In Freud's day, telling your parents how you felt about them would not have been encouraged. Today, professionals think it is a sign of good mental health to be able to discuss how you feel. Yet answer A is built on a secret rule that doesn't allow you to change the dynamics: *It is wrong to express my true feelings to my mother if my words are going to hurt her.* You want to honor your mother, and you know that even if you combine honesty with tact and politeness, it is quite possible that she will take offense. While your secret rule displays your sensitivity and compassion, it might be deeply harming you. So what if Mom gets a little bent out of shape? Maybe you need to have a good fight to clear the stale air that surrounds your relationship! Is it always better to stifle your feelings than create conflict?

It is important to consider whether you apply this rule to everyone, to loved ones, or just to your mother and father. If it is a general way of behaving, then you will begin to feel the effects very soon, if you have not done so already. It is fundamentally unhealthy in every sense of the word to keep your feelings bottled up inside. If you apply this rule to your mother in particular, then the advantages of a stilted relationship must be weighed against possible estrangement. But maybe you are overestimating how your mother will react to your newfound self-respect. Increased self-esteem is priceless, and you have every right to pursue it. You can go about asking your mother to reevaluate the way she treats you without sounding obnoxious. If you are hurting, why not start small and try to let a little of the pain out?

The secret rule for answer B takes an aggressive approach: *I do not have to tolerate continued criticism from mother—or anyone—and am willing to go to extremes to express that.* You have reached the point where you are ready to tell Mom just what you have been sitting on for the last few decades. If you start, it won't be easy to stop. You are even prepared to throw her out if she can't behave. If you chose this secret rule, consider the possible downside. Taken to its fullest extent, this rule could result in anything from rejection to retaliation—even ganging up on someone. Would you take it that far?

As you apply your rule, remember that self-expression is not necessarily the same thing as pummeling "mommy dearest" into the ground. People usually have to learn how to be thoughtless and uncaring, and your mother undoubtedly had a good teacher. Your resolve to express your feelings is very healthy, but tempering that expression so that it is powerful but not offensive is even healthier.

The secret rule behind answer C is akin to the "slow and steady" approach: *I will respond to criticism tactfully and politely.* You realize that if you are able to keep your cool and express yourself without a blaming attitude, you might get your point across. When you can feel someone else's pain—that is, when you empathize with that person—it is hard to want to hurt her. If you have chosen this rule, it sounds as if you have already developed a good deal of empathy and don't wish to make your mother feel as she makes you feel. So you are taking an approach that nicely asks her to stop. This is a healthy secret rule because it allows you to avoid impulsive and offensive behavior.

Of course, not everyone responds to a nice guy. So be aware that this rule will not always get you as far as you want to go. If the pattern that this rule highlights has served you in the past, it seems that the rule works in your life. You avoid guilt and regret; you never lower your own standards or lose your dignity in anger. That's all good. But if you continue to harbor resentment, it's time to beef up that rule with a slightly more aggressive approach. Also recognize that it is not sinful to show anger. If you are hurt, you are important enough to tell the person who is hurting you to stop. And if you need to get a little miffed about it, there's no harm in a stern word or a heated tone.

4. Your present career has been fairly successful and you have made a good living. It's a practical, honest, and reliable career, but you are so

good at it that it doesn't present much of a challenge anymore. Recently, your creative side has been itching to get out. You find yourself musing about an old dream of being a chef. In the limited amount of cooking you have done, you have found it fun to invent new dishes and get the compliments of those who enjoy your creations. While watching a cooking channel the other day, you saw a commercial for a local culinary school. You could train to be a chef there! What will you do?

A. Work is something to support yourself, not something to enjoy. I better stick with security.

B. I am getting out of my present job as soon as possible and signing up.

C. I'll stay in my career for now; I know it and I do well. However, I will take some cooking classes and plan to retire early so I can pursue my interests in cooking.

Can you do the same old thing backwards and forwards indefinitely just because it pays well? Is it better to make a good living at an uncreative job and express yourself only through hobbies, or to take a risk and find a way to incorporate your creative side into your work? What were you taught about work and personal expression? If you chose answer A, your secret rule separates career from creativity: *Work is not an expression of creativity but a way to earn a living.* You have come to believe that work is equivalent to money, not a way to develop the aspects of yourself that you most like or your true passions. If you chose this rule, look deeply at your life. Do you suffer from a sense of frustration? Who told you that work has to be something you tolerate as best you can? Who said frustration was normal?

If finance allows, why isn't it all right to do just what you want to do? It may well be that your notion of contentment at work is making money without a lot of struggle and giving the best support you can to your family. If you are satisfied with your present profession and just need a little personal change for variety every now and then, then keep your rule. But if you find yourself vaguely or not so vaguely dissatisfied, you may want to work on changing your secret rule. Perhaps a lot of your anxiety comes from stifling your creativity.

Within answer B is a secret rule that demands a certain amount of personal expression: *I do not have to tolerate a stifling professional life; I can change it to suit my creative drives.* You have discovered that work is not just a place to be for a third of your life, but a place to gain satisfaction. It has dawned on you to live a little. You are prepared to make some serious life changes and have already discovered that stimulation and interest can be as important as security and comfort.

Sometimes we need to get out of our comfort zone to grow to our full potential. If you have chosen this secret rule, then you are a risk-taker, which can be a very good thing. The chief consideration for you is whether you have a habit of making quick decisions and tend toward impulsiveness rather than well-thought-out plans. Are you really prepared to go through all the training and start all over at the bottom? Confirm that you are not just reacting to boredom instead of acting from a desire for self-expression.

The secret rule associated with answer C realizes the value of creativity, but doesn't prioritize it enough to make a complete change: *Personal expression at work is important, but it's not important enough to risk comfort and security right now.* You know that you want and need a change, but you are unwilling to make any quick moves in your life now. It is the middle path and it is safe and sensible. If this safe approach has worked for you and not resulted in feelings of resentment, then keep it. But answer this question: Will you keep the promise to yourself and *really* pursue your interests later on?

When the initial impetus to change is gone, will you keep up your enthusiasm? If you chose this secret rule, you are prepared to delay gratification. If this is a lifelong pattern, then you must consider whether you are fooling yourself. While there are many factors to think about when making a major life change, you may want to review your options more seriously so that you don't let another opportunity for self-expression slip away.

5. You are enjoying a delicious dinner and great service at a local restaurant. But the calm atmosphere is interrupted when the person at the next table begins to berate the waiter. The angry customer claims that his appetizer was not brought to the table in a timely fashion. He becomes inappropriately nasty, yelling and hurling insults at the waiter. What, if anything, will you do?

A. It is not my problem. I will not get involved.

B. I will confront the obnoxious customer and defend the waiter.

C. I will tell the irate customer that he is disturbing everyone around him and preventing them from enjoying their meals. I will then urge him to take his complaints quietly to the manager.

What are your secret rules regarding public expressions of personal opinions? Your involvement or lack thereof is a clear reflection of your level of expression. Who hasn't, at some point, wanted to say something when an angry mother yanked the arm of her toddler? Yet many of us just walk away. Well, unlike that time when a screaming baby roared for three hours in the airplane seat beside you, you *can* do something when placed in the above-described situation. Were you taught to mind your own business or to get involved where even angels may fear to tread? It's certainly the former if you chose answer A. Your secret rule claims, *I don't feel the need or the right to express my opinions on things that do not directly involve me.* It is understandable; it is not your problem. But does this rule really work for you? Will you carry a little guilt into the night? Will you feel like a failure or a weakling for not saying something? If you have these residual effects, the rule simply does not work.

Moreover, how extensively do you apply this "keep to yourself" rule? Is there any circumstance in which you would offer a strong opinion or defense? If someone were shoplifting right in front of you, would that prompt a comment? If your friend wanted to leave his dog in a hot car, would you say something? There are a million scenarios we could construct. Look carefully at your rule and consider how much you are motivated by privacy and good manners, and how much is really based on fear. To feel right with yourself, you must believe that you have been true to your highest values.

Answer B's secret rule comes head-to-head with looking the other way: *When I am offended by a person or behavior, I have a right—if not an obligation—to express my discontent.* You certainly have developed a strong sense of self. If you chose this secret rule, you are more assertive than most and may well see your involvement as a simple question of right and wrong. Of course, you could also get yourself deeply involved in situations that could turn very ugly.

Has this rule served you well? The answer is "yes" if you feel cleansed and useful at the end of an involvement. The answer is "no" if you feel more frustrated and uptight because your verbal reactions often get you into altercations. Decide whether you need to tweak this rule.

Perhaps you could give yourself some parameters—for example, you might speak up only if the victim is defenseless or if you think a serious wrong is involved. Maybe this rule also highlights that you are a bit of a control freak who has to have a hand in everything. While standing up for the little guy may be noble, be aware that everyone does not have the same moral code, and that cultural and group norms may necessitate a more tactful, low-keyed approach.

Answer C's secret rule says, *I should respond when something offensive occurs around me, but I should remain as neutral as possible.* This is the middle path found somewhere between rushing away from the fire and running into the burning building. You feel the need to express your discontent when a disturbing situation is taking place, but you do not pass judgment or take sides. You do not necessarily seek justice, try to defend the innocent, or attempt to patch things over. Instead, you simply want to maintain calm and comfort for yourself and those around you. So you would rather the angry customer manage his complaints in a less public manner.

Is there any situation in which you would make a judgment call? Would you ever say more than, "Take it outside"? If so, your secret rule simply keeps you tempered and at a safe distance when things are not *too* offensive. But if you cannot think of a situation in which you would directly defend someone or make a moral call, then consider that your secret rule might be based on a fear of involvement. What if that customer started attacking the physical appearance of the waiter and making ethnic slurs? Would you still counsel him to take his complaints to the manager? The caution here is that you may feel the need to be more direct, but are too timid to do or say what you believe is truly necessary when the time arises.

6. One night you accidentally discover your lover's extensive adult video collection. It includes tapes about various fetishes—the likes of which you have never seen! You confront your lover, who explains that this is a matter of personal enjoyment and private expression. You are encouraged to "share in the fun," if you'd like, but your lover makes it clear that he or she will continue to enjoy the tapes either way. What will you do?

A. There are certain things that are just wrong, and this is one of them. I cannot be with a person who wants to watch these things.

B. My lover and I are separate people with separate needs. It's fine for my partner to watch the videos, but I won't join in.

C. I like the fact that my lover is now willing to share such a secret desire. I would like to give it a try.

This situation involves a very important aspect of self-expression: sexual habits and tastes. Do you expect your partner to share sexual expression with you in every way? Could you be with someone who enjoys things that are out of your range of normal activities, yet still within the range of legal and nonthreatening activities? If you chose answer A, you have a strong sense of right and wrong when it comes to sexual expression, and you demand that your partner be identical to you in this area: *I cannot accept a partner who deviates from my notions of normal sexual expression.* You feel unable to let your lover pursue sexual expressions that you find distasteful. Are you satisfied with the limits you place on your relationship? Is it very important that you see eye to eye on every aspect of sexual expression?

Maybe you are comfortable with certain boundaries and truly need to be with someone who shares them. If that is the case, then stick with your secret rule. But maybe you simply have inherited certain values without truly questioning them. Or perhaps you have adopted a certain conventional stance on sexuality but, deep inside, feel frustrated and deprived. If that is the case, your secret rule is causing resentment and anxiety that is probably manifesting itself in other ways. In addition, you are entitled to your preferences, but must you call the shots for your partner? Without arguing for any particular sexual behavior, consider whether you could stay with someone whose personal sexual expression is different from your own. The answer might help you to avoid a destructive relationship.

The secret rule behind answer B says the following: *I can allow my partner to enjoy personal sexual expressions that I don't understand or share.* You don't get it, but that is all right because you still accept it. It seems you have an open and accepting attitude towards things that are unusual to you. You are content to live and let live. Flexibility is the mark of a healthy psyche. Regardless of your own sexual tastes, your lack of jealousy about something that is nonthreatening shows a good sense of self, and should make you a stronger relationship partner as well. But for some people, there is a catch.

Does your secret rule come from your head or your heart? It is easy to rationally tell yourself that your partner should be able to have sexual preferences that differ from yours. But are you happy with that rule? Are you "secretly" hurting or uncomfortable because you don't share the same sexual tastes as your partner? If you feel that you are doing the just and mature thing but still feel wronged somehow, then you need to adjust your rule. It works on paper but not in your heart.

Answer C's secret rule shows a strong desire to link your personal sexual expression to that of your partner: *I should attempt to share in whatever sexually satisfies my partner.* How far you commit to this rule is going to vary, one might suppose, according to what "whatever" actually is. Nevertheless, you are declaring yourself open to trying new things. You are also declaring your willingness to be involved in another aspect of your partner's life. If you chose this secret rule, you are either very much in love or very willing to experiment. Your choice also shows that you feel a need to play a part in everything your partner does. It's commendable that you allow your partner to explore personal expression, but realize that you don't have to express yourself in the same way.

There is a song or two about loving someone so much that you make bad choices. Remember that you have a right to establish certain personal boundaries; you do not have to match someone else's personal expression completely in order to have a healthy relationship. It is okay to say no. Trying out new things can be the best part of life, but you don't need to push yourself to a point of discomfort. Personal expression is about saying "No thanks!" as much as it is about saying "I'm in!"

7. You are told that you have the potential to develop one of three talents to a world-class level: chess playing, piano playing, or swimming. Training will require five years of practice, two hours per day. It is a big commitment, so you should really enjoy the talent that you pursue. Let's assume you are up for the challenge. Which talent will you choose?

A. I will choose chess playing.

B. I will choose piano playing.

C. I will choose swimming.

This question tries to identify the area of life in which you'd like to seek further expression. If you haven't made the effort so far, it is important to find aspects of expression other than being good at work or good at serving your family. Answer A's secret rule says, *I value mental abilities and want to increase my mental challenges.* You have decided it is worthwhile to train and study to become a chess master. Stereotypes claim that the world of professional chess is peopled with eccentrics and geniuses. Does that attract you? Do you desire to be a mental marvel? If you chose this secret rule, you either long for great mental abilities or already feel most comfortable in that arena.

If you have not been using your mental faculties all that much, you are yearning to do so now. Do people not respect your mind or your intelligence? When you become a grandmaster, no one will ever doubt you again! An attraction to high-level thinking and strategy is almost always a sign of a wise and thoughtful person. Since you recognize that something is missing in that sphere, what are you doing now to expand your horizons? It may be time to break out of the mold and into something that will challenge your mind.

If you chose answer B, your secret rule respects the excitement of the performing arts: *I value musical abilities and want more of a creative challenge in my life.* You would like to become more deeply involved in expressing yourself through rhythm and movement. Moreover, piano playing is a skill that offers social benefits. It would allow you to create something beautiful not only for *your* pleasure, but also for the pleasure of those around you. So your answer reveals a desire to be the source of entertainment for others as well.

Do you practice any of the performing arts as a form of personal expression? If not, you don't have to wait to be reborn as a musical genius. You can do it now, in this moment, bringing a new level of joy to your life. Whether alone or in public, the power of a musical instrument is hard to match. Of course, the piano is only one of countless possibilities. Consider the cello, flute, clarinet, or saxophone—just to name a few. And while you are deciding, here's something extra to think about: Since you did not choose a form of expression that focuses on either the strategic mind or the muscular body, do you already feel comfortable in those areas, or are you scared of those areas? Maybe you like being the center of attention, getting the crowds to clap their hands, but don't feel so at ease when faced with focused and quiet pressure.

The secret rule that serves as the foundation for answer C reveals the following: *I value athletic abilities and desire to enhance the physical activity in my life*. You wish to nurture your physical self as never before. In reality, professional sports training is long and difficult, and the opportunities to show your stuff to others are few and far between. But you chose this answer anyway. You are drawn to exhausting challenges and sweaty triumphs. Perhaps your secret rule has already motivated you to become healthier and better fit. Maybe you never paid much attention to this part of your life and now feel inspired to do so.

Do you have other forms of expression—mental outlets or artistic interests—as well? Answer C might point out that you feel most comfortable in the physical realm. Perhaps you veered away from the mental and artistic worlds because they cause anxiety or fear. Examine the motivation behind your choice. Did you select sports because you already know and are good at them? If that's the case, your answer tells you something about fear, rigidity, and what is underrepresented in your life. Try to make sure that each area—mind, creative soul, and body—is stimulated and nurtured at least a bit for optimum health and happiness.

8. After years of searching for spiritual meaning in your life, you have found a religion that provides comfort and understanding. You intend to convert within a brief period of time. Your family, however, is unhappy with your new spiritual home and is opposed to your conversion. They threaten to reject you and your friends, cutting you off socially and financially if you leave the family faith. What will you do?

A. I will convert. My faith is the most important thing in my life. No one can interfere with what is spiritually right for me.

B. I won't convert. My family is more important than my religious expression.

C. I will convert to and practice the religion of my choice, but I will not let my family know about it. I'll just have to keep that part of my life to myself.

We are looking at one of the most basic areas of personal expression—that of faith and religion. In this country, there are few things we hold dearer than the freedom to express this critically important aspect of ourselves. In this day and age, though, it is not the government or the religious authorities, but our very own families, that often object most to a change in religious affiliation. Answer A's secret rule reveals your sense of conviction: *How I choose to express my faith is more important than my fami-*

ly's comfort level with it. You are willing to risk rejection by your family. That is a very big step. If you chose this secret rule, you have courage when it comes to the personal expression of your spirituality. This shows that spirituality comes first and foremost in your life.

This secret rule is very noble, but it can also cause a lot of problems in your life. So confirm that your spiritual practices are authentic and important enough to justify risking your family circle. Is there any hidden element of rebellion against the family and how it has treated you in general? Could this be the only way to feel independent? Only you know if you are doing the right thing for the right reasons, but nevertheless, it is your privilege and right to express your spiritual convictions in any way you choose.

The secret rule behind answer B asserts the following: *Pleasing my family is more important than religious expression.* You have found something that gives you peace of mind and spirit, yet that is not enough. Do you suppose your faith would need to grow more before you could finally make the break with your family? How much does support, convention, or money play a factor in your decision? How much does being shunned affect you?

If you chose this secret rule, you are willing to sacrifice something that gives you great joy for the sake of family acceptance. Have you ever stood up to your family—about anything? What price are you paying for toeing the line? You should feel lucky to have found something that gives your life meaning and joy. Family togetherness is a wonderful thing. But if you should find yourself depressed and frustrated or sabotaging yourself in various ways, it may be a sign that you need to reconsider the rule and return to that which gives you greatest personal expression.

The secret rule upon which answer C is based says, *I am afraid to be honest with my family about my spiritual desires, so I must hide or reduce my religious expression.* You are trying to practice the age-old custom of hiding one's religion so that the "powers that be" don't find out. Well, sometimes it works and many times it does not. Certainly it is understandable to try to get the best of both worlds. Moreover, you show great concern for your family's security and hopes. But is it healthy to be afraid of being honest?

What is the primary fear that keeps you from expressing your personal faith? Is it hearing hurtful things from those you love? Do you fear being abused? Do you fear hurting or disappointing others? If you chose this secret rule, it is unlikely that this is the first time you have tried to keep something important from your loved ones. You ask a lot of yourself, and deprive yourself the joy of truth and expression. Realize that this rule is a compromise that may work for a while, but if your new religion is what gives your life meaning, you will one day be forced to choose. Why not deal with the truth now?

9. When you were growing up, your father always said that tears were a sign of weakness. Every time you cried, you were punished. Your father even believed that it was undignified to cry at a funeral! You have had a few decades to decide whether shedding tears is a good thing or a bad thing. What do you feel now?

A. I still prefer to stifle my tears. Crying is uncontrolled emotion, which is weakness.

B. Tears are not a sign of weakness, but a normal human expression of emotion. It's fine to cry and express how you feel.

C. It is normal to cry at funerals, but not on a regular basis or in response to day-to-day events.

This question concerns an overlooked but vitally important part of personal expression—your ability to express yourself emotionally. It is one thing to say how you feel, and quite another to actually express how you feel with tears and sorrow. Gender is often the first place we see a difference in the ability to vent. "Boys don't cry" is the traditional adage, but is it really so wise to make people tough and unfeeling? If you chose answer A, you believe that emotion makes you vulnerable: *Crying and other emotional expressions are signs of weakness, and I prefer control.* For whom must you maintain an appearance? You have practiced long and hard, steeling yourself against the pain of life. Has such denial served you well? Do you feel healthy when you hold your emotions inside your body?

You have learned or persuaded yourself that shedding tears is a character flaw. Crying shows how hurt and needy you are. And you probably think that "needy" is not good. It makes you vulnerable and allows people to get to you. Does that sound familiar? It is not easy to let the tears flow after they have been turned off for a long time. To determine if it pays to change, ask yourself if you're happy with your present state. If you feel estranged or disconnected, inaccessible and pent up, it might be time to rethink the rule and reach out to someone who can let you cry.

Answer B's secret rule says, *I am open to expressing tears whenever it feels right.* You are able to use tears in all their various forms. In fact, you have come to recognize the value and honesty of emotion. If you chose this secret rule, you intuitively understand that it is healthy to let your feelings flow. While others may find your ease with emotional expression a weakness, it has probably worked very well for you.

As in all things, however, one can overdo. The downside of being totally free with one's emotions is the tendency towards obsession, over-reacting, and maybe even insincere sentimentality. It is best to find a middle path—self-control, yet self-expression.

The secret rule associated with answer C reveals, *I feel comfortable crying, but only in the face of loss.* You accept crying in the face of great pain. However, you are still unaccepting of tears—or the showing of general vulnerability—except when absolutely necessary. Tears are appropriate in dire times, such as at the loss of someone important. But otherwise, you keep a tight lid on your emotional expression. Has that served you well?

Realize that you do not have to deprive yourself of periodic emotional release. If you chose this secret rule, you are not comfortable letting yourself experience the range of emotions available to you. You are concerned with appearances or roles. But spontaneous emotion, such as tears, makes us beautifully human. Not being in complete control can be a good thing at times. If you have never cried at the movies, you have missed something.

10. You have been invited to a very prestigious party with people you always wanted to befriend. If you are well received, you might be able to make business contacts as well. As you charm your way around the room and the night wears on, the conversation begins to turn more and more stimulating and controversial. Everything from abortion to capital punishment to human cloning is discussed. You find yourself among individuals whose opinions are almost completely opposite from your own. You want very much to be accepted by them. How will you handle these controversial discussions?

A. I will tell these people exactly how I feel. If they are the kind of people with whom I should be friends, they will respect my honesty.

B. I will avoid saying much so that I don't sound too convicted. I don't want them to know a lot about what I really think; I don't want to blow my chances.

C. I will agree with whatever the group is saying. I want to be in with these people and that is the best way.

Are you willing to express your true feelings when the group believes very differently from you? How much are you willing to express yourself when disagreeing might hurt your chances of "getting in with the crowd"? On the other hand, maybe these fabulous people will respect you more if you speak up for yourself. They might value an independent thinker rather than someone who seems to be mindlessly agreeing for their benefit. The secret rule for answer A states, *I prefer to express my opinions and take the consequences rather than betray my opinions.* You are uncompromising. You detest when people go along to get along. If your goal is to gain entrance to this desirable circle of important people, you might be sabotaging yourself by telling everyone just how you really feel. But experience or insight must have shown you that you would rather disappoint them than yourself.

If you chose this secret rule, you are determined to let the world know that you are your own person. You are proud and seemingly confident in your beliefs, and that can be a very good trait. On the other hand, sometimes people who try too hard to establish their independence secretly fear losing their individuality and being just like everybody else—mediocre. Hopefully, you feel strongly about your opinions and are not just an attention grabber. You are probably feisty and proud, but also confirm that you don't unnecessarily confront and irritate others.

The secret rule behind answer B argues the following: *It is more important to blend in than to express my personal opinions.* You have a goal in mind and that overrides any need or desire to express yourself. Often, your rule works well for your large agenda—say nothing and others might assume you are one of them. You play it safe. But does it allow you to develop your true self? Is it working as well on the inside?

You advocate the school of thought that says, "Discretion is the better part of valor." You might also think that no one really needs to know what you consider to be your personal opinions. Why, indeed, does anyone—especially a stranger—have to hear your innermost feelings? But what if you are put on the spot, no longer able to say, "No comment"? The positive aspect of this rule is that it gets you in the door. But in the end, does it place you where you *really* want to be? If this has been a life strategy, it will eventually catch up with you, creating trouble and anxiety. Perhaps you should try asserting your opinion and see how it goes.

Answer C's secret rule states that *personal expression is less important than getting what I want from others.* You prefer acceptance for personal gain, not truth for personal expression. There is nothing wrong with wanting to be accepted and wanting to do well. But you seem willing to say almost anything to get in with the group. Have you ever taken the time to figure out who you really are?

When, if ever, do you reveal your true self? How does it feel to say things you don't really mean? Is this pattern of insincerity just for new contacts, or do you find that you frequently ignore your own feelings and say whatever the situation requires? If this is a life pattern, you bury your true self deeply inside. If you find yourself increasingly depressed, anxious, or mistrusting, you truly should consider actively changing your secret rule.

CONCLUSION

Personal expression is who you are in your work, your clothes, your music, your politics, your friends, and your playtime. It is not enough to have a good job and loving relationships anymore; we are encouraged to truly express ourselves and fulfill our dreams. It is healthiest to be who we authentically are. We must find and give expression to our deepest passions and interests. In the end, *that* is what life is all about.

7. Friendship

"Friends are good medicine," proclaimed a California public service campaign. As a doctor, I can't think of a truer statement. Friendships can bring us great joy and the priceless feeling of belonging. They can also do the opposite. We have all been disappointed or hurt by our friends at one time or another. In addition, we have all harmed a friend in one way or another. And the closer we are, or the longer the relationship has gone on, the more hurt we feel.

We all *think* we know what a friend is and what a friend does, but do we really? Are you a good friend or a "fair-weather friend"? Do you actually have a best friend? Do you encourage your friend to be the best she can be, or would you rather see her fall short of the mark so you can have the chance to pick her up? Would you lie or cheat for a friend? Would you fight for a friend to protect her from harm? What is the difference between a friend and a companion? Do you really know who your friends are?

Friendships are our first relationships beyond family. They predate our earliest romantic encounter by many years. The quality and depth of our friendships very often reflect our moral and ethical code in a way that few other life issues do. You may live a full and happy life without romance, but without a friend, chances are you are going to be very lonely. So let's take a look at a few of your secret rules that may get in the way of finding and keeping good friends.

1. You and your friend are both single and looking for that special someone. At a social gathering, you find yourselves attracted to the same person. This individual seems very nice and has a lot to offer, but while your friend is completely smitten, you are casually interested. Over the course of the evening, it becomes apparent that the object of affection is more interested in you than in your friend. Considering that your friend is more anxious for this person, what will you do?

133

A. I will downplay my own assets and encourage this new love interest to take a second look at my friend.

B. I will pursue the new possibility for myself. I might find that I really care and would hate to miss a potentially great opportunity. This person might be the one for me!

C. I will not make great efforts either way. I will simply let nature take its course.

How do you behave as a friend when you are in competition for a romantic partner? Is all fair in love and war? If there is anything that can destroy a friendship, it is two friends competing for the same love interest. Invariably, one gets more attention. Is this new flame—who might not be there for you in a week or a month—worth the risk of losing a good friend? Behind choice A, the secret rule says, *I would gladly encourage someone that I have no deep interest in to pursue my friend over myself.* You would like your friend to have someone special, and are willing to turn that individual's interest away from yourself. You see no point in competing with your friend, whose interest seems so strong. If you chose this secret rule, you clearly value the friendship over a potential romance. You are logical and realistic in romance. Moreover, you do not need to flatter yourself with someone else's attention. That shows that you are secure.

Have you found that friendship lasts while romance comes and goes? Your answer signifies a tremendous respect for friendship *or* a tremendous lack of faith in romance. Whether you care for your friend or have a somewhat jaded attitude toward flirtation, your ultimate decision is to let your friend enjoy some excitement and hope. While competition may be good for sports or academics, it can often be deadly for a friendship. In the end, your practicality will allow you to have the best of both worlds and, most likely, you will be a happier person.

Answer B is built upon a secret rule that states the following: *When someone is very interested in me, I will risk a friendship to take advantage of the opportunity—even if I am not initially that invested in it.* You are not as interested as your friend, but you think you might be missing something that your friend sees in this new person. You have learned that a person can grow on you and that it is not wise to let a good chance for romance slip away just to be the "good guy." If you chose this secret rule, you are hungry for love, and maybe too hungry. Your willingness to pursue someone you halfheartedly care for, just to have someone in your life, speaks of an emptiness that is unlikely to be filled by this new person. In the meantime, you have not considered the fact that your friend *does* have energy and excitement for this new person. Wouldn't you find some satisfaction in encouraging that?

While it is true that people can grow on us after a while and that love is often better when we fall more gradually, you are not focusing on the good deed you can do for your friend. You also have a sports mentality when pursuing romance—fight to win. Is your goal simply about winning the acceptance of a person, whether you are interested or not? If so, think about how much more energy you could be placing into your first-rate friendship instead of a second-rate attraction. If love doesn't last long and friends seem to come and go too, maybe you are trying too hard for yourself—and not hard enough for your friends.

The secret rule for answer C asserts that both you and your friend should just go with the flow: *The pursuit of love should not be complicated by ideals of friendship, for love works best when it is allowed to develop in an environment of honesty and truth.* You have decided to be yourself and let the experience of the pursuit unfold naturally. You realize that you can't sell someone else by diminishing yourself. If you chose this secret rule, you recognize that love is not a game to be played but an experience to be enjoyed when the moment is right. You have learned that love cannot be staged like Shakespearian drama. While the desire to help a friend may be quite selfless, you probably realize it could also be quite ineffective. Stepping aside might be noble and kind, but it also might not help your friend in the long run. It may be trite, but it remains true that being yourself and honoring your friends may be the best way to have the best of both worlds.

We are often attracted to one another for reasons that are less than rational. You may find that, if pursued, you have more in common than you think with this new person. If you are honest with your feelings and it doesn't work out, your friend may still get the chance to date the love interest. Meanwhile, you can maintain the friendship *and* still find someone with whom you are truly compatible.

2. Your friend is not as smart as you are. Both of you are taking a college final and your friend desperately needs to pass this course in order to graduate. He has always looked to you for help in a jam. This is an especial-

ly big jam, as he seems unable to comprehend the material even with a good effort at studying. You have done your best to act as tutor in hopes that your friend will just cross the pass line. But as the morning of the exam dawns, you realize that there's really no chance that your buddy will make the grade on his own. In a panic, your friend asks you to cheat. How far will you go to help him?

A. I will not cheat, under any circumstances, to help my friend pass.

B. True friendship means helping my friend pass, even if it means cheating.

C. I will let my friend cheat as a last resort, but if he gets caught, he must take full responsibility and not involve me in any way.

Friendship inevitably involves integrity. How much are you willing to bend your moral code to help a good friend? Answer A's secret rule says the following: *I will not compromise my personal morals for my friendship.* You believe it would be wrong to help your friend, regardless of the circumstances. You have set your standard, and you plan to keep to it. If you chose this secret rule, you value your integrity over friendship. It is a strong statement.

Now it is time to check your motivation. How much of your motivation stems from integrity and how much of it from fear? Does getting caught have anything do with how you feel? Also consider how you would respond to your friend's begging. What if you friend pleaded with you and told you that things would never be the same if you graduated and he didn't? Would you be willing to lose the friendship over this issue? If you remain firm in your beliefs, then clearly you are a person of high moral values. Unfortunately, you may well pay a price for your code of conduct. People often expect their friends to endorse and participate in questionable conduct. Your ability to maintain your own rules in the face of criticism and possible rejection makes you an exceptional person. You probably also realize that a person who expects you to change your personal standards is not truly a friend at all. In such a case, the loss might be disappointing but not as painful as expected.

Answer B allows you to compromise your personal integrity: *Friendship is so important to me that it seems reasonable to compromise my standards for someone who has worked hard and tried his best.* You honor friendship above even your own rules of integrity. You can rationalize helping a friend, especially if that friend has really tried hard. Does it make any difference that the course means little but the consequences could be large?

The problem with agreeing to cheat is the question that inevitably comes next: Where does your compromising end? It can be a slippery slope. What if, years later, your friend needs you to bend the tax code or the law to keep him from harm? How long are you obligated to protect your buddy from life's responsibilities and consequences? Without over-dramatizing the effects of a college exam or implying that you will both turn to white-collar crime, realize that from small events there are consequences and that one day you may regret what you have done. If you are ever to bend the rules in this way, it is best to know from the start just how much you are willing to compromise and when you will stop, lest you create something you cannot control.

If you chose answer C, your secret rule plays the midline: *I will put myself at some risk for a friend, as long as I will not be tied to his actions in any way.* In other words, if you are the very silent partner, you can go along with the program. How much of a guarantee do you have? What if, to mitigate his own punishment, your friend brings you into "the crime"?

If you chose this secret rule, you could politely be called *naïve.* When it comes down to it, cheaters often try to save themselves. The care you feel toward your friend might quickly turn to anger as he tries to save himself at your expense. Yes, in theory, your friend might admit it was all his idea, and you could tell yourself that you at least tried. On some level, it is a noble gesture to help your challenged friend to get through. But here's the missing part: Anyone who would ask you to cheat is just as likely to lie as well, if the need is there. Are you really sure the friendship is as strong and as protective as you need it to be? Ultimately, then, helping others to get away with stuff may not be the best way to serve your friends.

3. You have just seen your best friend's spouse having dinner with someone and it appears to be very cozy. There is a lot of touching, and it certainly doesn't look like any business meeting you have ever seen—unless it was monkey business. Your friend may not be aware of this dinner, and maybe she will never find out! But who knows? All you know is that you want to help the best way you can. What will you do?

A. I will tell my friend what I saw as soon as possible.

B. I will confront my friend's spouse and tell him what I saw.

C. I will mind my own business.

How can you best help a friend who is being betrayed by her spouse—or who, at least, *seems* to have been betrayed? What are the boundaries we set for ourselves? When does something become our business so that we feel the need to insert ourselves in the middle? If you selected answer A, your secret rule says, *I help my friend best by exposing someone who would hurt her.* You feel the best way to help a friend with an unfaithful spouse is to get involved directly by revealing everything you witness. If you chose this secret rule, you tend towards impulsive action and often do not think through matters and all the consequences that follow. In desiring to serve your friend, your heart is in the right place. You feel right and righteous and are certain of your own morals and ethics. But you also might be jumping to conclusions.

This secret rule might already have caused conflicts because of your quick black-and-white, right-or-wrong judgments. While you may be watching a romantic interlude, in fact, you don't know the whole story. Helping your friend or protecting her from emotional harm can be a loving act, but don't be surprised if the messenger is confused with the message and you lose rather than keep a friend in the end. Consider doing more thinking and investigating before you jump into the water.

Answer B is built on a secret rule that you should actively but cautiously protect your friend: *When I feel a friend's important relationship is threatened, I confront the involved individuals directly to solve the problem.* You don't like misunderstandings and confusion, so you cut to the chase. If you chose this secret rule, you are direct and forthright almost to a fault. You feel that total honesty and hot pursuit are the answers to relationship problems. On the surface, it sounds like your approach is a good policy—honest and proactive. But what if you confront that seemingly errant spouse and you get a half-truth. What do you do then? Suppose you are told that he needed to comfort an old friend who had suffered a terrible loss? Do you accept that? Do you report it back to your friend? Ultimately, is it your responsibility to smooth out the bumps in your friend's relationship?

While answer B seems to be the clearest, most heartfelt response, you might find it difficult to decide what to do with the information you glean from your confrontation. It may leave you in a difficult position and with more responsibility for your friend's happiness than you actually wanted. Think back to times when you directly went probing to protect someone you love. Does this secret rule work for you? Have the outcomes been helpful, or have you gotten your nose dirty and your feelings hurt? Only you can decide whether this rule is working in your life.

Answer C's secret rule takes the hands-off approach: *It is not my responsibility to protect my friend from any romantic problems she might be having*. In other words, you feel it is best to stay out of situations with friends and their lovers. If asked, perhaps you will tell. But to take a direct role as an informant is not your style. You have found that such behavior offers little reward and often makes things worse. You probably prefer that others butt out of your life as well.

Is there *any* time when you would say something to either member of the couple? Not being the "little birdie" who tells is often a good choice. It is, however, dependent on many factors, and your rules should allow for some flexibility in your response. The worst rule would be inflexibility and the complete unwillingness to do anything, at any time, to help a dear friend.

4. You notice that your good friend's personal hygiene has deteriorated lately. She has been going through some tough times and seems to be letting herself slide. Her breath is bad and she has strong body odor. Others have commented behind her back, but your friend is completely oblivious to the problem. What will you do?

A. I will confront her directly and gently explain the problem to her. I wouldn't be a friend if I couldn't be entirely honest.

B. I will not say anything. You accept a true friend, even with her imperfections.

C. I will try to drop hints, but I will not create an awkward or hurtful situation by addressing the problem outright.

This question addresses, in a much different way from the previous question, how best to help a friend. Here, we suspect your friend is either having some kind of physical or mental breakdown or has decided to take "going natural" to the extreme. It has reached the point where she is becoming the object of ridicule. You may tolerate her changes, but is it enough to tolerate something that you know is fundamentally unhealthy? If you chose answer A, your secret rule puts you in the driver's seat: *My friend is hurting in some way and I must intervene and help if I can.* You have taken the direct approach. You recognize friendship as more than companionship—more than just doing things together. You recognize friendship as an obligation to help as much as you might aid a beloved family member. Your first step is to state what you see and to explain that others see her behavior as well.

Does it concern you that you might hurt her feelings? Could you get a negative reaction, a defensive response? Absolutely! Do you care? Hopefully not too much. One of the hardest things a friend can do is an "intervention." It can get ugly, but it is what is required to save someone from himself at times. We have many levels of relationships—we have pals, buddies, and companions, to name a few. And then there are all-weather, fair-or-foul friends. Your secret rule places you in the last category. It impels you to action. You are a good and brave friend. Just be sure to use sensitive language!

Answer B leads to a secret rule that asserts, *I care for my friends best by accepting them unconditionally.* You feel that you serve your friend and friendship best by looking the other way. You feel that true friends must be uncritical and nonjudgmental. One of the hallmarks of friendship is, in fact, that we accept certain things about our friends that we don't necessarily like. Practically speaking, everyone has one or more friends that have annoying habits. While it is true that constant criticism doesn't make for great friendships, you must learn to find the middle ground in your acceptance of others. In this scenario, ignoring your friend's situation might lead you to ignore a serious health problem.

Furthermore, are you sure that your choice is based on absolute acceptance, or is there a part of you that just doesn't want to get involved? Would you really let a friend destroy herself just because you espouse an uncritical attitude? If you don't say anything, who will? You are to be applauded for learning to love a person and ignore her flaws, but consider how you would feel if harm came to her and you could have prevented it through definitive action. If courage is the problem, adjust your secret rules to motivate you to speak up.

Answer C's secret rule highlights a fear of creating any discomfort in your friendship: *It is not my responsibility to correct my friend's behavior, but*

I will subtly let her know that something is wrong in an attempt to help her out. You want to be diplomatic and to avoid hurting anyone's feelings, yet you also desire to convey a message that something is very wrong. Let's acknowledge it: You have trouble with confrontation and intense emotional responses. You tend to avoid situations in which deep feelings and distressing problems are likely to come out. You want both your friendships and your life to be perfectly smooth, despite the fact that bumps are part of the game. Are you afraid that you will be criticized or rejected in some way if you tell what is what? Why is it necessary to treat your friend with kid gloves?

You still have not differentiated between a friend and a companion. When you recognize the rights and obligation of friends, you will see that, as in any profound relationship, there are going to be unpleasant moments when a truth comes out. You will find life more satisfying and relationships more meaningful when you finally understand what makes a friend a friend.

5. You have noticed that your longtime friend has had a severe cough lately. He gets red-faced and, at times, can't seem to catch his breath. You have also noticed that he struggles to get up a flight of stairs. Things seem to be getting worse. When you suggested that your friend go to the doctor, at first he made light of the situation, telling you not to worry. Then, as you persisted, he became annoyed and angrily told you that he is capable of taking care of himself. What will you do?

A. I will keep urging him to see a doctor, even if it means enduring his anger.

B. I will leave him alone now. I already tried to help and he wouldn't listen to me. He's not really my responsibility.

C. I will enlist the aid of others and take him to a doctor. I'll even pay, if that is what it takes!

This question is about the ever-deepening role of a friend and how much we are obligated to help another, in spite of his resistance to our entreaties. When individuals know something is wrong and refuse to face facts, we call that denial. The two major areas of denial that most people are unwilling to face are substance abuse problems and a serious illness. Statistically, men are much more likely to wait until the last minute—and possibly until too late—to face up to what is really going on with their bodies. It is difficult to know when to draw the line between helping and intruding in such cases. This will be determined by how much your friend is a companion and how much your friend is family. If you chose answer A, your secret rule tells you to keep pushing: *I will continue to nag, pester, cajole, and say whatever is necessary to get my friend the help he needs.* You are not afraid of a little yelling; you feel committed to helping your friend whose very life might be threatened. Even without being a doctor, it sure sounds like his heart or lungs may be compromised. Still, after all is said and done, the most you feel you can do is nag him. You feel responsible enough to push, but not to take any more action.

You are certainly a loyal friend, but the fact that you are aggressive only in speech shows that you still refuse to get deeply involved in the life of your friends. Maybe you respect a certain boundary between friends, or maybe you don't believe that adults should push each other too far. Regardless, you still think it's more important that your friend likes you than that you save his life. You still want to be the good guy on the outside, offering your heartfelt encouragement, but not going any further. Has this rule helped you in life? Or do you carry regrets for not pushing your dear friends more? You certainly don't give up on your friends, but you also keep a safe distance. Consider being brave and taking other paths of action.

Answer B's secret rule argues, *I can't and won't try to help someone who won't even try to help himself.* You have clearly defined your boundaries concerning friends. Moreover, you have concluded that adults really know what is best for their own bodies and minds. It also may mean that you have tried harder before, but your efforts failed and you do not want any more responsibilities like this on your conscience. Your answer shows that you have some sort of fear of rejection, possibly due to conflict in the past. Are you satisfied with succumbing to this fear, or are you riddled with anxiety inside?

If you chose answer B because you really don't like to upset your friends and experience conflict, maybe you are being too sensitive. So your friend told you to buzz off and leave him alone! He's angry, but not truly angry with you. Only you can decide how much effort is enough and when to absolve yourself of further involvement. But thickening up your skin for a larger purpose might leave you with less upset in the long run.

The secret rule for answer C says, *I will override the will of my friend and help him despite himself.* You feel so strongly about your friend that even if he doesn't want your help, you are going to give it to him. Isn't he entitled to make a mistake or be sick if he wants to? Your answer indicates that you take control of situations and assert your will often in the face of serious objections. Is that because you are a control freak or because you are beside yourself with worry? At your worst, you are overbearing and *so* right it annoys people. At your best, you are a natural leader who knows when and how to do the right thing.

You like to set things and people straight. While your heart is in the right place, you cannot set everyone straight. Yet it is unlikely that you will stop because that is your nature. Since it will bother you to no end if you don't at least try to force your friend to a doctor, you are compelled to do so. Picking up the tab just completes the gesture. It is important to remember, however, that while ostensibly you are doing it for your friend, you are also doing it very much for yourself, because you won't be able to live comfortably in your own skin until you feel you have done everything you can.

6. You and your best friend are men, and the two of you and your spouses go out one evening. The ladies go off to the bathroom and when they return, your wife appears upset. You ask why and she puts you off. Later, at home, she shares that the other wife revealed that she is being physically abused by your friend. You have known this couple for a while and never suspected anything. Your wife also tells you that she was sworn to secrecy and that if it got back to the husband, he might take it out on his wife. She is frightened and doesn't want you to say or do anything. You are stunned, but feel you can't ignore what you now know. What will you do?

A. I will say nothing. It's not our business and our friends are fun people. We should carry on the friendship as before.

B. As a couple, we should no longer associate with either of them.

C. My spouse should remain friends with the other wife and, in so doing, try to get her help somehow. I will support from the sidelines and try to keep everything looking as normal as possible.

Friends that we think we know sometimes turn out to be quite different. With new and upsetting information, can you still be friends with people? Do you have a responsibility to remedy a friend's life? Is it any of your business to get involved in good friends' marriages—especially when you are good friends with both members of the couple? The secret rule for answer A allows you to remain removed from an ugly situation for the sake of a comfortable routine: *I don't have to like everything my friends do or to get involved in their personal relationships in order to enjoy their company.* If you hadn't heard that your guy friend was a wife abuser, he would still be your old buddy. And in truth, this couple is still the same fun pair, right? They just have a little secret that need not involve you. If you chose this secret rule, you place a much greater emphasis on people's entertainment value than on their character or morals. Is that truly being a friend?

Perhaps you have seen or experienced enough pain and now have adopted denial as a life-coping strategy. Maybe you have tried to get involved with friends' problems in the past and have gotten burned. Staying out of this couple's abuse case is certainly one way of continuing the safe norm, but doesn't it bother you, at least a little? Your drive to maintain the friendship is very healthy. The lady, in particular, desperately needs some continued normalcy in her life, without judgment. Many people might be appalled at the situation and shun the couple entirely. There is a definite argument for maintaining the façade and allowing the abused woman to have an outlet for her frustrations that will not be compromised. And perhaps continuing the relationship allows her a little joy and respite from what must be a very difficult situation. But also make sure that you won't beat yourself up in the long run for not encouraging more change to take place. By letting everything continue as usual, on some level you are accepting the abusive behavior. You are certainly not obligated to fix people as others might try to do, but doesn't this couple now seem different in your eyes? Is there *anything* you can do—without breaking your wife's confidence—such as telling your male friend that his wife seems particularly uneasy or hurt? Maybe you could also casually tell him how much his wife means to you and your wife. A small "heads-up" might spark a change.

Answer B's secret rule tells you to cut ties completely and right away: *If I am truly offended by an individual's behavior, I cannot be his friend or associate with him in any way.* Your male friend, much to your surprise and possibly horror, has been physically abusing his wife. You cannot accept that. If you chose this secret rule, you have a clear moral code that will not allow you to associate with individuals who violate your norms of decency. It seems reasonable enough that if his behavior offends you, you will have nothing to do with him. But what about her?

If anyone needs old friends right now, it is the wife. Why must she be cut off because you don't want any part of a nasty situation? Are you afraid to stay involved? Are you happy with being so self-serving? If you care that much about right and wrong, maybe there is something you can do to help. How will you feel knowing that you could have done something about it? There are laws against such things, so aren't you letting a criminal go free because it doesn't suit you to help? Answer B is clearly the easiest way out. The question is when, if ever, does your secret rule make an allowance for helping a friend who might desperately need you?

The secret rule behind answer C is a safe middle ground—for you: *I won't abandon a friend in need, but I will take the least conflictual route possible.* Lying low and supporting from the sidelines seems reasonable in this case. You will continue to protect the lady by not making a big show and also by being available to quietly help—through your wife. If you chose this secret rule, you are idealistic, committed, and willing to stand up for your values without being impulsive or reactionary. You will swallow your own anger and stay friendly with the abuser, for his wife's sake. Hopefully, this quiet acceptance will not last too long before the situation is remedied. What if the wife gets the courage to leave? Will you cut ties with the husband then? Is your motivation largely concern for the wife or fear of creating conflict with the husband?

There are pitfalls, of course. You may get angry at yourself for not being more active. You may feel the need, at some point, to distance yourself from your male friend. But, for now, you are tempering your upset because if you betray the woman's confidence, it could be disastrous for her. Has this rule worked in your life? Do you often play a safe middle ground? Think about times when you have chosen a quieter, safer role. Did such a rule produce contentment or anxiety in your life? Answering that question will confirm whether this secret rule is indeed a healthy rule in your life.

7. You and your friend are playing in a charity golf tournament. You notice that your friend is cheating by taking the ball out from behind a tree and taking a good lie. Your friend does not realize that you are watching. Because of the pressure and the audience, you decide to wait until after the tournament to deal with what you have witnessed. Several hours pass and the scores are turned in. Your friend is the winner by one stroke and is scheduled to receive a trophy that evening! What will you do?

A. I am offended that my friend is cheating and will confront him right after the round is over.

B. I will say nothing to my friend. Although my respect for him will change, he is the one who ultimately has to live with himself.

C. It is no big deal to cheat at golf; everybody does it. We are only amateurs out for fun. For all I know, others cheated too.

What level of honesty or morality do you expect from your friends? Is it fixed and rather consistent, or are you more flexible and forgiving of your friends? A friend is a special category of person. We often allow a friend to say and do things that we would not allow a stranger to say or do. How far does that special relationship go and where is that boundary? Answer A's secret rule tells you to hold your friends to your usual standards: *Just because a person is my friend doesn't mean that I should make exceptions for him or allow him to cheat.* Your friends get no special deals from you. If you chose this secret rule, you demand a high level of integrity from others. You live by a code and try to stick to it. You are, on one hand, moral and honest, but at times you can be a bit rigid, perhaps demanding more than others can comfortably deliver. Can someone cheat a little and still be your friend, or would you refuse to have a relationship with such a person?

There are many kinds of cheating, from actively breaking a rule to just looking the other way. Without attempting to defend dishonesty, look at your secret rule for any flexibility in what you expect from your friends. Perhaps you are comfortable with holding your friends to universal rules. You like boundaries and maybe that works for you. But if you have suffered from regret and anxiety because you never bend rules for friends, then you might want to reassess your sense of justice versus friendship.

Answer B's secret rule relies on adults to be adults: *My friends, like all others, must use their own conscience to decide what's right and wrong.* You are willing to let your friend claim the trophy even though you know he didn't win it. Are you so sure that he will eventually learn to make the right choices through trial and error? Through karma? If you chose this secret rule, you have a confused and ambivalent attitude towards right and wrong. On the one hand, you are annoyed or offended. Yet you don't think it is worthwhile to be honest regarding what you expect. You also have problems with confrontation and take the easy way out: "It's not my business." Clearly, it is your business on many levels, including allowing the entire field of players to be cheated because of your laissez-faire attitude.

You might think you are being open-minded and even noble to allow friends and others to make their own choices. But you are also letting a lot of people down. Your friend may have developed his attitude because no one ever took the time or energy to demand integrity. Moreover, if you let others get away with things and then resent them for it, you may wish to rethink this rule and see if it has served you and your friends all that well.

Answer C branches out of a secret rule that allows exceptions and deviations from your usual standards: *There are times when a little cheating is permitted, especially among my friends.* So a little cheating is okay, but big cheating is not okay? How do you know the difference and where do you draw the line? If you chose this secret rule, you might have an overly permissive attitude towards dishonesty, along with an acquired talent for self-deception. You don't expect much from anyone, including your friends. Are you sure this rule works for you? Are you comfortable believing that your friends should not be held to certain standards? After all, doesn't that give them a lot of room to trick and betray those who love and respect them?

If you are really convinced that cheating is widespread and acceptable, especially among your own friends, you can also expect to be artfully swindled in the future. By not ranking honesty as a priority, you will end up surrounding yourself with people who might not even understand the concept of friendship. When invoking your secret rule about minor cheating, remember that it can be a hard habit to break and that you must be most careful in extending the line of what you are willing to let yourself or others get away with.

8. Your friend has been accused of embezzlement. She has been hiding from the authorities for a week and has just contacted you. Your friend claims that she is innocent. She needs your help to gather information, money, and time to prove her innocence. You are aware that aiding and abetting a fugitive is a crime. What will you do?

A. I believe my friend and will help her in any way that I can. I am willing to take certain risks on her behalf.

B. I will turn my friend in to the authorities. I believe that justice will be done and that this is the safest and wisest road to travel.

C. I will not turn my friend in, but I will not offer any aid. In fact, I will ask her not to involve me further in her problems.

How much do you trust your friends, and how far will you go to back that trust? Maybe you feel it depends on who the friend is, what the alleged crime is, and your relative vulnerability to legal consequences. In general, though, do you think that friends are *supposed* to protect each other from the law? The answer is a hearty "Yes!" if you chose answer A and, therefore, its accompanying secret rule: *I will do whatever is necessary and take great personal risk to help a true friend.* For you, great risk is the true test of friendship. You expect yourself to be a committed, loyal friend no matter what the accusations. Maybe you are so secure in your own instincts and choices that you *know* one of *your* friends would not actually commit such a crime. On the other hand, maybe you have some doubts about your friend, but want to help her out of a jam anyway. In any case, you believe in standing by those for whom you care, even in the foulest of storms. Your answer reveals that it is also in your nature to be loyal to other causes as well, making you a strong ally and determined foe.

Your absolute dedication to your friend is admirable. Everyone should have a loyal friend like you! But aren't there lines to be drawn? If your friend is really guilty, you cannot offer blanket aid for anything and everything before you jeopardize some of your own core values. This question has pointed out that you are headstrong and determined to stick by those you love, but it also highlights that you might need to temper some of the expectations you place on yourself. You can be a friend without compromising your own life and values. It is okay to tell someone you love her and are there for her without directly aiding in possibly criminal business.

Answer B's secret rule is the following: *I can help my friend best by holding her to common legal standards.* You believe in the law, which you see as unfailingly seeking and finding justice. You feel that you will serve your friend best by letting the authorities have her. If you chose this secret rule, you have a relatively rigid moral code, which could be either healthy or harmful. You also place very clear limits on friendship. Do you much prefer a world of black-and-white to confusing shades of gray? You apparently feel your friend is better off being assessed by the law. That might be true, but then again, we know that is not *always* true. Sometimes good guys and gals are falsely accused. Sometimes things occur that are out of our control; it can happen to anyone, anytime.

In addition, this secret rule might have a partner rule that tells you not to jeopardize yourself in any way. In your answer, isn't there a real concern—first and foremost—for your own liberty? In an ideal world, we would never have to risk very much for our friends. They would always be enjoyable companions. But the standard of friendship is matched against family relations, not pals and buddies. Don't we stick with family through thick and thin? Should good friends be any different?

Answer C allows you to escape deep involvement: *My friends must be accountable for their actions and I won't help them escape justice.* You don't want to get further tied up in this mess. You are not going to interfere, either way. Even for your very best friend, there is no aid and no quarter available. Would you at least get her an attorney? If you chose this secret rule, your credo is, "Mind your own business." You believe that you can live life by avoiding hard choices and walking away when times get rough. You have probably lived this way all your life and hope that you never get put in a position where you might have to risk something great, let alone for a friend. But is that realistic?

What if there was no risk to you? Would that make any difference? If that doesn't change anything, then your answer is really more about not getting involved than about any fear for the self. You much prefer living life safely in the middle and avoiding the edges. If you are happy with your safe position, stay there because it works for you. If you feel bored, alienated, or disconnected, your "hands-off" secret rule probably doesn't serve you any longer.

9. Your longtime friend needs to come up with a large sum of money within a few days. He has a gambling problem and, although he gets professional help for his addiction, he occasionally falls into serious debt. The last time this happened, he borrowed several thousand dollars and has not paid all of it back. Now he needs even more money. If he doesn't pay off, there is no telling what might happen to him. You have always treated this friend like a brother. It hasn't bothered you to dig into your pockets in the past. But recently, you have been trying to pay off your own medical bills, so you don't have extra money to hand out. Will you help him out of the hole this time?

A. I will help my friend out of his debts, even if it means that things will be a little rough for me during the coming months.

B. I will refuse to lend my friend more money to pay his debts. I'm finally making myself a priority. I need the money desperately, as well.

C. I will not lend my friend any more money—not because I don't want to or can't come up with it, but because I am feeding his problem.

How much must we sacrifice for the dearest of friends? And what if the sacrifice we are asked to make is not to help someone with love, health, or career, but instead to get a friend out of the trouble that he continues to create? When must even the best friend say enough is enough? If you chose answer A, you have decided to put yourself out, once again, because you cannot stand to see your friend in need: *I will help a good friend for as long as he needs me, at whatever sacrifice I need to make.* You are able to have friends so close that they become like brothers. In that sense, you are a rare individual. Moreover, you are a passionate individual. But that is both your strength and your weakness; you are loyal to a fault.

Sometimes we have to give all to our brother, and sometimes we have to apply a little tough love even if it hurts us. You are in a bit of a dilemma because if you don't pay off his debts, there will be some unspoken consequences that could be grave. On the other hand, we can't allow even those whom we love most to continue self-destructive behaviors without feeling the sting of future consequences. You are not yet ready to let him feel the sting. Maybe this will be the last time and he will learn his lesson, but if not, will you keep kidding yourself and aiding him in the future? You certainly cannot be faulted for your loyalty and commitment, but sometimes as hard as we try, we cannot save the ones we care most about, even with all the money and time we have to give.

Answer B's secret rule says, *I will support a very good friend only to the point where my own security is threatened.* You have helped in the past. He still owes you money and now it is time to make sure your lifestyle is not further compromised by this dear but troubled friend. You are practical by nature and generally recognize the difference between being selfish and being self-protective. This time around, emotional arguments or feelings of guilt will not sway you.

Your answer shows that there is a bit of regret and anger in you. You have sacrificed yourself many times before and are *finally* willing to rank yourself as a priority. Use this self-study to guide you in the future. Avoid letting events in your life get to the point where you feel that you have ignored or disrespected yourself and your own needs. It would feel better to make this choice out of compassionate thinking, instead of financial frustration.

The secret rule behind answer C argues, *I won't enable my dearest friend to maintain self-destructive behaviors, even if it is painful for both of us.* In other words, it is not about the money; it is about your friend's health. Gambling is an addiction for many people, and you obviously feel that your friend is ill and needs help. If you chose this secret rule, you have personal knowledge of the consequences of self-destructive habits and want to prevent one more tragedy. You feel deeply for this person and it undoubtedly hurts you terribly to let chips fall where they may. But you strongly believe that giving him money one more time and allowing him to evade the consequences of his actions will do greater harm. Your heart is in the right place.

But what about your friend? He is in a very precarious position. Is this truly the only way for him to learn his lesson? Is there no compromise, perhaps even one more time? This secret rule is usually developed over a period of trial and error. It is one approach to the problem of "diseased" or flawed friends who have come to rely on you when they are at their worst. It is not easy to find a balance, but it seems that you have done as well as you can. You have offered help, but you also know when to call it quits. First, you are respecting yourself enough to listen to your instincts. Second, you are truly helping your friend. He is on a destructive path and needs to face the facts. While you may shed some tears for your friend, you will probably also feel healthiest and most content with your final decision. We all have to learn where to draw a line. That is part of life and part of friendship.

10. You are the manager of a nonprofessional team of athletes and are charged with picking your team. The object, of course, is to select the best players so that your team can win the league championship. There are many more athletes vying for positions than there are available spots. Your good friend—who is not the best of the bunch—desperately wants to play. You know that he doesn't really deserve to be on the team, but you have the power to give him a place. It is your decision alone. What will you do?

A. Friendship and sportsmanship are more important than winning. I will give him a spot on the team.

B. My duty as team manager comes first. I will not give my friend a position at the expense of another, more capable player.

C. I would like to give my friend a chance, but I can't jeopardize the team, so I will tell him that the decision is out of my hands—that I am not allowed to create any situations that might cause a conflict of interests.

Is it more important that the team win or that you enjoy sportsmanship and camaraderie with your good friend? Do you owe your friend a special opportunity, in spite of the fact he may be athletically challenged? Answer A tells you to place the loyalty of friendship above all: *I will use my advantages and authority to benefit my friends because that's what friends do.* You value friendship over leadership integrity. Clearly, winning isn't everything. In fact, it is more important that your friends like you and are happy than that a bunch of strangers feels that justice was served.

At some level, you don't take your leadership responsibilities too seriously. Is that generally true or only when it comes to games? Would you hire your friend for a job, as well, even if he would be much less competent than another? Perhaps you are not the best person to lead and should rightfully let others take charge. There is nothing wrong with being a feeling person, but if it is not in your nature to put personal feelings aside, you might consider letting others do the dirty work. Choosing your buddy will possibly create dissension and challenges to your authority if he turns out to be a lousy player. And you will have to deal with that. There is no right or wrong action here, however. If you care deeply for your friend and you have developed certain standards of friendship that cannot be breached, it is clear you must follow your secret rule and take full responsibility for what follows from it.

Answer B's secret rule places leadership responsibility over friendship: *When in a position of leadership involving many, I owe my allegiance to the greater group, not to my friend.* You are the captain and you must act on the team's behalf. Your friend loses out. If you chose this secret rule, you honor integrity and responsibility. You have little sentimentality and recognize that your friend's hurt feelings go with the job. If not already a leader, you would do quite well in a position in which you were required to make hard decisions that many would balk at. Due to your abilities, you will get positive feedback as a fair and equitable leader. The greater group will like you and it is important to be liked.

Hopefully, your friend knows you and will not take your decision too personally. You have made your priorities, and in order to feel best about yourself, you should stick by them. Your answer also displays a strong desire to win. In that sense, there is a vulnerability and some insecurity about how you are perceived. You want to please the greatest number of people possible and show yourself as the best. You recognize your friend as a weakness or liability, and winning is more important than smiles from your buddy. Your secret rule can serve you well in positions of leadership, if you can also learn to show some empathy for the feelings you will hurt.

Answer C's secret rule finds a compromise and, quite frankly, uses dishonesty to get you out of a bind: *I will lie to my friend to protect his feelings when there is no alternative to hurting him.* He's your friend, and if it was practical or reasonable to put him on the team you would, but people are counting on you to do the right thing. You feel it is better to lie and save his feelings than to give him the hard truth: "You're just not good enough." You try hard to do the right thing, but only if you can get away with not hurting anyone, including yourself. You avoid confrontation and often fail to take responsibility for what must be done. You tell yourself it's the best for everyone, but it is really best for you.

Your heart is often in the right place. And at times you have undoubtedly gotten away with this balancing act, but it will eventually backfire and the truth will come out. You will be exposed as a liar and might feel a fool. Why place yourself in a position of dishonesty? Why allow yourself to feel upset and torn apart? We are all guilty of white lies now and then, but if you must use them, do so sparingly and when you are sure they are absolutely the last resort. Otherwise, you will find yourself suffering from anxiety and guilt. Being the bearer of bad news is not easy. Maybe your friend *would* resent you or hold a grudge. But is that so hard to work through, if you are truly friends?

CONCLUSION

In this chapter, we have tried to look at typical life situations that challenge and define the meaning of friendship. Your secret rules largely depend on the quality of friendships you have now. If you are satisfied with what you have, then you are blessed. And if you realize you don't have the kind of love and closeness that you desire, it may be something you wish to work on in the years ahead. Few aspects of life are more satisfying than loyal, healthy, devoted friendships.

8. Spirituality

Almost everyone has a viewpoint concerning the spiritual realm, the source of creation, birth, death, and the afterlife. What's it all about? Why are we here? Is there a God? And how can we know for sure? How mankind dreams of being something larger than earthly, of being immortal! We want to go on forever and ever. Even life extension would help! If we could just live 200 years instead of the average 70-something, imagine what we could do and learn! Yet would that be enough? Is it ever enough? In the end, we are still left to face the unknown. And no one has ever returned from the unknown, so it is the most natural thing to want to stick with the sure bet—this lifetime.

For our human minds, the unknown looks like the end of the ride. What if it turns out that this isn't true? Doesn't that change the whole ballgame? What about the idea that you reap what you sow—karma? Could what you do today come back to haunt you or reward you? If you knew that your present actions would definitely influence your spiritual future, would you make different choices today?

Throughout the ages, people have gone into deserts and up on mountaintops to search for what is beyond the physical world. They have come up with some pretty amazing ideas. Many mystics, for example, have proclaimed quite surely that there is continued existence for us, as sentient beings. All the religions, in some way or another, have described an afterlife. The difference between the true believers and the majority is that the majority only hopes, while true believers have a high degree of certainty.

Though most of us do not retreat into hermitage, we struggle with spiritual questions. And the way we handle those questions largely shapes our daily existence. Your secret spiritual rules of how the universe operates are bringing you either great peace or continued anxiety. Let's examine some of these rules and find out how to enhance the spirituality that gives your life meaning.

1. You are seventy years old and have been diagnosed with terminal lung
   ◆ cancer. Your spouse and two adult children are alive and well, and you
have no financial worries. In other words, you have everything to live for. But
due to the cancer, you have been given only one year to live. As you gather
information on your options, you find out about cryogenics—the science of
freezing organisms for preservation. You could be frozen at the moment of
death in hope that a future cure would be found and you could be brought
back to life. Will you choose to be frozen?

A. Yes, I will request cryogenics. I know only this life and want more of it.

B. No, I have faith in an afterlife and have no need or desire to be frozen.
I will still be alive somewhere else.

C. I am not interested in cryogenics and am uncertain about any afterlife,
but I do realize that everyone dies, and I accept my fate as comfortably
as I can.

As human beings, we not only struggle to prepare for tomorrow but
also think about what will happen after death. Does a belief in an afterlife
structure your secret rules, or do you believe that earthly existence is as
far as we go? Answer A's secret rule refuses reliance on an unproven
afterlife: *The only life I know and trust is the present one, so I will do what I can
to avoid death.* You have no true faith or belief in a spiritual world. In simple terms, you believe that when you are physically dead, all awareness
and life ends. You are well grounded in the physical world and place little faith in gut impressions or intuitive explanations. They come from the
same invisible, unreliable place that people refer to as "the spiritual" or
"God." You have probably been described as logical and reasonable. That
approach may serve you very well in certain areas of your life, such as
business, but has it left your emotional and spiritual life a bit threadbare?

At times, we must rely on what we cannot see or feel. For example,
we often rely on our instincts when it comes to choosing friends or trusting a stranger. Well, when you put aside the scientific perspective that we
are all taught to use, what does your *deepest* self tell you about spirituality and the afterlife? And what does your refusal to consider an afterlife
tell you about yourself? Do you tend to be close-minded, to consider
things from one angle only? Do you try to exercise control over everything and never quite let go? There seems to be no harm in trying cryo-

genics, but before you do, you might try experiencing the world more intuitively. Maybe there is a spiritual perspective that will fulfill you and diminish the terrible fear of death that causes you anxiety. You never know. With a new spiritual outlook, you just might wind up somewhere you never expected to be!

Answer B's secret rule states, *I have no need to preserve my dead body, as I know my spirit will live on somehow.* You are pretty certain that there is a spiritual world ahead, and you are content to die a natural death. Choosing answer B signifies that you are very open to what you cannot see or touch. You accept what you know through intuition. Your life is enhanced by an active faith that allows you to look outside of the box that we term "logic." If you can balance both the intuitive and the verifiable, you should remain levelheaded and content, with little anxiety over the future and with a great appreciation for the present.

Explore the authenticity of your belief system to assure yourself that this is the secret rule for you. Is your secret rule *really* based on a developed system of faith? Have you pursued your spirituality and found that a continued existence in an afterlife is the deepest truth for you? If so, your rule is authentic and healthy. However, some would choose this rule out of wishful thinking. They have not come to peace with death or to any serious conclusions about an afterlife, but are in denial of death so that they rationally choose to opt for the less painful belief. This secret rule would not be effective in such a case, because it would be based on trying to trick the self into trusting that another world is to come.

The secret rule that serves as the foundation for answer C is as follows: *Death is a natural part of life; what we believe does not matter because it has no bearing on where we wind up.* You accept the inevitable earthly end and care not to prolong it artificially. Your approach shows that you are not suffering from a fear of death, nor are you obsessed with controlling every aspect of life. You also recognize that you lack the requisite faith and belief to care much about what your final destination might be. If you chose this secret rule, you are a realistic, down-to-earth individual who is rarely given to flights of fancy. You don't rely much on guardian angels, but you have developed an appreciation for the natural world. You peacefully accept the cycle of birth and death in all that is around us.

A profound spiritual understanding might be alive inside your "I don't know or seem to care" attitude. You find it presumptuous that others believe that they know what cannot be known. Instead, your form of spirituality recognizes that you are a tiny being in a vast universe. The cycle of life and death tells you that there is a plan, a system, a method to the madness; you dare not second-guess the Who behind it all. You are dust in the wind and are humbled by it. If that sounds familiar, then your secret rule works for you. However, if you experience any anger, despair, or depression at the thought of your death, you are not fundamentally content with your secret rule. There are unresolved fears that you are desperately trying to cover up with a confident and carefree answer. If you are in that position, you might find that spending time on your spiritual life will allow you to reach a more satisfying conclusion.

2. Freedom of religion is one of our most cherished rights. There are some spiritual rituals, however, that are considered illegal by the government. Specifically, peyote—a hallucinogenic cactus—is allowed to be used only by certain Native American tribes, for spiritual rituals. Any other person, regardless of intent and sincerity, is forbidden to use this substance. In addition, Rastafarians believe marijuana is sacred to their religion, but they are not allowed to smoke it in the United States. The use of mind- and mood-altering substances for religious purposes has occurred since before recorded time and is accepted throughout most of the world. Do you think, then, that if a religion uses mind- or mood-altering substances as part of its ritual, any individual who desires to practice should be allowed to do so?

A. Sure! Freedom of religion includes any dogma and rituals that your heart desires, as long as no one is injured or damaged in the process.

B. No. When a group decides to make up a religion so its members can use drugs, that is not a real religion.

C. Rituals and ceremonies are just entertainment for the followers. Organized religion, official or unofficial, gets in the way of authentic spiritual experience and is a complete waste of time. All these strange practices should be outlawed.

Does religion provide a good reason to use substances that are otherwise considered publicly dangerous or offensive? Is there one set of rules for spirituality, and another set for secular living? If you chose answer A, you believe that a religion and its spiritual practices do exempt a person from the legal sphere of rules: *People should be able to do anything that they believe brings them closer to God.* Allowing individuals to find God in any way they can is important to you. You feel that spiritual pursuit ennobles and enlightens people, and you want to encourage that. You recognize that not everyone fits into the most common religious practices, and that is part of what makes this world a great place to live. If you accept this attitude toward religion, you are likely to be open-minded about other issues as well.

Your selection of answer A reveals that you are frustrated with the boundaries that government has set. Government is too involved in people's lives and it needs to live and let live, unless there is a legitimate concern for the safety of its citizens. It sounds reasonable enough, but, really, aren't some people going to take advantage of the religious loophole for selfish reasons? Isn't it likely that if the government let people smoke marijuana as part of their religion, it would really be an open invitation to use drugs without any of the real tenets and practices of a religion? Can getting high be a major part of an authentic religion? Won't it give new meaning to being the "high" priest? And won't the high priest also become the head dealer? And what if individuals wanted to do other now-banned practices, such as animal sacrifice? Would you support that? Is there any limit to what you call a religion? While your secret rule is very permissive and encouraging of honest spiritual discovery, taken to its logical conclusion, there are still practices that would make some kind of defining controls ultimately necessary.

Answer B's secret rule places certain restrictions on spiritual practices: *A religion must have standards and guidelines; it cannot be a collection of random beliefs or desires strung together for personal gain.* You can't accept a religion that has, as one of its foundational practices, the use of illegal drugs. If you chose this secret rule, you tend to be dogmatic about what constitutes "proper" religious beliefs and judgmental about the habits and customs of others. If you are very certain about what a religion is, you are also certain about how other individuals' lives ought to be lived. You feel like you know what is a reasonable custom or ritual, but do you? Some might find *your* customs offensive or upsetting. For example, if you practice Christianity, try to understand how a person who is unfamiliar with your beliefs would feel about eating a wafer representing the actual body of a Man-God. And if you practice Judaism, you probably never considered the cutting off of infant boys' foreskins to be offensive because circumcision is a long-held custom. But a person from a different culture might find that offensive.

Shamans and native healers have used mind-altering substances for centuries without the culture becoming lost in a hallucinogenic frenzy. Native Americans seem to have shown great restraint and responsibility with the use of their psychedelic substances. Why, then, fear that unfamiliar religious practices will be dangerous? Certainly do not pursue these paths yourself if you find them inauthentic, but judging others might bring you anger and upset. Maybe you just need a little more *faith*. While there are some who might abuse the freedom to call their practices "religion," history shows that wisdom more often prevails and only those practices that meet spiritual needs survive over time.

Answer C claims that we should throw the whole idea of religion out and keep spirituality separate from group or institutional practices: *Organized religion tends to inhibit and interfere with true spiritual experiences.* You believe that neither organized religion nor the government is qualified to make judgment about what is and is not a legitimate spiritual experience. If you chose this secret rule, you're a rebel in many areas; religion is just one. You see religion, with its many rules and customs, as giving individuals the false impression that they are having a true spiritual experience. That leads us to the big question: How then is a spiritual experience different from a religious experience? What is a spiritual experience? Your conception of God or spirituality seems at odds with standard religion. You want some pure experience of the divine without all the trappings of ceremony and ritual. But how is this achieved? And is what's right for you also right for everyone?

Whether through marijuana, meditation, or begging in the streets of Bombay, people find their paths in ways different from yours. What is it that makes your spiritual experience pure and unadulterated by religion? You have unnecessary anger towards tradition. If lack of clergy and rituals suits you, by all means go for it! But remember that many, throughout the ages, have sought and received spiritual nourishment from group religions and they continue to do so—even with the trappings of ceremony and ritual. Whether as formalized religion with all the pomp and circumstance of a royal coronation or chanting a mantra on a dirt floor, each individual is trying to find what it all means and where we fit into this life. Judging others' practices leads only to stress and anger.

3. After your close friend is killed in an auto accident, he starts appearing to you in your dreams. He tells you not to worry, that he is in a beautiful place. Moreover, he describes the tragic accident in details that you have never heard before, directing you to an important piece of evidence about the accident that has not yet been found. In these dreams, your friend also relates messages from other deceased friends, such as, "Joe says, 'Hi,'" and "Everyone wants you to know they're fine." Do you believe that the communication with your friend could be real?

A. Yes. Dreams allow communication between spiritual planes. I'm going to search for that new evidence.

B. No. Dreams are just dreams; they have no spiritual meaning. I am not going to seek out this "new information."

C. The dreams are all reflections of my inner mind, but they do have meaning. The dream uses the vehicle of my friend to get me to look inside myself and find information buried deep in my unconscious. Part of me already knew the information but just couldn't access it.

Does inter-dimensional communication happen? Do you put faith in your dreams? The secret rule behind answer A allows you to believe that there is more than what we see with our eyes: *Souls from other spiritual planes do exist and can communicate with us.* In essence, you believe that your friend is really still "alive," and you can receive valid information through the mental state that dreams create. You clearly accept the survival of the soul after death, as well as its ability to make contact with the earthly plane.

It helps to get questioned by the devil's advocate: If souls can do as you believe, why are you being contacted *now*? Could it be that your grief has affected your perceptions in any way? If you are entirely honest, isn't there an element of wishful thinking on your part? You want your friend to tell you he is okay. Yet this dream seems to include some verifiable facts given along with greetings. Might you already have this information in your subconscious mind, and the dream of your friend is just bringing it back? Or is this proof that your friend still exits? Turn inward and find the answers that leave you most at peace. Most important is that you feel a sense of completion or lightening of your emotional burden.

Answer B's secret rule does not allow you to find significance in the "visit": *Dreams are only products of our anxious minds.* You believe that dreams contain feelings and ideas about the everyday world, but they don't contain any spiritual information or communication. If you chose this secret rule, you believe spirits—if they exist—remain in their spiritual home and do not cross over. This is a logic-based belief that is more aligned with most people's interpretation of how things work.

Your unwillingness to follow up on this new information, however, says you are fearful of discovering that something more may exist. You are, in that way, reluctant to leave your comfort zone. Why not follow up? If the information turns out to be accurate, you might require an expanded view of the universe. Is that so bad? If the information is worthless, you have lost nothing. And if, up to this time, you did not believe that souls live on at all—let alone talk to us from beyond the grave—how would it affect you to change this belief and become more spiritual or metaphysical? You might be shaking your head and thinking all of this is just the mushy New Age thinking of people who are afraid to die. Before you dismiss this dream entirely, however, consider that there might be something very positive that you needed to hear.

Answer C's secret rule gives significance to dreams without linking them to celestial communication: *Dreams have psychological meaning and are a key to unconscious knowledge and feelings.* You view dreams as a source of information about what is going on in the depths of your mind. You are open to examining your own mind, but reluctant to discover if any greater mind exists. Perhaps you are unafraid to probe your deepest self as long as that self doesn't have a soul connected to it. At most, you consider some vague notion of the beyond, but all you really know and care about is the present existence. That reasoning has served you well and keeps order in your world, while allowing you to be rather liberal-minded and open to new ideas.

This choice sounds good, except that you have to struggle very hard to maintain a rational façade to your mental investigations. You know that you can't really find the depths or limits of your mind, no matter how deep you go, so why not consider that your personal mind is just an extension of a greater Mind that shares information with you? In your attempt to be scientific and rational, you may miss a chance to connect to one of the great mysteries of the universe.

4. You are a community clergy member. One of your roles is to act as spiritual counselor, lending a kind ear, offering helpful advice, and always maintaining confidentiality. But someone has just confessed a murder to you, and furthermore has revealed that he is about to commit anoth-

er one. According to your code, you are not permitted to tell the police—or anyone. Clearly, if you don't say anything, another person might die. What will you do?

A. All I can do is advise the person not to commit the next murder. I cannot break my oath of confidential service.

B. I will alert the police and tell them what I know. I choose to save a human life, and I know God would want me to do that.

C. I will warn the police about the plan for murder, but I will not tell them about the confession concerning the previous crime.

What happens when a religious commitment conflicts with justice and safety? Answer A says that religious vows win out: *My code of ethics as a person of God forbids me to violate a confidence, even to save a life.* If you chose this answer, you have a strong conscience and a firm, if not rigid, sense of right and wrong. You are loyal to those you serve, and probably also to those with whom you are personally involved. In an age of shifting values, you are in some ways a rock that others rely on. The community needs individuals like you, because you are a trustworthy friend come hell or high water.

Unfortunately, your strict and at times unyielding value system can end up trapping you in the corner. Despite the surety of your responsibilities as a spiritual leader and friend, there might be doubt and conflict in your own mind as you find yourself in moral dilemmas created by the same strict code. You must consider whether your secret rule, made at an earlier life stage, serves you and others best now. Decide if God might indeed favor saving a life rather than sticking with a tradition.

Answer B allows you to shape your action according to particular circumstances: *My code of ethics, despite any oath I have taken, must always choose life.* You feel that confidentiality is relatively less important than life. If you immediately chose this secret rule, you have a fluid value system in the process of change. If you lingered and thought long and hard, you would still feel ruled to a large degree by guilt and punishment. Whether quickly or slowly, you have come to the conclusion that you best serve your fellow humans and God by shaping your actions to individual situations. That displays the ability to be flexible and to compromise, which are generally healthy traits.

It is doubtful that many would fault you, but how loose have you become? Is it only murder that would change your code of ethics, or would other crimes and misdemeanors become fair game? For example, would you turn someone in for sexual abuse? How about a doctor who is addicted to drugs, yet still works on patients—even though he is known to have made life-threatening errors? One role of the clergy is to allow someone to have a place to speak his or her mind without fear of punishment. Test yourself by trying out other hypothetical situations, and see if this rule continues to work.

The secret rule behind answer C offers a way to compromise some— but not all—of your spiritual duties: *My religious oath allows me to save a life, but not to intervene for deeds already done.* It is acceptable to prevent something from happening, but it's not your business to see that justice is done. If you chose this secret rule, you are still fairly rigid in your ethics but are willing to make exceptions to religious obligations. You are clearly still conflicted, however, as you would prevent a crime but still remain silent about what has already occurred.

In your ideal world, congregants would turn themselves in after a good talking to. But if the criminal does not own up to his previous crimes, do you have any responsibility to the community? You realize that a certain amount of flexibility is necessary; that is healthy. But once that change starts occurring, you will be called to reassess your boundaries in general. Is God's punishment enough, or should there be some earthly consequences for past crimes as well? The answer will not be found in the writings of philosophers and theologians; you alone must find which code and which secret rule really fits best.

5. While watching television, you come across a program on the possibility of dark forces at work in our world. A couple reports that someone is attacking them with evil. They believe that someone has invoked the devil to torment them. This couple describes how they become suddenly weak and ill, and smell foul odors. Their home is being affected too, as objects fall off shelves and senseless accidents occur. The terrified people are convinced that black magic has been practiced on them. Do you believe that a devil or evil forces could be behind these occurrences?

A. Yes. A dark force contrary to the force of God—a Satan—is doing them harm and could do any of us harm.

B. No. I do not believe in good and evil forces. There is a rational explanation for all that we see. Life is not subject to the whims or control of supernatural forces.

C. I don't believe in evil powers, but I believe in the force of good. Bad things happen when goodness is absent.

While studying spirituality, we must address the possible presence of evil. If you believe in unearthly forces that can purposely work against us, then you chose answer A. Your secret rule is as follows: *There is evil and darkness that can affect any of us.* You acknowledge an opposing force to God, by whatever name, and you believe that it causes harm and must be respected. When you look at the world, you see the work of God or Satan being done. You probably also believe that it is possible for people to wield the force of darkness or evil in a direct attempt to hurt other individuals.

Your understanding of evil and why it exists says a great deal about your metaphysical and religious beliefs. Both wise men and fools believe in the dark and the light, but it is in the interpretation of what they see that makes the difference. Dark forces can be considered a part of our very own nature. Each of us has a dark side that is natural and does not make us evil, but human. There is indeed free will in choosing the dark over the light, and some believe that we can study and use our power to harm others. If, after considering this option, you still feel certain that outer, evil forces do exist, then your secret rule works for you—as long as you can maintain this belief without getting paranoid and living in fear. On the other hand, if you find yourself unhealthily dwelling on the dark forces around you and experiencing tremendous anxiety, perhaps you have to work on a change in perspective.

The secret rule for answer B argues: *The world is neither good nor evil, but a series of sequential events based on laws of science.* Life is amoral—neither good nor bad—by design. There is no one making us do good or evil; we have only ourselves, the human race, to condemn or congratulate for what we do. If you chose this secret rule, you are the ultimate rationalist. Whatever happens is neutral in value and just a matter of interpretation. In your universe, the couple under discussion has things happen to them because of strict physical and psychological laws. If we don't understand it today, we shall tomorrow.

Individuals who deny any force outside them are determined to retain control of their lives at any cost. If "forces" are used to explain events, then how can one maintain control? Then we'd all be at the mercy of the invisible and unexplained. Do you resist feeling so vulnerable? The upside of such thinking is that such individuals take responsibility for their behavior and have few superstitions. The really big downside of such thinking is that without good and evil as points of reference, where is the moral compass? How do you decide if a behavior is more harmful than good? Where is the conscience about right and wrong if there is no such thing as good or evil, God or Satan?

Answer C tends to diminish the question of evil altogether: *There are no dark forces, but goodness—the true universal force—is not everywhere.* There really is no evil, but a place or person without love around him can become this thing we call "evil" or do "evil" things. If you chose this secret rule, you are an advocate of unconditional love as a path to personal growth. You no longer see the world as dark and light, but rather as really good and less good. Individuals who negate evil sometimes seem simplistic, wanting to deny the unpleasantness and misery that is around them. But they are not simply naïve or overly optimistic. They believe that the best way to help the couple described is to send love to them and their household. And that's not a bad reaction.

At one level, it is a beautiful concept to believe only in the best. Unconditional love without thought of evil is a wonderful idea in theory— throw enough love someone's way and all will be well. If love really is the answer, then maybe it is not Satan or evil we need to fear most but apathy, greed, and selfishness, which bring out the worst in humankind and constitute the real evil we face. If this is your perspective and you feel fulfilled by it, you have found a wonderful answer to the age-old question of evil. But make sure that your answer is not simply a means of avoiding dark and mysterious things out of fear of the unknown.

6. At the summer county fair, you stumble upon a psychic's booth and decide to have a little fun. The gray-haired old woman looks into your palm and begins to tell you true things about your past. She seems to know about your divorce, your surgery, your mother's death—all of it. How amazing! You always thought that psychics and palm readers were a hoax; now you are not so sure. She then warns you that an accident will occur at your home on a certain date. If you and your partner are there, both of you will die. If you are not in the house, the danger will pass and you will be safe. She cannot be more specific. What will you do?

A. I will not leave the house on that date. Only gullible and fearful people listen to psychics.

B. I will not be home on that fated day. The psychic was sent to save my life.

C. I will make my schedule more flexible and will be prepared to leave the house at a moment's notice on that day.

Can horrific events be predicted by gifted people? And if so, were we meant to avoid death? If you think foretelling events is all guesswork, you follow the secret rule behind answer A: *There is no predictable future; it is all what we make it to be.* People put stock in psychics because it enables them to feel more in control of their lives, right? You are practical, well grounded, and ready to take responsibility for your life. You are a reliable person who makes no excuses and offers none. You create your own luck—no need for you to get the lotto numbers. It is all well and good, as they say, except that you are in denial of what has shown to be predicted and true. A countless number of individuals have made predictions that have come true. That is a fact. It is also on record and common knowledge that many predictions do not come true. There are phony psychics and false predictions. But is everyone either a fraud or a lucky guesser? That is more the question.

The possibility of predicting the future wreaks havoc on your understanding of the world. If the future can be seen, it must exist. If it exists, where does it exist and how can it be known and seen? It means there is an invisible world where things are evident before they happen, and there are those who are able to enter this realm. This is where it gets scary, if this is your secret rule. It now sounds as if there is a fate or destiny for you. Does that make you panic, feeling a loss of control? Consider that you might be shaping your spirituality around an obsession with control instead of authentic beliefs and insights.

Answer B's secret rule poses a strong belief in prophecy and foretelling: *Predicting the future is not only possible, but a gift sent to save us.* According to your spirituality, many psychic predictions of the future do come true, and a wise person respects that the future can be known and seen. You accept that the spiritual realm is accessible. Most likely, you draw predictions frequently from various sources—for example, astrology, tarot cards, palm reading, and other forms of "psychic readings."

Your challenge is to separate the wheat from the chaff. You have probably gotten readings in which something was predicted that never came true. In fact, it has happened more than once. You have also gotten contradictory readings, and still you persevered to find what was "real." Taken to the extreme, individuals with this secret rule will often not make assertive life choices or take any risks without getting a reading to determine if the planned move is a good one. The more you rely on others to guide you, the more you disempower yourself. You lose confidence in your own intuition and wisdom. If there is anything the New Age movement was supposed to do, it was to get individuals to take responsibility for their own actions, blame others less, and come to believe in their own inner guidance and wisdom. Do you believe in yourself?

Answer C's secret rule considers prediction without wholeheartedly relying on it: *It may be possible that the future can be known, and I feel that such advice should be at least listened to.* It is possible that someone might have some foreknowledge of events. Yet you will not entirely count on such prophecies. If you chose this secret rule, you rely on intuition more than you would readily admit. Most of your friends and colleagues are nonbelievers in such things, but you have your other side—your spiritual/metaphysical side. You know that there is more to life than what you can see and touch. You are conflicted now because you consider yourself rational and realistic, yet you do not discount the possibility that something—somewhere—is sending you a warning.

Sometimes seers are right, but many times they are wrong. So you compromise and choose a safe middle path. If you find yourself comfortable with being open to both sides, then your secret rule works. You are not a control freak; you don't need all the answers, and you aren't given to panic either. To take the next step, however, try trusting your own intuition instead of some psychic's words. What precautions do *you* feel are either necessary or unnecessary?

7. Throughout history, and certainly within the last two thousand years, there have been innumerable wars between nations. Often, the driving force behind these wars has been religious discord. Even today, the major religions are actively in conflict with one or more other religions. Traditionally, each side believes that God or Goodness is on their side, to the point that some will gladly sacrifice their lives and expect a greater heavenly reward for having done so. Is God on anyone's side?

A. God is on the side of the people who promote equality and peace.

B. God, if He exists, is neutral and doesn't take sides in a war.

C. God is angry with both sides and will probably punish both sides in some way.

In your opinion, is there one real Truth, one right way? Answer A's secret rule suggests that this is so: *God is on the side of those countries that believe in liberty and equality for all people.* According to your beliefs, God assesses the beliefs of various cultures and then sides with one or two. In fact, God probably supports *our* interpretation of spiritual law. In times of war, then, you believe that God can and should be giving us a helping hand, an advantage in some way. What are the signs that God favors one country or group over another? Is victory assured when people are on the "right side"? Ironically, the other side feels that it receives divine support, too.

Do you feel that certain other cultures and religions are in league with evil, with Satan? Does God excuse the deaths of innocents because we really didn't mean it? Is anyone's hands clean? It's nice to think that God watches over us and helps the good guys defeat evil. The problem with this thinking is that it negates the other side's belief in their God and gives us a feeling of superiority that is, in some ways, inconsistent with the very values we espouse, like equality. We don't know, of course, what God is really up to, but hopefully He is at least giving us the wisdom to do the highest and best thing for all humankind.

Answer B's secret rule states, *God is not subject to human emotions and loyalties; He does not take sides.* In other words, God is a neutral force. You feel that mankind and mankind alone is responsible for resolving the problems it creates. Obviously, if you are a nonbeliever, then there is no godly intervention at all. But if there is God in your life, He seems to be a distant observer. He is there in some capacity but refuses to involve Himself in petty, earthly conflicts. Why is this so? Is there no right and wrong in absolute terms? Is there not a better way to treat humanity, a more righteous way to be? A more godly nation?

In some sense, if you subscribe to answer B's secret rule, doesn't it seem as if God doesn't care? Or maybe we are here to learn a lesson: "Learn to get along and solve your problems." Once again, we cannot know the mind of God when we barely can figure out our own secret rules. While neutrality seems a nice safe position, this rule implies that God may not be actively involved in any of our problems on earth. Are you fundamentally comfortable with this understanding of God?

Answer C's secret rule suggests an angry God and, perhaps, a tragically flawed human race: *God is not neutral in war, but angry with both sides for not obeying His commands.* God is livid at the endless, senseless loss of life that He sees happening day after day. If you chose this secret rule, you are a highly moral, if not somewhat unrealistic person. You also believe that there can be no righteous or acceptable killing, that all of it is equal. You feel that humanity has failed to live up to sacred laws, and that God no longer sees any "good guys."

Your choice of answer C reflects a pessimistic spiritual outlook. You probably suffer from guilt and fear because of your secret rule. You have lost a sense of right and wrong, disbelieving that there could be a better cause or a moral side. If we turn our heads away and do nothing when we see immoral actions like the killing and subjugation of a people, wouldn't that be wrong? Are there no justifiable wars? No good guys? Can you live a healthy life with this viewpoint? Your disdain for war is healthy, but your perception of an angry God is likely to make you live in fear.

8. Recently, you have had a run of "bad luck." In a short period of time, you have lost your job, broken your ankle, had a best friend move away, and finally, had your car broken into. It feels like the bottom has fallen out of your life. How do you interpret your present turn of events?

A. This must be a karmic lesson. When so many things happen and none of it is my fault, then I am paying for things I did in the past.

B. Life is about suffering, which is supposed to be good for your soul. It is God's will and there is little that can be done.

C. The random hand of chance or fate is simply manifesting itself in my life. There's no other explanation.

Do you believe in the world's retribution and/or in the virtue of suffering? You follow answer A's secret rule if you think that there is some sort of price to pay for past decisions and actions, whether they occurred in past lives or past years: *When bad things happen to a good person, it is karma—a lesson in the form of payback.* You reap as you sow, and this law of the universe means that bad deeds from the past will haunt us in the present. Along with that belief comes a whole series of associated beliefs that you use to make choices in your life. If you really believe that you did nothing during this lifetime to cause a bad string of events, then you are a student of reincarnation as well.

Karma is the balancing of a score from days gone by. As a believer in retribution for past misdeeds, you are, on the one hand, trying to take responsibility by not blaming others but accepting your present state as part of the greater cosmic plan. On the other hand, when you are steeped in these spiritual and metaphysical beliefs, you become helpless and must stoically accept your fate. You must be very careful not to ascribe every misfortune to bad karma, as if you had nothing to do with your present-life experiences but are only a passive sufferer of centuries-old original events. This thinking will weaken your initiative and give you an excuse to avoid making the requisite life changes.

Answer B's secret rule finds value in misfortune: *Suffering is a natural part of human existence, and I expect it to be part of my life at sometime.* It is how God taught the saints, and it teaches us to be humble and compassionate towards others. If you chose this secret rule, you feel that you are taking on a role that God has chosen for you. You feel fated to have this suffering as part of your development as a person. In this role you expect to carry out difficult tasks for a greater good. This is how you view hardships in your life. The events described are tests set up by heaven to see if you are worthy. There is no complaining for you because, as part of the test, you must accept your fate gracefully.

But is every bad thing a test? Aren't there things that are chance or coincidence? How do you really know that any event is part of the great cosmic test just because it makes you suffer? Is it all God's will, or do your fellow humans have any part in what happens to you? The problem with your fatalistic beliefs is that they can lead you to take no action to correct the things that have gone wrong. Why bother to fight the lawsuit or look for another job? Maybe you deserve it. And is the next lesson to become homeless and totally penniless? Maybe you aren't supposed to find another job until you have completely hit bottom. If you accept the premise of suffering for your own good, it leads to absurd notions of what you should or should not be doing. No one can say with any surety why bad things happen to good people. It is one thing to see a certain benefit in hardship or suffering—it might teach you to be more sensitive, to appreciate life more, or the like. But to rely on suffering and accept it as God's wish will prevent you from helping yourself and learning other valuable lessons along the way.

Perhaps you believe that events simply unfold. If so, you chose answer C and its secret rule: *Bad things are just happenstance without any great cosmic meaning.* There is no method to the unfolding of events, good or bad. Some individuals experience better fortune than others, and that's life. If you chose this secret rule, then you are realistic and self-determined. You do your best and expect the best, but you realize that the worst can still happen. Getting fired from your job was a manmade event—your boss's doing. Likewise, the crook who broke into your car was not a messenger from God or a force of retribution from your Louis XIV days; your car was available and easy to get into.

You call it chance. The advantage of this secret rule is that, on any given day, things can turn around. Good fortune can follow bad fortune as day follows night. There are no lessons to be learned or karmic debts to pay off. If you can work hard and maybe catch a break now and then, you are satisfied. It is a lot more spontaneous and effortless than trying to figure out the meaning of every parking ticket. The only real downside is that you never probe into possible reasons behind a chain of unfortunate events. If there is no overarching philosophy, then it is much harder to connect the dots and see a pattern you can change. Indeed, if there are things that just happen, then there very well could be events and experiences that happen for a reason, based on other secret rules that you have failed to look into.

9. You and a friend decide to attend a stadium-size prayer service with a famous evangelist as the main speaker. There are literally thousands of fervent individuals praying. There are speakers reading from the Bible, but mostly a lot of prayer. Your friend, who suffers from severe arthritis and walks with a cane, has always been deeply religious. At the present time, he needs several medicines to function, but he feels that the prayers of thousands will help heal him. You also have some medical problems, including emphysema and severe migraine headaches. Several hours after the service concludes, your friend states that he feels much better and notices that he

can now walk without his cane. He is excited but not that surprised. He says it proves that if you have faith, you don't need medicine—only God. You don't feel any changes in your condition, and nothing happens over the next couple of days. How do you understand what has happened to you and your friend?

A. Prayer can heal if you have enough faith. Most of us lack that unyielding faith, so healing doesn't happen as much as it should or could.

B. Prayer is beneficial to some extent, but should not be counted on. One should still largely rely on Western medicine.

C. Prayer makes devotees feel better, but in reality it has little if any long-term effect on the outcome of the illness. People think they will get better, so they do for a while.

Do you rely on—or at least believe in—prayer as a source of healing? You believe in the power of prayer if you chose answer A and, therefore, follow its secret rule: *Prayer is an effective method of healing if you have enough faith in God.* Prayer works, as has been shown time and again, but will not work for those who lack the proper faith and trust in God. If you chose this secret rule, you are a religious person who also feels deeply flawed. You did not have enough faith, so how could you be healed? Actually, you feel unworthy of being healed. You also judge yourself and others by a rather strict system of good deeds and bad sins. As a result, you chronically find yourself and others unworthy. Underneath it all, you also have many questions about God and His relationship to man. You want desperately to believe more sincerely than you do, but you can't.

Your faith has given you as much anxiety as peace of mind. If God's intervention proves your faith, what does no action or change in one's health status prove? How do you know that it isn't God's will to let you suffer as part of His greater plan, no matter how hard you pray and believe? As your rule stands, you feel like a failure, which you also project onto others. Consider changing your rule so that your religious beliefs give you comfort and encouragement. Otherwise, you will continue to struggle, judging others and yourself much too harshly.

Answer B's secret rule asserts: *Prayer can be a healthful adjunct to traditional medicine, but is not to be relied upon for real cures.* Prayer works sometimes, for some people, but it is unrealistic to expect miracles no matter how deep your faith goes. You see yourself as an open-minded, practical, religious or spiritual person. You want to believe in prayer, but fundamentally don't. You will first take any traditional treatment available and aren't about to wait for prayer to start working. You may have seen some instances of prayer at work, but mostly your experience with prayer is what you have read or heard about secondhand.

Your practical attitude is apparently functional: If prayer works, you will take it like another drug. Yet you forget that sincerity in and real acceptance of prayer may be necessary to make prayer really work as a treatment. Prayer is not just another drug that you drip into your veins. It involves a much more active belief and open heart, which you might not presently have but can certainly work on. Maybe it only works if you really believe that God is there for you. Do you? Can you just pretend that, or might you have to search your soul and find out if there is indeed even an ounce of true faith? So if you really want prayer to work and not just hope it's an occasional adjunct, you may have to do more than you ever have to discover what your true spiritual feelings are. Today is as good a day as any to begin.

Answer C's secret rule considers prayer a trick of the mind: *Prayer is nothing more than a placebo effect or self-hypnosis.* According to your beliefs, prayer works as well as a sugar pill—a placebo—or much like the power of suggestion. You don't see God as being active in the lives of human beings, and may wonder if God is really "out there." If you participate in religion in any way, it is strictly for ceremony, ritual, community, and maybe even appearance. Praying to some invisible God to get well seems, if you are honest, pretty silly. You can always rationalize that any healing which takes place as a result of prayer is either suggestion or a spontaneous healing. You have all the bases covered.

Ask yourself whether religious healings are not the only thing you find hard to swallow. You may find holistic medical treatments bogus and foolish. In fact, any new scientific or social discoveries that don't fit into your preconceived world are likely to be rejected. You are the ultimate skeptic. Therefore, we can only assume that it would be silly for others to pray for you, should you become ill. Well, try to be *completely* honest. Would you dust off your prayer book if the doctor said, "There is nothing more we can do for you"? If you can admit that to yourself, why not re-examine your rule as to why you struggle so hard against your natural desire for a spiritual connection.

10. You are alone in your living room, and you begin to feel light-headed. You sit down on the couch and soon pass out. The next thing you realize is that you are floating towards the ceiling and feeling perfectly fine. Without any distress, you find yourself floating above your body and can look down and see yourself slumped on the couch. You continue to drift farther away from your body, toward a bright light. A tremendous sense of peace and calm fills you as you rise higher and higher. Then suddenly, and with a severe thump, you are back in your body and sitting on the couch. What happened to you?

A. I had an authentic near-death experience. There is life after death!

B. The whole thing was just a dream. It's a fantasy of what many wish would be true.

C. My experience is a sign that I have potential which I never realized, but it certainly does not promise an afterlife.

If you had an "unearthly" experience, would you accept it as truth or chalk it up to a dream? The secret rule behind answer A places a lot of faith behind spiritual experiences. Acknowledging that you had a near-death experience, you also acknowledge that life after death occurs: *Our spiritual selves can separate from our bodies, which proves that we survive death with our minds intact.* The only explanation possible is that you emerged from your body and floated toward the spirit world, only to return to earth with new knowledge. For argument's sake, let's explore this understanding. Does this experience *prove* that there is life after death? Some people whose hearts have stopped also report the "light," but they could never say what happens beyond the light. Could the light you saw simply be the light you have heard and read about? Don't you really want the light to be there?

If you had an out-of-body experience, would it change the way you live your life now? Would you take more risks if you were sure of a future existence? If you are a true believer in a separate, sentient spirit flying off to meet its maker, then one might expect profound changes in your attitude towards life and death. But if the thought of a near-death experience leaves you feeling a little alarmed or confused, your secret rule is not consistent with your deepest beliefs. You clearly want to believe in the world beyond and would benefit from some counsel with those wise in the ways of the spirit world to maximize this very profound experience.

Answer B's secret rule is a rational, safe answer: *There is no evidence that we can separate our physical and spiritual selves and ultimately bring them together again; it's all in our minds.* It is a dream of many that our souls can leave our bodies and return to them again. Certainly, it is easy to dismiss your experience as a dream. But why start out assuming you were dreaming? What is it about your spirit and body as separate entities that seems so impossible? You have read or heard stories of people who were clinically dead and then came back and reported seeing their body as they floated upwards. These appear in all cultures, as told by children and adults. What, in your present religious beliefs, dismisses such events? Do you disbelieve because they are not proven in a scientific way? Are you happy choosing rationalism to the point that you cannot open your mind to other possibilities?

If you chose this secret rule, you may be terribly frightened to leave the safety of your present belief system. While your secret rule keeps spirit and body tightly glued together, it may be that some additional readings or classes are in order. You will not feel any inner peace until you resolve some of the fundamental issues that your "dream" is trying to show you. Your experience and the questions it triggered are leading you to learn something. If you claim you are agnostic or atheist, all the more reason to question that as your true belief system!

Finally, answer C's secret rule gives significance to your experience but still roots it in the individual instead of God or a Greater Spirit: *I have the potential to explore other forms of consciousness and tap into greater levels of existence.* You are comfortable with the understanding that we, as individual spiritual beings, have a lot more potential than we realize. But you do not push the envelope by further exploring connections, the afterlife, or God.

Your secret rule shows that you are open-minded and curious. Since you believe that there is more to us than what we see on the surface, why stop there? If you are willing to acknowledge that there are greater levels of existence, why not take it a bit further? What is the purpose of such levels? Are you afraid to venture into religious questions? Perhaps that is why you temper the out-of-body experience by claiming it shows *individual* potential and power. Do you fear the responsibility if you recognize that God or a greater force might be involved in your life? Of course, if you are satisfied with your present understanding, stick with it; your secret rule has provided you with balance and contentment. But chances are that your supernatural experience will start you thinking about the larger questions of spirituality, and if that is the case, do not let fear get in the way of grasping not only greater consciousness, but also greater connection.

CONCLUSION

You have thought through some difficult spiritual questions and completed a profound self-search. If you find that you tended toward two, not one, of the answers for certain situations, you are not wishy-washy or weak. Most of us are still in the process of spiritual discovery, and that quest continues throughout life. The fact that you are trying to come to terms with the "big questions" is admirable and healthy. Most importantly, after finishing this chapter, realize the benefit of having an open mind and a courageous spirit that is willing to look at life from a variety of perspectives.

9. Sex

Sex is about getting touched. Doesn't "being sexy" mean that you possess a quality that makes other people want to touch you? This kind of touch, let's agree, is the placing of one's hand on another with purposeful intent. Touch is the stimulation of a physical part of us that has been, in some way, asleep. Awakened from numbness, we cry out, "Don't stop until I'm finished and complete."

Since puberty, we have discovered that it is very important to be touched. By being desired and touched, you connect to someone, if only momentarily. You are not alone, left out, forgotten, or unwanted. The pleasure of being desired and touched makes you feel so alive! You get affirmed and acknowledged. But what, exactly, is sex? It is a form of touching that leads to a unique series of sensations that may or may not end up climaxing in one gigantic sensation. The power of this touch is so enormous that individuals will go to the greatest length to experience it. They will risk life and limb, reputation and fortune, all for the magical feeling that we call sex.

And you must have it, right? Must everything have sex appeal? If so, why? Why do we need to buy things that make us feel sexy—lingerie, seductive music, perfumes and colognes? Could this obsession be one of the few ways in which most of us transform our everyday experience into something extraordinary? Or do you not really prioritize sex anymore? Is good conversation as delightful as good sex to you? Would you rather have a great friend and mediocre sex or great sex and a mediocre friend? Do you know your most secret rules about sex and being sexy? Let's look at a few of your possible secret rules to make sure you are getting what you truly want from this thing called sex.

1. You recently ended a long-term relationship. It has been a while since you've played the "single and available" scene, and you are in the

mood to have some fun. You gather a few friends for an evening at a trendy dance club. This club is known for its celebrity clientele, so you are not completely shocked when you see your favorite movie star up on the dance floor. However, you are completely shocked when, toward the end of the night, that same star offers to buy you a drink. Within half an hour, the two of you are dancing closely. It is not long before this movie idol invites you back to a hotel room, presumably to have a night of passion together. You have the opportunity to have sex with the object of your fantasies! Most likely, this will be a one-night stand. You have no expectation of a profound love affair. What will you do?

A. I will go back to the room and have the sexual romp of a lifetime.

B. I will politely end the evening. This person is pursuing loveless sex and that means we would just be using each other.

C. I will go back to the room and fool around a little, but I am doubtful that I will go "all the way." Just being together in the same room is quite enough for me.

When it comes to sex, are you ever into plain old fun, or does sex always carry a deeper emotional involvement? Answer A's secret rule goes for a rousing good time: *If I have the chance to have sex with someone that I have always desired, I will take the opportunity.* Your dream has come true and you are apparently unconcerned with where it will lead. If you chose this secret rule, you like to experience sex as an adventure—at least sometimes. Desire overrides thoughts of commitment, emotional involvement, and possibly—but not definitely—even safety. There is a freedom to your spirit which others admire. You are uninhibited and courageous. But that carefree spirit can get you in trouble at times. Are you cautious enough to protect yourself, or do you just jump in? Do you suffer from regrets after you make an impulsive decision based on the pounding of your heart? In other words, has this secret rule helped you?

If you generally tend to grab an opportunity for sexual pleasure—*full* sexual pleasure—when unattached and have no serious regrets, then your secret rule does work for you. Simply consider some less-obvious reasons why you might take such a risk as to have sex with a person you barely know anything about. Is it really about serving yourself well, or is it about boredom, revenge, or being too drunk to care? Are you just getting back at someone who left long ago, or do you genuinely feel that a one-night stand will satisfy you? By answering these questions, you will learn whether or not you need to adjust a rule that prioritizes immediate pleasure.

You have firm notions concerning the higher purpose of sex if you chose answer B and its associated rule: *I don't have sex with people I don't know, no matter how attractive or famous they might be.* You don't have sex without feelings or commitment. In fact, you have a strong moral code that overrides your sexual desires. You take your relationships seriously. It may be a simple matter of having grown up with a certain code; sex without love or marriage is just wrong. If it is wrong—period—then would it create too many bad feelings for you to attempt to push yourself into something that is against one of your most basic rules? Is your decision to abstain from this sexual encounter based on religion or fear? What is the main motivation behind your decision not to enjoy a night of intense passion with an object of your fantasies?

By choosing answer B, you also express a strong determination not to feel used in some way. Do you often feel that the other person is getting more out of sex? Maybe the issue is not so much that uncommitted sex is wrong, but rather that you don't get what you want from it and feel taken advantage of. It is important to identify any less-obvious motives behind your answer.

The secret rule behind answer C attempts to allow pleasure without fully giving in to your sexual urges: *If I am attracted to someone special, I will touch that person but feel uncertain about having sex too quickly.* You want some kind of contact, but you are not ready to engage in full intercourse. So you hesitantly decide to continue the evening, probably worrying that your movie star will become angry at being teased, but willing to take that risk. If you chose this secret rule, you are conflicted about sex; you struggle between pursuing pleasure and feeling shame or confusion by doing so. There is a part of you that imagines you are a free spirit, ready to experience great sexual adventure. Yet when the time comes, you cannot yield to your impulses because, someplace inside, a little voice is telling you that it is wrong to take total pleasure for pleasure's sake.

Think about it. You have your chance of a lifetime, totally unencumbered, but choose to go for a little *cuddling* instead of the fireworks. Who is really telling you "no"—your feelings or part of someone else's conscience? Hopefully, it is the former. If you are truly abiding by someone else's rules, though, your secret rule is not as authentic as it may sound. It seems you stop short of what you desire, and this may reflect a deeper pattern worth examining if you are to enjoy your life to the fullest. That being said, your restraint might also come in very useful. Perhaps you are cautious about disease, pregnancy, and future emotional pain. If that is the case, then your secret rule works for you. You do not deny yourself all fun, but you put a limit on it because "the big picture" is never far away.

2. ♦ Your lover has been invited to a bachelor(ette) party with a group of friends. You know these friends quite well and consider them a wild bunch. There is no doubt in your mind that there will be strippers and sex acts at the party. To the best of your knowledge, your lover has not agreed or disagreed to go yet. Now is the time to say something—if anything—in case you are uncomfortable with this situation. What will you do?

A. I will forbid my partner to go to the party.

B. I won't say anything. I'll let my partner make the decision alone.

C. I will explain that I am uncomfortable with the situation and ask my partner to consider not going to the party.

How much do you seek to control your partner's sexual desire? If you feel you have a strong right to keep the sexual focus on yourself, then you chose answer A and its secret rule: *I will not allow my lover to be in a situation where sexual acts are likely to occur.* Assuming you even have that power, isn't your lover mature enough to make these decisions? Consider that you are too controlling and often have little trust in others, even those you know well. It would be one thing to protest if you knew your lover was definitely going to the party and was certain to cheat on you, but to flat out forbid it in advance indicates a serious lack of trust and some serious deficiencies in the relationship. If you know your lover is that unreliable, what are doing with this person in the first place?

For you, a committed relationship does not mean committed sex only. It also means committed sexual desire, sole sexual context, and maybe even wearing figurative blinders when around the rest of the world. It is clear you feel threatened, but of what? Do you fear that your sweetheart will have sex outside the relationship because your partner is dissatisfied with your sex life? Has this individual cheated on you before? And if you forbid one party, remember that your prohibition doesn't prevent things from happening at other times. It is not like sex for free, let alone for money, cannot be had elsewhere. Your need to control and dominate means you already feel threatened and things are out of control in your mind. Rather than forbid your lover to go, it would be better to find out what you might do to strengthen your sex life and then let go of the reins before you kill the thing entirely. Attempting to completely control another's sexual situations is not healthy for anyone. Your secret rule is bound to create anxiety and anger in your life.

Answer B is built on a secret rule that says, *I trust my lover to not jeopardize our relationship with casual sex, and I have no reason to assert my opinion concerning sexual matters that don't involve me.* You will let your lover decide the best thing to do. If you chose this secret rule, you are capable of a trusting relationship. As an adult, you realize that you have no right to control another person's sexual decisions. Surely, you have an opinion one way or the other, but you have decided not to voice it at all. But are you comfortable enough to at least vocalize your opinion in a nonthreatening way? It sounds like it could be a pretty wild party. Is your partner capable of using restraint when faced with temptation? If your lover did participate in some way with one of the strippers, what would that mean? Would you be resentful if your lover decided to participate?

Your resolve to avoid outward attempts to possess someone's entire sexual life is admirable. But there is no reason why you shouldn't calmly express concerns to your partner. Maybe your lover is shocked that you have no opinion on the matter. Maybe your mate would like to know what limits you see as healthy. If you truly don't have a care, then your answer is authentic and your secret rule functions well for you. But if you suffer fear and upset inside, yet hold back because you feel you have no right to speak up, then your secret rule will sabotage you in the end. Consider being a little more vocal—albeit maturely and respectfully—about your expectations and hopes when it comes to your sex life.

Answer C's secret rule takes a healthy, open approach to your sexual concerns: *When I feel my relationship could be threatened by a sexual situation, I will be honest and express my concerns and expectations.* It sounds like the party could get pretty wild, and you feel the need to tell your partner that you are scared that something might happen. If you chose this secret rule, you have the beginnings of an honest relationship. It is the beginning because the first part is being honest; what you do next will make all the difference. Your lover is invited to a traditional rite of passage, but you are entitled to be anxious and to communicate your feelings. Maybe you will even make a request: "I would feel better if you didn't go." It is fine to be so honest, but do try to avoid the ever-manipulative, "If you love me, you won't do this."

By requesting that your lover not attend, or at least that your lover stay very restrained if attending, what message are you giving your lover? Are you fearful that your relationship won't survive the party? The great fear in most relationships is that the other person can't really be controlled and that he might do something damaging to the present relationship. If your honesty can be followed with the honest expectation that your lover will do the right thing, you have hit an ideal balance. In return, you will either know you have a "keeper" or, equally productive, you will discover that this person is not right for you and save yourself further problems down the road. Your efforts to be honest and mature are applauded.

3. It is the beginning of a romantic relationship with a friend, and you are deciding on the sexual ground rules. Both of you are aware that the other has been recently involved, but you have not been very specific about the past or your expectations of the future. You are excited about this relationship and think it may have long-term potential. But right now, you are most concerned with reaching a comfortable agreement about your sexual practices. Which of the following statements best describes your ideal situation?

A. We will start building a sexual relationship but also continue seeing other people.

B. We will be each other's exclusive lovers and develop an intimate relationship.

C. We will agree to develop an exclusive partnership, but if a really good opportunity with someone else comes along, I'll allow myself to explore it—on the side.

When you decide to forge a new sexual relationship, how exclusive do you want it to be? The secret rule behind answer A says, *I reserve the right to be sexually active with more than one person until a commitment seems warranted.* In other words, while you are starting this relationship up, you will continue to date and sleep with other people. If you chose this secret rule, you struggle with having real intimacy with your lover. Perhaps you are afraid to rely completely on someone, as that might make you vulnerable. It may be that you have been hurt and are now trying very hard to avoid pain. Explore the reasoning behind this rule, even if it is a bit unsettling to think about. Understanding why you follow this rule will allow you to adjust it, if you desire.

When you are just beginning a new love, there is a transition time between multiple partners and commitment. As individuals mature, though, they find it is generally harder to be intimate with more than one person. When will you know that you are ready for monogamy? A lot will depend on your history, of course. For some, there is never a time to be fully committed; it seems limiting, suffocating, and intolerable. If you are content and fulfilled with managing several lovers at once, then your secret rule functions healthily in your life. Hopefully, though, at some point, you will find that you *can* commit to someone, as it is the only way to develop the kind of intimacy that most people desire. If you find that no one ever seems to be quite enough, then it is time to revisit the rule and look more deeply at why you tend to keep your options open.

Answer B's secret rule seeks monogamy from the start: *When I find someone for whom I deeply care, I want and expect a committed relationship.* You have already decided that this person is special and worthy of your monogamous affection. If you chose this secret rule, you are quick to commit and seem to know your mind and heart very well. You also take precautions, reducing your risk of disease and lack of intimacy by choosing one lover. It is your ideal to form a quick and tight bond with someone. Now answer this question: Is your relationship ready for such commitment?

You may naturally tend toward an exclusive relationship, but many people do not. Is it your partner's desire to be monogamous as well? If you don't get your new lover to commit quickly, is the relationship over? Sometimes people are not in the same emotional space at the same time. If you wish to be monogamous and committed and your lover does not, can you handle that or will you feel betrayed? And are you ready to have sex at all? Obviously, you take sex very seriously. That being so, you should be very confident in a relationship before jumping into a full sexual dynamic. While there is often emphasis on those who find it hard to commit, there is an equal danger for those who are too willing, too quickly, to declare their undying sexual commitment. While your early decision to declare your special interest in your newfound friend may seem mature and desirable, it also may be premature and may put too much pressure on the relationship.

Answer C's secret rule states, *I will commit to the person I have until someone better comes along.* Yes, believe it or not, that is what your secret rule says. You feel strongly about the person you are with, but you seem to have no delusions that this is your final life choice. You desire your partner thus far and prefer to be monogamous, but you have left yourself an out. When it comes to realism, you are the most practical of persons. Some might even call you cynical. You are always scanning the horizon, aware that somebody might come along who is even more wonderful than the person you are with presently. That can be called "trading up." Do you always try to trade up?

Think about this secret rule. Has it made you happy? Has it produced mature and healthy relationships? It is hard to build something intimate when you always have an eye on the back door. While no one would suggest that you stay with someone who makes you unhappy or with whom you seem to have no future, people are not mutual funds to keep trading for higher returns. Your approach to this new relationship is a bit pessimistic; you are already half-expecting to find someone better. At some point, you have to look at your behavior and see whether you are being fair to yourself, as well as to your host of lovers. Maybe there is nothing wrong with any of these people; you just don't know what you want. If that's the case, consider not necessarily becoming sexually committed to someone until you are sure they are something you truly want. Perhaps that will diminish some of the fear you feel about being wholeheartedly sexually committed.

4. You and your lover are fighting about sex again. This time, one of you is in the mood but the other is not, and complains about the emotional versus physical elements of your sexual relationship. You realize that you both must start exploring the love/sex connection. In your opinion, how do sex and love fit together?

A. Love is related to sex but much more profound.

B. Part of real love is great sex; the two are inseparable and equal.

C. Love and sex are separate. You can love someone and not have great sex; you can have great sex with someone you don't particularly care for.

If you and your life partner are not sexually compatible, you certainly will have to start asking yourself questions about love and sex. It is not an easy task to articulate the connection between the two, but our secret rules actually hold the answers by which we abide. Answer A's secret rule claims: *Love goes deeper than physical pleasure, but sex is an important expression of that love.* You have learned that love can exist without sex and that love has a special pleasure of its own. Still, sex is a part of expressing love to your partner. If you chose this secret rule, you know that great love will surpass great sex every time. You are clearly the romantic, excited as much by poetic words or a loving deed as by a passionate embrace. Perhaps you adopted this secret rule because at one time, you loved someone with whom you could not have a relatoinship—someone with whom, perhaps, you could not even share your feelings. In such a case, you might have learned to find great pleasure in a simple conversation or a silent glance. Or, quite differently, maybe you currently have such a rich love that one act—the act of sex—could not even come close to tapping into its fullness. Yet you still understand sex as a key part in communicating love.

You possess a beautiful notion about love and sex; it is not something that anyone should ask you to change. Implicit in your rule is the belief that you can love someone dearly and yet not have the strongest passionate connection; other criteria make your relationship just as loving and romantic as the sexual fireworks. Your realistic rule gives you the flexibility to find balance and should make you a solid and loving partner, as long as your partner feels the same way. You might have problems when you are in conflict with a lover who is more attached to physical pleasures than you. Can you put your "all" into a lovemaking experience, or is it always just a part of something else? Could your emphasis on deep love as the primary goal be making your partner less likely to instigate spontaneous sex—no restrictions—for sheer pleasure once in a while? Talk to your lover about your understanding of love versus sex, and try to compromise so that you can share the passionate, sensitive actions that you crave.

The secret rule behind answer B ranks great sex right up there with great love: *Real love is part of and equal to great sex.* You can only conceive of loving someone if the sex is great as well. Does that mean that if you aren't having great sex, you are not in love? If you chose this secret rule, your heart opens most when you are in the throes of passion. You need that intensity and excitement to tell you that this is love. You have, so far, judged love by the passion it generates in you.

You may have been lucky and enjoyed decades of unbridled passion along with the kindness and selflessness that is love as well. It is also possible that you have never had a relationship outlast the sex. Once the passion is gone, the love seems to go. How often must you change partners? If your partner is not as interested as you for a given period of time, then that person is not in love with you anymore? Your emphasis on great sex and great love as synonymous is likely, ultimately, to be a limitation. It may be news to you, but the intense passion of a new love may fade in years, let alone months, and yet something that others call "love" remains. Such people may be compromising or settling, or maybe they just recognize that romantic love has more dimensions than bedroom compatibility. Without judging your very personal secret rule, if you have found that you fall in and out of love as the excitement fades, you might consider that you are missing much that love has to offer. You are missing other joys and pleasures of the heart that come from a more expanded, less physical view of love.

Answer C's secret rule is as follows: *Great sex doesn't prove how you feel about a person.* You have experienced both romantic love and great sex and, for you, they are not really related. You have recognized that great sex, while very persuasive in making you feel intense emotion, can also be fleeting and is not sufficient in and of itself to make you feel great love.

You are not alone in your view. Actually, the idea of a connection between love and sex is a relatively new concept. Not so many years ago, women were taught to tolerate sex, while men went to women of "ill repute" if they wanted real pleasure. Bad girls gave you pleasure and good girls gave you families. Nowadays, we hope to strike a more reasonable balance. While your secret rule might be very real according to your life experience, it is possible for sex and love to be intertwined. Sex can be made "greater" when spiced with a true love connection. Consider opening up to a relationship that honestly unites great sex and profound love—at the same time. Do not be afraid to expect everything. You just might get it!

5. Your lover, who is also your life partner, wants to experiment with some new sexual techniques in order to recharge your sex life. While you love each other very much, both of you recognize that a certain amount of routine and boredom has set in. You never consented to nontraditional sexual practices in past relationships. Previous partners had asked you to do unconventional things in the bedroom, but you refused. Then again, you never really loved them. This time, your true love is asking you, and you definitely want to keep this relationship alive. Are you willing to change your old "do and don't" list?

A. Yes. For someone I love, I would be willing to try something that I previously rejected.

B. No, odd sex practices are for perverts—not for me. I have a moral code and this violates it.

C. While I love my partner, I don't believe in making myself feel too uncomfortable. It is not a moral issue, it is about what feels good, so I'll make an attempt, but if I feel cheap or embarrassed, I'll stop.

In a safe environment, are you willing to adjust your sexual practices in order to spice up your sex life? Or do you think that anything other than traditionally performed sex is deviant? You are rather open-minded and risk-taking if you chose answer A and its accompanying secret rule: *Any sexual practice between two consenting adults is fine, especially when trying to please a love partner.* According to your secret rule, unconventional sex practices are worth a try within an exclusive, loving relationship. You desire to keep the relationship fully functioning, and therefore you are willing to go where you have not gone before. You seem to understand how precious love is and have decided that it is worth pushing the envelope to keep the flame of passion alive.

Do you have a new set of limitations already in mind, or are you willing to try almost anything your partner imagines? Often, our sexual interests and practices are limited by our early experiences, and unless someone literally takes us by the hand and shows us differently, we tend to stick with what we know is acceptable. Now is the time to show some flexibility and realize that many of your limitations were just preconceived notions. Those notions can be broken through if there is enough motivation and encouragement. But how far will you go to please your lover? You are not going to abandon all your morals and personal tastes just to keep someone happy, are you? There is a balance you will have to find between pleasing someone else and pleasing yourself. If you can open up this very personal area, it is likely to bring you closer together and help to keep your relationship alive.

The secret rule behind answer B does not allow you to experiment and explore new means of sexual pleasure: *There are sexual practices that are just immoral and disgusting and that I would never participate in—for anyone.* You have a set of moral values with regards to sex and you are intent on sticking to them. In our scenario, we have not specified what you might have to do, but you have already decided that moving out of your comfort zone is forbidden. You have a rigid moral code that, if broken, will bring you guilt and shame. Family, culture, or religion has probably heavily influenced you. It is difficult to break away from these institutions and still feel good about yourself. You have your beliefs, but there is also the issue of your relationship. Your partner wants something more, and it will be difficult for your mate to excuse your refusal to take risks.

If there is any possibility that you can open up—even a little—and still feel okay, it will help the relationship immensely. Your partner is frustrated, and if your relationship is as healthy as you hope it is, you want to relieve some of that frustration. In this situation, you are in a safe environment with a committed partner. Do you have anything to lose by being a little unconventional? Your secret rule might be keeping you from showing a new and exciting side to the person you care most about.

Answer C's secret rule argues, *I'm willing to experiment with sex, but I won't embarrass myself or let myself be exploited for someone else's pleasure— even someone whom I love.* You hear your partner's wishes and will try to accommodate them up to a point. If you chose this secret rule, you might have been used or manipulated by others and are still feeling resentful. You are fearful of being made a fool or somehow shamed by your actions. Exploitation comes when one person takes advantage of another for selfish purposes. But in this case, the other person is your life partner. If you love this person dearly, how can any sexual experimentation be shameful?

We have not specified what new games might be played, yet you are already suspicious and defensive. Your answer states that you are going to try mutual exploration with someone that you love. But do you trust your partner? Do you really trust anyone? You have given yourself an out so that you will not feel too trapped or vulnerable. Have you been hurt already and feel the need to maintain control by saying, "I can stop this at any time"? If you can break through this barrier and approach your sexual explorations with a more positive attitude, you may add to your self-esteem and trust. Assume that something good will happen and that, most likely, you will be richly rewarded. Then, if you are uncomfortable during your "experiment," consider why you feel this way. Is it physical discomfort or is it your secret rule? Openly discuss your feelings with your partner and see if you can reach a compromise.

6. You are about to get married and are completing a premarital counseling course. The head of the course is married herself and is very knowledgable about modern marital issues. During the final meeting, she emphasizes that partners often do not have equal sex drives. The amount of desire and pleasure is not likely to be the same between the two mates. She also emphasizes that the number of times you have sex does not say anything about the level of pleasure. It is quite possible to have frequent sex and get little pleasure from it, or to have rare sexual experiences that are, nonetheless, outstanding. She asks you to consider your thoughts regarding these issues. Which of the following statements most closely expresses your reaction?

A. I would rather have infrequent great sex than frequent mediocre sex.

B. I would rather have frequent mediocre sex than infrequent great sex.

C. As long as we feel close to each other, I am not hung up on how frequent or pleasurable sex is.

How important is it for sex to be *great sex*? Answer A's secret rule says it's very important: *Great sex once in a while builds a healthier relationship than frequent mediocre sex.* Simply put, you prefer quality over quantity. If you chose this secret rule, you seek intense and powerful life experiences, even if they are few and far between. Sex is just one of the "highs" of a life worth living. You are probably also the type of person who saves money all year so that you can have one great vacation at a daring ski resort or ride the rapids of the Colorado River. Just the anticipation makes the wait worth it. You also have the patience to nurture and bring forth all the glorious experience of a fantastic sex life; you don't mind taking the requisite time for its proper development. If this rule has left you feeling satisfied, don't change a thing. But do make sure you choose a partner who thinks of sex in the same way. Many people like the security of frequent sex with a partner, even if it does not always involve an astonishing physical climax.

Your capacity for intense, unforgettable pleasure is also a statement about your ability to let loose and be out of control. It is wonderful that you want sex to be a thing of wild abandonment at very optimal times. But try not to underestimate the power of frequent, albeit sometimes routine, sex during certain times of need. You might find that your relationship goes through a period where your partner—or you, for that matter—needs a lot of touching and attention. The sex does not have to be earthshaking; it's just desired for the intimacy and release that it offers. If you set sex up to be phenomenal every long-awaited time, then you have to produce magic each time. That puts tremendous pressure on you and your lover, and does not leave room for those quiet, relaxing sexual moments that may serve simply to make you, as a couple, feel connected.

The secret rule that serves as the foundation for answer B claims that frequency is the key: *Frequent, if only mediocre, sex is much more productive than rare but great sex.* You enjoy quantity over quality. We have not defined how infrequent the arrangement would be, but the thought of being without sex for too long is not to your liking. If you chose this secret rule, you are more comfortable with the known and predictable. Patience is not your greatest virtue, and a slow, steady release is preferable to prolonged waiting for the great explosion. It is neither better nor worse than waiting for the occasional earthquake. But it is best to be matched with someone with similar tastes, lest you feel frustrated and disappointed.

Your answer reveals that you are less likely to be a risk-taker or an adventurer. You are, however, reliable and consistent. Your love of pleasure is no less than others', but you may be unwilling to give up the control afforded by habit in order to experience the great crescendo. Like chocolate or vanilla, it is all a matter of taste. Just be aware that you have built a firm reliance on the act of sex. Without your steady quota of love, you are likely to be irritable and unpleasant. Be careful that you don't start equating love with sex and charge your partner with not loving you if that person goes through a dry spell of sorts.

Answer C's secret rule places sex as a far second to plain old affection: *Touching and being close to the one I love is more important than the frequency or intensity of full sexual pleasure.* When a person is right for you, there is a magic in touch. This is what you hold in highest esteem. You are more sensual than sexual. You gain as much pleasure from rubbing elbows as many do from touching more erogenous areas. You also feel more secure with slow, gentle touches; you like to cuddle. It doesn't mean that you cannot or do not enjoy passionate lovemaking; it is just not a priority.

You are patient and gentle by nature, and you serve yourself well by working these traits into your secret rules. If you try to be any other way, you will lose a very precious part of yourself. As long as your partner has a similar understanding of sex, you will enjoy many cozy nights sipping wine and watching good movies in each other's arms.

7. You have been steadily dating a great person of the opposite sex. In fact, you are starting to consider marriage with this person. You don't live together but have keys to each other's homes. One night in your lover's apartment, waiting for your partner to return, you hear the answering machine click on. To your utter amazement, a person of the same sex as your partner leaves a long message, ultimately saying the following: "I know we haven't spoken in several years, but our relationship was the most authentic love I have ever experienced. Is there any way we could get back in touch?" Your lover has not discussed much about prior sexual history, and you certainly were not informed about bisexual or homosexual tendencies. What will you do?

A. I will confront my lover with the information. If my lover can promise that he is now thoroughly secure in his heterosexuality, then we can make this relationship work.

B. I will leave immediately. I am offended by my partner's prior history and can no longer feel comfortable with his sexuality.

C. I won't say anything. My lover is entitled to his past, and I am entitled to mine.

Quite obviously, our world contains more than "boy-meets-girl" love stories. Homosexual relationships, from dating to marriage, are becoming widely recognized and accepted. And there is a reasonable chance that if you are heterosexual, your chosen partner might presently experience homosexual feelings or have experimented with homosexuality in the past. If you gained such knowledge, how would you react? Answer A's secret rule reveals that, knowing homosexual behavior was part of your partner's past, you would still desire to continue your heterosexual love relationship: *I will accept a lover's past homosexual tendencies as long as I can trust that this person's heterosexual desires are now dominant and secure.* You do not feel terribly threatened by a sexual orientation that is different from your own. You also believe that a person's sexual orientation can change over time. Your secret rule allows you to keep an open mind and a nonjudgmental attitude about sexual history. But you must also completely trust your partner's honesty and desire in order to feel at ease with this secret rule.

Homosexual activity is expressed on a wide spectrum, from extremely exclusive to rare and occasional homosexual acts performed by predominantly heterosexual people. How will you know where your lover is located on the spectrum? Talk about it. Clearly, if your partner struggles with both hetero- and homosexual desires, you might not be able to feel secure. In addition, you might be unable to fulfill each other's sexual needs. The other possibility is that your partner is completely content with your relationship and can make you feel fine. Whatever the outcome, your forthright approach is a healthy one. Instead of burying fears or making quick calls, you decide to work on the situation. Due to the motivation you have to preserve a good relationship, you are capable of being a great partner. But also be wary of asking too much from yourself or another. Keep an open mind in both directions.

Answer B's secret rule labels homosexuality a deviant practice: *Homosexuality is contrary to our human nature; I want no part of anyone who would participate in it.* You find homosexual acts fundamentally disturbing. Moreover, you do not feel that a person's sexual orientation can change; it is a fixed characteristic. As explained in the analysis for answer A, homosexual activity is expressed on a wide spectrum, from exclusively homosexual behavior to rare experimentation. Homosexual acts do not necessarily make someone a homosexual. Your lover could be 95 percent heterosexual with an occasional desire for someone of the same sex. But you probably would still feel alienated from such a lover.

You know yourself. If you could not enjoy a relationship with someone due to that person's past homosexual tendencies, then it is better not to continue the relationship. Both partners would end up feeling angry, hurt, and threatened. Such dynamics would prevent a healthy love relationship because trust and comfort would not be present. But there is a possibility that your answer reaches past love relationships and creates a prejudice toward homosexuals in general. Consider if your reaction is simply about your preferences in a lover or about an unhealthy fear of homosexuality. If you suspect the latter, seriously consider working on this fear. Why judge the lifestyle of homosexuals and bisexuals, ultimately creating anger in yourself?

Answer C's secret rule reveals, *I have no right to question my lover about sexual history or feel concerns about differing sexual orientation.* Your answer shows an attempt to avoid prejudice and to erase the past. Your open-mindedness and fundamental trust are impressive. But your answer also highlights a passivity—even a possible denial—that is unhealthy. Why *don't* you have the right to discuss sexual history with your partner? Are you afraid of what you might find? Are you afraid of being questioned yourself? Considering issues from disease to fulfilling your partner's desires, a healthy relationship—hetero- or homosexual—involves honest sharing of experiences, desires, concerns, and lifestyle needs. If your relationship is healthy, you will be able and willing to address this issue instead of pretending it is not there.

Your secret rule allows you to build something new and exciting with your partner. You do not have to rid yourself of any residue from the past; you suspect that ignoring it will work just as well. On the other hand, be aware that your rule requires a lot of energy. Realistically, it would be hard to forget what you heard and feel confident that you truly know your partner. Why not take the honest and open route? Are you simply avoiding something that makes you uncomfortable? Once the information is in front of you, it cannot be erased. Chances are it will surface in your mind on more than one occasion. Being proactive—confronting the issue in a calm and nonjudgmental way *now*—is one way to fight conflict and anxiety in the future.

8. Your young niece has a boyfriend and they have strong feelings for each other. She is too embarrassed to talk to her parents about sex and feels you could be more honest and objective. She asks you to explain when a young woman is ready to have sex. What do you say?

A. You had better be married, engaged, or pretty darn close before you become sexually active.

B. If you are in a loving and supportive relationship and know that it will mean something to both of you, then you are probably ready.

C. You have to be physically mature, be responsible for your behavior, and have covered all the bases such as disease and pregnancy prevention. Then you might be ready.

What are your feelings about premarital sex, especially when it comes to the younger generation? If you tend to think that marriage is the marker, then you follow answer A's secret rule: *A female is ready to be sexually active when she is committed to her marriage partner.* You want your niece to be sure that she is not being used for someone's gratification and then left without the promise of a future relationship. You maintain an old-fashioned and safe value that protects girls from sex-hungry boys. Or maybe you see sex as a sacred act between two lifetime partners.

There is no arguing that the younger the girl, the less wisdom and experience she may have to make the right choices. Your niece may be many years away from the kind of relationship you are describing. And if so, your secret rule might be the healthiest advice for her. But what if she *is* in a mature relationship? What should she do until marriage? Is kissing okay? How about petting, and how far should that go before it is over the line? Suppose she doesn't want to commit to anyone until she has finished college or even graduate school? And what is your greatest concern about a girl who becomes sexually active too early? Will "decent" men no longer desire her? You hold a value system that was prominent decades ago and in some ways didn't work badly. But in this day and age, many young women are having sex, and it is probably most important to fill them in on the facts first. In an ideal world, it might be desirable for young people to begin their sexual experiences in the bonds of a warm and loving relationship that ends in marriage. Maybe your niece can hold to the advice you give her. But if she cannot, you must understand that the world has changed and that young women are not the dependent damsels of yesteryear. They are free to make choices, just like a man. What they need most is clear information and encouragement to seek healthy love partners.

The secret rule for answer B asserts: *Sexual activity should begin when a girl is in a supportive relationship in which sex has meaning.* You don't require a ring or promise thereof, but you would ask that she be with someone who really cares and will continue to be with her after they begin their sexual explorations. If you chose this secret rule, you place a great deal of emphasis on the depth of the relationship. Can a girl be in a deep relationship at fourteen? Sixteen? Does the fact that she is in a relationship give her wisdom and maturity? Could she be positively childlike and immature and still have a caring boyfriend? Are there any other criteria you would like to add to your list of reasons to have sex?

Suppose your niece is in this supportive relationship, has sex, and finds out that it didn't feel as good as she had hoped. It was actually a disappointment. What do you suppose was missing? Should she have gotten her sex education from the boy, a book, a video, a teen movie, or anyone who might have been helpful? While it is best to have one's first sexual experience with a loving and caring partner as opposed to being drunk at a party and half-conscious, there may still be something missing—education and maturity. While guiding your niece through the rocky shoals of early sexual experiences, you might need to expand your rule to factor in how ready she actually is beyond the fact she has a nice caring boyfriend—an element that is necessary but not sufficient in the best of all worlds.

Answer C's secret rule says: *A young woman is ready for sex when she is past puberty, emotionally stable, and fully informed.* Responsibility now becomes more relevant than love. And this, in no way, is meant to diminish the meaning and power of love, but young love is based more often on sizzle than substance. Excitement often translates into love in the inexperienced heart. If you chose this secret rule, you recognize that sex requires maturity and responsibility as much as any emotional preconditions. You expect your niece to bear at least half of the responsibility for the sexual experience. You have a proactive and healthy idea when compared with many who would have the female remain the victim of unscrupulous boys.

No one knows for sure when anyone is truly ready for the first sexual experience. But your approach seems very helpful. You add responsibility to the understanding that sex is about shared feelings. After talking with you, your niece may just have enough understanding and wisdom to make it safe, pleasurable, and meaningful.

9. You are doing an Internet search on your home computer, looking for information on a work-related issue. When you click on one of the suggested web addresses, you are surprised to find a pornography site pop up before your eyes. Unexpectedly, you are now looking at graphic sexual images! Your search was in no way related to this material; one of the "key words" in your general search must have tapped into this site. What is your reaction?

A. I am horrified and will immediately exit this site.

B. I will explore the site for a few minutes, but I admit that I feel some discomfort and embarrassment in doing so.

C. I think the site is fascinating and stimulating. I'm going to have some fun with this lucky find!

In our culture, pornography is available at the click of a mouse or the press of a remote control. Because pornography is within any adult's reach—to the point where we may even be unexpectedly exposed to it at times—each one of us must make a decision about our comfort level. If you selected answer A, your secret rule clearly denies any comfort with or acceptance of pornography: *Pornography is morally offensive and destructive.* From where does this viewpoint stem—your religious or cultural background; your interest in women's rights; your own independent code of ethics that you have developed through personal experience? By contemplating the source behind your secret rule, you will understand your strong conviction more clearly.

If you are being 100-percent honest with yourself, you do not need to change a thing. Your secret rule anticipates your upset at pornographic images and tells you to stay far away from them. A secret rule functions optimally when it brings comfort and satisfaction to your life. If you feel most comfortable by avoiding any of the sites that offer graphic sexual images for entertainment purposes, by all means, click out or click off. Of course, if you are frustrated or angry with yourself for obeying this secret rule, it may not be functioning well in your life. In such a case, you have the option of reevaluating your rule.

If you selected answer B, you have a mixed opinion on the use of pornography: *I find pornography arousing, but my notions of what is socially or spiritually acceptable keep me from taking too much pleasure in it.* You are honest enough to accept that pornographic images excite your sex drive. However, you also associate pornography with negative concepts, such as immorality and sexual deviancy. As a result, spending considerable time enjoying the images is not an option for you; your shame far outweighs your pleasure. You were probably raised to believe that pornography of any type is both morally offensive and spiritually destructive. Even though, as a mature adult, you can come to your own conclusions about what is desirable and undesirable, you are still influenced by prior lessons and warnings.

Ultimately, your secret rule might work just fine for you. Perhaps you allow yourself to dabble a little, but then you leave the pornography behind so as not to lose yourself in its world. If you believe that you will be drawn deeper into a reliance on pornography and eventually be angry with yourself, listen to your secret rule. However, if you continue to feel frustrated and confused by your "sneak a peek" approach, consider adopting a revised secret rule that allows you a firmer stand on the issue, either way. Your feelings of shame might be telling you that pornography is fundamentally unhealthy for you; or your curiosity might be telling you that you are ready to open yourself up to new sexual rules.

The secret rule associated with answer C tells you to explore and enjoy the images on the screen: *Pornography is personally entertaining and ethically acceptable.* If you did not feel that pornography is appealing and useful, you would not waste your time looking at it through a computer screen. In order to understand yourself better, explore *why* you choose to spend time in front of these graphic images.

Are you merely having some fun? As long as you feel contented accessing the pornographic images, the rule works. You can enjoy yourself without feeling any residual guilt or self-loathing, which is a sign that you are secure in your own judgments and values. But if you are accessing these sites because you are sexually frustrated or even addicted to the pleasure they bring you, you should examine related areas of your life. You might be relying on pornography to fill a need that warrants attention. If tapping into this type of sexual material will make you feel more frustrated, angry, or resentful, then it might be best to reshape your rule on pornography.

10. Your spouse was in a terrible fire and sustained serious burns on over 80 percent of the body. After undergoing intense treatments in the hospital for ten months, your partner will now be moved to a rehabilitation center for another year. You visit your spouse at every opportunity and do what you can to maintain a healthy relationship. But when you are at home, you suffer from extreme loneliness and sexual frustration. You know that it will be at least another twelve months before you share your bed with your mate, and even then, things will be very different for the two of you. After discussing your concerns with a trustworthy friend, he suggests contacting a reputable escort service and gives you the phone number of one. What is your reaction?

A. I am repulsed by the suggestion and will immediately reject it.

B. I will accept the phone number but never use it.

C. I will call the number at the earliest opportunity.

Prostitution is an age-old business. Here is a situation that involves more than sexual desire; it includes despair and loneliness as the motivating factors. Is there any situation in which you would define the purchasing of sexual activity as an acceptable option? Probably not, if you selected answer A. Your secret rule reveals: *Prostitution is an inexcusable business with no redeeming features.* You make no exceptions to your opinion on prostitution, even when it is used as a last resort. The given scenario removes the risk of disease and lack of confidentiality by explaining that the particular escort service is recommended by a trustworthy friend. Therefore, you are not holding back for those practical purposes. It is your personal moral code that objects to sex for money and keeps you from even considering the option. You would rather remain committed to your mate than to relieve your loneliness and frustration with a hired partner. In other words, you cannot divorce sexual activity from your exclusive love relationship.

If your secret rule is healthy for you, then you will feel content and strengthened by your decision to remain celibate. You have not chosen an easy path, but you are convicted enough to manage it. In the past, you realized that betraying your own moral code for a quick fix or an exception did not work. Therefore, you have decided to stay in your comfort zone, and that is a safe place to be. But to confirm that you are following your secret rule for the best reasons, check your motivation. If you decide against hiring a prostitute because you are afraid of what others would think and say if they found out—not because you wholeheartedly want to remain exclusively involved with your spouse—then you are not being completely honest with yourself. You will remain deeply conflicted and anxious, even if it doesn't show on the surface.

Answer B's secret rule displays that you have a flexible opinion of prostitution: *Prostitution is acceptable and useful in a limited number of cases, but I don't want to turn to it myself.* You are not offended at the thought of hiring an escort for sexual excitement, at least as a last resort. However, it is certainly not your first choice, nor is it a turn-on. You are realistic about sexual loneliness. For you, sex is an important link to true love and, ideally, you want to keep it exclusive with your mate. But you also see sex as a basic physical need that can, under certain circumstances, be separated from love. In fact, you believe there are times when it is healthier to enjoy the paid-for release of sexual frustration than to maintain celibacy out of shame or guilt.

You consider yourself strong enough to avoid this last resort. You do not feel it is personally necessary—yet. Notice that you *keep* the card. Somewhere inside, you know there may come a day when you must turn to this option. You do not seem to struggle with the anxieties that naturally come when we demand black-and-white answers of ourselves. If you truly are content with refusing the service yet keeping it in mind for the future, then you have found a comfortable way to get through the moment. If, however, your secret rule brings upset and regret into your life—for either considering the service or disallowing yourself its benefits—then this secret rule is not serving you particularly well. Instead of being most content on the middle ground, you are most uncomfortable there and are seeking some conviction, one way or the other.

Selecting answer C is a sure sign that you see some forms of prostitution as valuable: *Under some circumstances, there is nothing shameful about buying sex.* You understand prostitution as a legitimate service—at least in some cases. Moreover, you see sex as a basic physical need, not necessarily an act that is largely associated with emotional love. According to your values, there is nothing wrong with serving this need through a business transaction; that would be more constructive than allowing yourself to become frustrated to the point of obsession or despair.

If your moral code allows you to hire an escort without any residual feelings of guilt and personal shame, then your secret rule is consistent with your deepest needs and beliefs. There is the possibility, however, that you hold yourself to one secret rule in desperate situations and another when the deed is done. Confirm that you have thought through this issue enough to know that you will not punish yourself with notions of betrayal once the sexual frustration is not consuming you anymore. It is helpful to explore your secret rules to the point where you can apply them in tough times and in good times.

CONCLUSION

Sex and sexy are everywhere. Everything seems to shout, "Look at me . . . want me . . . crave me . . . you know you have to have me." Walk past the checkout counter at any grocery store and look at the dozens of magazines that tell us what we should look like, dress like, and desire in order to be sexy and have a great sex life. Hopefully, this chapter has helped you figure out your *own* answers, instead of being force-fed by someone else's ideas. Perhaps you do not have a large sexual appetite. That's perfectly fine! Simply find a suitable partner. Or maybe you like old-fashioned sex without all the glimmer and trappings—literally—of eroticism. That's fine too! Of course, maybe a little experimentation is your thing. Whatever the case, you should be able to explore and articulate your needs freely so that you can enjoy the most contentment in your life. Sex can be invigorating, moving, therapeutic, and stress relieving when practiced in the right way with the right person. If it can offer all that, then why not figure out if your secret rules about sex work for you!

10. Love

Is there any subject that has been given more attention in music, art, and literature than love? What artist, poet, or novelist has not weighed in on the good, the bad, and the ugly of love? In fact, such creative minds can articulate feelings that we could scarcely express in words. But the truth is that everyone who thinks and feels is an expert on love. If you have lived life at all, you have tasted the sweetness and the bitter disappointment of love. You may or may not have the gift of words, but you know what you feel and you have established secret rules around those feelings.

The love we are talking about here is romantic love—the love born of passion. Romantic love can make us climb the highest mountain or sink to the lowest depths. We could debate at length what an ideal or true love is. But who can say, in more than the vaguest idealized terms, who or what is good for us? We are left to discover for ourselves what we want and what feels right. If only finding our soul mate were as simple as feeling the magic and excitement of desire! But alas, so many frogs and so few princes and princesses!

It is a fairly common if not universal experience to face challenges when finding and establishing that special love connection. Either one partner is not attracted enough to the other, which creates conflict, or there is good chemistry but incompatibility in a number of other areas, which also creates conflict. The proof of our struggles is evidenced by the thousands of books, seminars, and websites on how to make love succeed. Behind all of these markets are the counselors, psychologists, and psychiatrists who discuss the same problems with their clients in the confidentiality of their offices. The bottom line is that there is more to love than chemistry, as most of us have already discovered. A special love is likely to contain the deepest friendship, the collaboration of great ideas, and the shared struggle to make it through life. But it is easy to mistake something that feels good for a special love. Have you ever mistaken desire for love? Or, on the other end of the spectrum, have you played it too safe and avoided the passionate fire of love relationships? Have you found true love? To what lengths will you go to protect your love? Where are you most vulnerable? How much are you responsible for the success and failure of love? Answering certain questions might reveal where you are stuck and where you are strong. Take some time to consider how you know love and why it is often not what you thought it would be.

1. While away on an extended business trip, you meet and fall in love with someone. But there's a catch—you have a significant other back home. When you return home, you realize that you are still in love with your long-time lover, too. Can you be in love with two people? You wish it were possible to have both. It is likely that you will return to this other place, due to business. That means that you can easily have contact with the new love interest. How will you resolve this tough situation?

A. I will have to decide on one partner and stick with my decision.

B. I will keep up both relationships as long as I can.

C. While it is possible to be in love with more than one person, a relationship is also about history and commitment. My loyalties should lie with my long-term lover, so I will have no more contact with this new flame.

Is true love exclusive? Can you be in love with more than one person at a time? Answer A's secret rule firmly denies multiple true loves: *Loving two people with equal intensity is not possible; one must be true and the other must be infatuation.* You have learned, through either observation or experience, that two powerful relationships cannot be truly equal—only one love can be real and the other an attraction or diversion. You know that attraction, even sexual passion, does not signify deep love. For you, there is one love, one soul mate, no pretenders to the throne. Your secret rule most likely functions very well in your life, allowing you to establish a secure and intense relationship with one partner.

Your choice of answer A also shows that you are eminently practical. You know instinctively that carrying on with two loves is most often a recipe for disaster. With this rule, you are less inclined towards deception. And if you are the clear-thinking romantic we suspect, you won't agonize or lead anyone on. You will choose your true love before there is more confusion and hurt.

The secret rule supporting answer B finds that more is better: *Loving two people is not only possible but desirable if it means that more needs get met.* It takes two lovers to fill your tank. Each person is special and, between the two, you can finally find the fulfillment you have always dreamed about. If this is your philosophy, you have never experienced fulfillment in a relationship. You spend a good deal of time shuttling between "loves," hoping that incessant attempts will somehow help you meet the mark. There is nothing wrong with getting your needs met; you are to be commended for going out and getting what you always wanted and needed. But on the other hand, why run yourself ragged? It is magical thinking to believe that maintaining two "true loves" can go on indefinitely. You will either hurt the involved parties or wear yourself thin with anxiety.

Maybe you just intend on taking what you can from this experience, knowing your time is limited. Just consider that someone will be hurt badly and feel betrayed and deceived. This secret rule might work for you, but it is more likely to sabotage the pursuit of a healthy, authentic love.

Answer C's secret rule states, *I can only make one love affair work, and shared history is more important than novelty or adventure.* You feel that two loves at once are possible and, for a brief moment in time, exciting and romantic. But you know that soon the reality will hit you and you will be forced to choose one over the other. So to avoid that awkward time, you have decided to go with the comfort of your original relationship. For you, an important part of true love involves shared experiences and longevity. You also value security and reliability.

Now check your answer against your deepest wants. Are you choosing the long-term relationship because you owe that person something? The other possibility is that you are just more sure that he will be there for you. There is nothing wrong with loyalty and keeping commitments you already have. That is a good thing. The question you must ask yourself is whether you are doing the right thing for the right reason. The ideal is to make your decision out of a personal desire, not out of obligation. If your secret rule is working properly, it should not only keep you out of trouble, but also make you very content. If you really feel more for the other person but are scared to make the leap, you might find yourself more regretful than forgetful regarding the one you left behind.

2. After a rocky relationship characterized by nasty arguments and what seems to be a complete inability to get along, you decide to leave your lover of ten years. It has taken much strength and determination to do so because you have been very loyal and devoted. A week after you move out, you get a desperate call from this ex-lover, threatening suicide if you don't come back. Will you go back, at least for a little while, until this person gains some clarity?

A. Obviously, this person is terribly in love with me. Out of love and loyalty, I will go back and try to help them through it.

B. I am definitely not obligated to go back and I will not be manipulated by this ex-love. I will remove myself completely from the situation.

C. I will not go back into this unhealthy relationship, but I feel obligated to get some friends and professionals involved.

What, if any, obligations do we have to those we formerly loved? How much does history count when it comes to obligation? If you chose answer A, your secret rule argues that your past controls your present to a large extent: *After a long love history, if someone really needs me, I am obligated to provide some care.* You obviously still care enough to help your old lover. But your caring is likely to come from guilt rather than love. If anything happened, you would feel responsible. You are struggling with some boundary issues. Each of us has a boundary, or should anyway, that allows us to act as honestly and selflessly as we can without feeling that our actions are pushed onto us. Anyone who thinks that it is all right to show up at your door day or night, invading your room or your life, when you want separation has a boundary issue.

While it is a noble and caring gesture to go back and stay for a while until your old flame finds his way, he has clearly disregarded your decision to separate—a disrespecting of the boundary that you have attempted to erect in order to get away. Sometimes we care best for a person by letting him fend for himself rather than trying to fix up every bit of discomfort that comes along. And if something were to happen to this ex-lover, you would not be responsible. An adult is in charge of his own actions.

The secret rule for answer B reveals that you have washed your hands of all involvement: *When I decide that a relationship is over, I will not be manipulated back into that person's life—for any reason.* You have made a clean break and intend to keep it that way. Do you have any obligation at all to this person? If you chose this secret rule, you have strong and firm boundaries. You are likely to be generally assertive and should not have much trouble saying "no" and meaning it.

Yet consider this: If you are so self-assured, then you should be able to help, even just a little, because you know you will not leave your own comfort zone. Would it invade your boundary to have mutual friends give you reports on his progress or, if they asked you, to make a call or send a card? If something happened to this person, how would you feel? Besides telling yourself it's not your fault, wouldn't you feel sad if he really did make a suicide attempt or, worse yet, succeeded? Separation is clearly called for; you have had enough, and it is not generally advisable to give in to someone who uses suicide threats as a way to restart a relationship. But there is also no harm in alerting a mutual friend or family member so that you have the peace of knowing that, out of compassion, you made an effort to help an old friend.

Answer C's secret rule offers a healthy balance between letting go and sending a lifeline: *I feel obligated to get some help for an old lover in pain, without deeply involving myself in the process.* You feel bad for your old lover, who cannot seem to move forward, but you cannot and will not allow yourself to be manipulated back into the relationship. You are using both compassion and sense, and that is a great combination. Your boundaries are secure enough to maintain empathy without pity. You have adequate self-esteem, which should help you recognize a healthy level of involvement in other situations where boundaries are being tested too. Because of your own sense of self, you do not put yourself in positions where you feel tricked or cajoled.

Your secret rule should give you peace of mind. You have found a balance between caring for yourself and caring for others. You maintain an open heart and avoid panic, as well as unnecessary pity. The right thing would be to help in some way; the only question is how much and how long. It may be that nothing short of getting back together again will satisfy your ex-lover. That must remain nonnegotiable. Should you attend therapy sessions with this person? Probably not. But alerting someone to the suicide threats is a great move. If he continues to threaten or make gestures, you have done all that is reasonable. A clear conscience based on empathic action should allow you to further separate, knowing you have done all that could be reasonably expected. It is the right thing for the right reason.

3. You were single for a while and have finally met a great person. It's the first time in a long time that you have fallen in love so quickly, and it feels very real. Once you declare your love for each other, the details about your lives start to come out. You find out that your new love just finished a program for addiction to cocaine and alcohol. While this person seems very appropriate so far, you are aware that addictions are difficult to overcome. You are also aware that you would be sharing in this complicated battle against substance abuse. Will you stay in the relationship?

A. Yes. I will gladly stay and play a role in this person's recovery.

B. No. While I understand the difficulties, I don't want to get involved.

C. I will give this person one chance. If there's a slip, I will probably leave.

Is love enough to carry you through health problems and potentially destructive behaviors, or does that now seem to be an adolescent notion? Do you really want to go to meetings and support groups just to make the relationship work? Is it wise to begin with someone who has a great deal of healing ahead? The secret rule behind answer A says that love means compassion and direct help from the start: *I will give whatever help and support necessary to make my love relationship work, even if that means taking part in a lifelong challenge.* You know how hard it is to find love, and have the strength and determination to make it work. Your idealistic and hopeful attitude will make someone very happy. But do you fully understand what you commit to when you take on a serious journey such as addiction recovery? Are you sure that you, personally, can provide the attention, stability, and commitment necessary, or do you tend to be impulsive and overly romantic?

You may not realize that sobriety is only the beginning. While your determination is admirable, you cannot love another person's problems away. You cannot, by yourself, give a person enough love so that she will never use drugs again. If your approach is *that* idealistic—in other words, if you have a savior complex—you are likely to get hurt. On the other hand, if you are prepared to be involved in all that the recovery process requires, including an occasional fall off the wagon, you may succeed. There is nothing wrong with loving someone with an addiction problem and giving everything you have to make it work. As long as you go in with eyes wide open and no illusions about the power of love to conquer all, your secret rule will at least provide you with motivation and energy.

The secret rule behind answer B instructs you to get out while you can: *I will not try to make love work with someone who already has problems, especially addiction, that could easily sabotage the relationship.* If you chose this secret rule, you have experienced how hard it is to make love work and don't want any additional burdens. That's a safe approach and certainly understandable. But, while anyone can comprehend why you might be gun-shy, do you really think that *anyone* will come problem free? Don't you believe that people can change? Don't you believe that your love adds something immeasurable to a person who may never have had someone like you? Overcoming addictions can be difficult, but people do it all the time. Programs do work and people can change.

Now that we have played the devil's advocate, if your secret rule still guides you away from remaining involved with an addictive personality, you need to honor that. Maybe you fundamentally know that you do not have the strength to endure such a battle at this point in your life. Maybe you have traumatic memories that will not allow you to handle the situation healthily. Have you poured yourself into someone only to find it went down the drain? Also, a person who suffers from an addiction should let a good while pass in recovery before she enters into a serious relationship. Maybe this new love interest is still in the initial stages of a big change and is not capable of developing a healthy relationship right now. You do have to look out for yourself too, as your secret rule instructs you to do. Only you can know what you are capable of and how much you can handle. Just be sure that your secret rule does not lead you down a path of regret and feelings of failure because you didn't give it a try.

Answer C's secret rule tells you that love is worth trying for, even in the face of a terrible challenge, but that it has limits: *For love, I am willing to begin a relationship with someone who suffers from problems such as addiction, give the relationship a chance to succeed, but establish limits if the situation gets too difficult.* You have been looking for love for a long time, and you are not ready to let a former addiction problem dissuade you from something good. At least you are willing to give her a chance. If you chose this secret rule, you have a realistic notion about love: Love can bring pain and struggle, yet also great joy that is worth fighting for. You have a less judgmental attitude towards addiction and realize that people do change. In fact, you probably are well-informed about addiction and recovery already, because your answer shows an intelligent approach to this situation.

While it does seem like a matter of character, there is clearly a biological component to addiction. If your love is doing what she can, the best she can, there will still be difficult times that will require patience and understanding. If you are willing to accept such a person into your life rather than decide in advance how many mistakes she can make, you'll have a good chance. It might be best to judge the success of the relationship on how much intimacy and honesty is taking place. Just like everyone else, people with addictions need to be loved and to give love. It is wise to give someone you love an opportunity to enjoy stability, warmth, and enhanced self-esteem. Most important, you must allow yourself the freedom to leave if you realize the relationship is hurting, not helping, the health of either partner.

4. Your lover wants you to visit his out-of-state parents again. It would be your second visit in as many years. You did not have a good time with your mate's family on a previous occasion, and you would prefer to stay home. So you politely explain that you don't want to join in the visit, but heartily encourage your partner to go ahead. Your lover then says, in effect, "If you loved me, you would do this little favor for me." What is your reaction?

A. I can't believe that my lover would use emotional blackmail to get me to go! I will certainly refuse to go and will not hide my anger about being put in this position.

B. My lover has a point. In the big scheme of things, visits with family are small requests. I'll go.

C. I see how important this particular issue is to my mate. So if my lover promises to stop trying to manipulate me and communicates honestly, I will probably go once more.

Do you have a problem going the extra mile for your lover? Do you think that one partner should not have to compromise for another? If you selected answer A, you think it is outright wrong for a lover to expect you to compromise on something you reject: *I will not allow myself to be emotionally blackmailed by someone I love; I will do what I want to do.* You are determined to maintain independence, if not power, in your love relationship. You recognize that if you can be coerced into doing things, there is no telling what you might be asked to do next. Your ability to express your wants is a positive thing. However, on the other hand, you are being asked to do a rather ordinary and usual thing—visiting the in-laws. Your anger seems a bit out of place and you seem not to take your partner's sincere desires into account.

Being in a healthy love relationship means making compromises. It will be very hard to succeed at love if you are immovable. Of course, there are certain things that will warrant a firm position; you should never compromise your deepest morals, beliefs, and instincts. But when it comes to a few hours with people you don't particularly like, or feeding the dog, or saving a little money, is that so bad when measured against your partner's peace? Your secret rule is bound to create conflict because of its inflexibility. Maybe what is needed most is an open discussion of what each of you expects of the other, so there are fewer surprises and less need to haul out the big guns. Examine how strong and effective your love really is if you are not willing to do small things for the person you love. While you cannot allow yourself to be emotionally blackmailed, both you and your partner deserve a nurturing love that offers a bit of self-sacrifice for the greater good.

You believe that love necessarily involves a certain amount of self-sacrifice if you relate to answer B and its secret rule: *There are times when loving someone means doing as your partner asks, even if it's difficult, just because you love that person.* You are willing to compromise on what seems like a small favor. You know that to maintain a healthy love, sometimes you have to do stuff you are not really crazy about. Your giving and peaceful nature is something special. And if you truly feel at peace with how this rule functions in your life, keep it. But do you suffer from unspoken resentment? If so, it may have a tendency to grow. Are you really going because you love him, or do you fear a big argument? Do you feed your partner's tendency to control you? Do you have a line to draw? The issue to examine is whether you are acting out of fear or love, because it makes a big difference. If you are afraid of losing someone and must do what he requests just to keep him, you are not in an equal and loving relationship anymore. In the end, you will resent your lover and feel ashamed of your own behavior.

Of course, your partner's nature has a lot to do with whether your secret rule is constructive or destructive. If this person is also willing to compromise, and if he is generally a giving and accepting person, then it's not so bad to give in—at least this time. But if your partner is chronically disrespecting your feelings and manipulating you with emotional blackmail, you have every right to say, "No more!" In the final analysis, there is nothing wrong with reconsidering a request because you didn't realize it meant so much to your mate. It is fun to make people happy, as long as you maintain your independence and get equal treatment in return.

If you chose answer C, your secret rule tells you to seek a give-and-take, bargaining balance: *I give a little when my lover gives a little.* You realize there is a flaw in the relationship when lovers have to constantly do things for each other to prove their love. You can always trump the other person's request by saying, "If you really, really loved me, you wouldn't ask me to do such a thing." To tackle this problem, you seek clear compromise. If your lover stops using such manipulative techniques, you will stop being so inflexible. Your approach will work in some, if not many, situations on one condition—your lover is willing to work with you. And both of you will get a chance to work on stubbornness, so you will be helping each other grow.

You recognize that a real love relationship is based on free will; once the choices stop being free, it starts becoming less and less loving. But you are also savvy enough to recognize that manipulation is a cry for help in some ways. Your partner can't seem to get his needs met the old-fashioned way, just by asking, and therefore must resort to less mature and more desperate measures. He does so because he is hurting and upset, not because he is mean. Your efforts to maintain your self-respect while sacrificing a bit for the person you love are admirable. Just don't lose too much of your intelligent, strong-minded self when you are bargaining. If your partner tends to be manipulative quite often, a fruitful discussion should take place.

5. You have been in a loving relationship with a man for the past three years. You were planning to get married in a couple of months. Everything seemed perfect. Then a month ago, your fiancé had a serious auto accident and presently appears to be paralyzed from the waist down. His mind is clear, his job will take him back, and he seems to be adjusting as well as possible to this rather sudden change in circumstances. But one change that frightens you is his lack of sexual feeling. He can use his upper body, but he has no real sensations in the lower half of his body. You used to have a great sex life and that was something you were really counting on. Have your feelings changed about him or the wedding?

A. My feelings haven't changed; I love him just the same and I plan to marry him as soon as he is well. Any life changes are just something to which we will both have to adjust.

B. Everything has changed. I suppose I still love him, but I can't marry him now. I don't intend to spend the rest of my life with a paraplegic.

C. I feel very confused. I definitely need some time to think about the marriage.

As much as we don't like to admit it, love can have limits. You can deeply love someone, yet also realize that you cannot take on his problems or habits, especially if they mean lifelong sacrifices for you. In a previous question, we studied whether you could commit to loving a person with an addiction problem. In this question, we are talking about someone who is physically limited, to the point where the limitations influence sexual activity and maybe even fertility. Answer A's secret rule prioritizes the agreement you made to this person before injury, and does not allow you to back out for physical limitations: *The personality and spirit of an individual are more important than physical abilities; an exciting sex life is a far second to a nurturing love.* Your notions of love are larger than the ability to sexually satisfy each other. Sex is only one part of your much larger concept of love, and it is not at the top. Moreover, technology has provided us with a lot of fertility options. So you will work around the physical limitations. You are capable of truly loving people for who they are and not for what they can physically provide. You are a most unusual person who has already mastered one of life's great lessons.

Apparently, you are prepared to live an altered lifestyle without complaint or resentment. There is no question that you are sacrificing a lot for love. But if this secret rule works for you, your resolve to make this love work will bring you fulfillment and personal peace. Your answer shows that you are a courageous, unconventional person who takes challenges in stride. Simply double-check that your decisions are based on authentic desire and commitment, not guilt or a sense of obligation. If you fit into the former category and not the latter, you have the capacity to love in a rare and beautiful way.

Answer B's secret rule instructs you to accept that practicality and personal desires can sometimes outweigh love commitment: *My love for an individual is based on who I think he is and who I expect him to be; when that changes, my love can change.* You committed to an able-bodied person who could do all the things you desire—one of them being sex—and now that person has changed. Your answer reveals that you place certain conditions on your love relationship, and that you can healthily work within the conditions you have chosen. You know your limits and your desires, and you don't force yourself to take on situations that impose upon them.

Indeed, you are entitled to live the life of which you have always dreamt. It would be foolish to try to persuade yourself that your fiancé is the same exact person as before. But to be sure that you feel okay with this secret rule, ask yourself the following question: If the situation were reversed, would I expect to be dumped as well? The point of this is not to induce guilt or to try to change your mind, but to explore a fundamental question about love. How much change can you tolerate before you decide not to love someone anymore? This scenario is premised on an extremely life-altering change, but what if your fiancé gained twenty pounds, lost his hair, or developed a limp? Is it the magnitude of change that affects you, or any alteration in your dream of a suitable love?

Answer C's secret rule allows you to put your commitment on hold, and gives you the option of leaving the relationship: *I believe in unconditional love for the most part, but there is a point when conditions can change too much and then it's okay to leave.* You are being honest. You want to make your committed love relationship work, but you also know that you have personal limits and personal dreams. What you don't yet know is how much you can tolerate.

If you chose this secret rule, you are still trying to find what a mature love really means to you. And for many of us, figuring out what love means and entails is a lifelong process, so do not feel underdeveloped or under pressure to find a set answer. You, along with many, probably have built your concept of love on sexual attraction, shared interests, exciting plans for the future, and assumed health. But maybe this whole talk of a "soul mate" and a "magical connection" falls away when the body significantly changes, even if the mind and spirit do not. Your answer provides the flexibility that you need right now.

6. You recently fell in love with someone who is very different from you— different religion, different ethnic background, different age bracket. Friends and family express concern that the lack of similarities will lead you down a difficult road, and that you will end up with big problems in the future. Yet you know that you share a deep mutual respect and caring with this person. Moreover, your personalities and intellects seem well matched. What will you do?

A. I have to be realistic and break up with my partner. Love is not enough to overcome so many differences.

B. I'm going to give this relationship my best shot. As long as we are true to each other, we can overcome any bump in the road.

C. It all depends on how willing my partner is to change. If my partner is prepared to make some changes in order to participate in my religion, my culture, etc., then we have a much better shot at succeeding.

There is no doubt that, in the history of love and commitment, many couples have overcome significant differences. But that doesn't mean that our secret rules tell us to encourage and support such relationships from the get-go. Some of us are more conservative, cautious, even pessimistic than others. Where do you stand on a relationship that starts out with built-in differences? If you chose answer A, your secret rule says that strong differences are likely to ruin a couple after a while: *Love is not strong enough to overcome large differences like religion, ethnicity, or age; it is best to stay with your own kind.* Your rule certainly has a statistical accuracy to it. Love, for you, is influenced by probabilities and averages. You feel you can learn by others' mistakes. If you chose this secret rule, you see love as a logical decision between two similar people. The fewer the differences, the more likely love will succeed.

Your understanding of love is similar to a good business arrangement. Romantic notions of building bridges between two worlds seem a bit naïve and foolish to you. You feel safe working within conservative norms. If your secret rule serves you well, you have no regrets and have been content with decisions to terminate any relationships that included a significant discrepancy in religion, custom, or age in the past. If your secret rule is not functioning well, you feel guilty, angry, and deprived at what you have sacrificed for safety's sake. In the end, you might blame society, your family, or your friends, but the decision is truly yours.

The secret rule behind answer B takes an optimistic approach: *If two people love each other, almost any kind of difference can be overcome.* You believe that it is the nature and quality of the love that allow a relation-

ship to succeed. In other words, you are the infamous "hopeless romantic." Your love decisions are not based on someone else's history or on
logic; they are based on faith that love can conquer any hardships. Moreover, you show that you judge others not by their class or ethnicity, but on
the content of their character. For you, love is less about social structures
and more about a spiritual connection.

Your secret rule allows you the widest latitude and greatest flexibility in making love work. Of course, it is always smart to confirm that your
secret rule truly works in your life. Have you experienced profound love
experiences with people who are very different from you? Have the differences enriched more than harmed your love life? If, after considering
how this secret rule has manifested itself in your life, you still feel content
and confident in your answer, then you have established a healthy secret
rule.

Answer C's secret rule reveals your faith in compromise and change:
*If someone is willing to accommodate me and compromise with me, then love can
work.* You are as practical as you are romantic. You know that serious differences in custom and generation can easily break up a couple, but you
also feel that flexibility is the glue that can keep two people together. The
power of working things out in a realistic and respectful manner is very
evident to you. And you probably feel that if someone truly loves you, he
will be willing to do what it takes to make you happy.

As long as you are willing to make equal moves toward compromise
and change, it is hard to anticipate how this secret rule could be anything
but positive. If you are as open to accepting and changing as you expect
your partner to be, then you have a healthy perspective that will give
your love the best shot possible. Your attitude is the "give a little, get a little" theory. Your partner is opening new vistas and new opportunities for
you to experience life. Your love is the portal to a new world. However,
track your reactions when these changes and compromises become a reality. Do you feel any resentment? Do you find yourself resisting? These
further questions will help you identify whether this secret rule is effective in your life.

7. You are committed to your lover and would never do anything to shake
the trust in your relationship. In fact, the two of you have just moved
in together and are planning to marry. But you are starting to feel uneasy
about a few new patterns. Your lover has been calling you more and more

at work. The latest request is that you be available by pager at any moment. And your lover has requested that you not see your old friends of the opposite sex anymore because "there is so little time for us." When you confront these issues, your partner says that it's just a little jealousy and that it's natural—after all, you are so attractive and that worries your lover. You explain that there is nothing to be worried about. However, the behavior continues. What will you do?

A. I will explain that this behavior is intolerable and suggest that we take a few steps back in our relationship.

B. I guess all of these efforts are a sign that my lover really cares about me. I will put up with the inconveniences in order to soothe my partner's mind.

C. I don't want to be under my partner's thumb, but I still think we can be happy together. The best way to handle this is to let my lover think that I am complying by making small gestures, but then continue to do what I like anyway. Once my partner realizes he has nothing to fear, he won't feel so jealous and think he has to control me.

Can you stay in a relationship that suffers from a fundamental lack of trust? Do you understand and accept jealousy, or do you shrink from it? You have no tolerance for distrust and jealousy if you selected answer A and, therefore, its secret rule: *Without trust, love cannot work.* You are an independent person who wants to maintain space and personal friendships. There is nothing wrong with that. However, if you have a partner who wants to be involved in *every* aspect of your life, you will feel forever trapped and frustrated. It is important to pay close attention to this secret rule so that you can choose a long-term relationship that serves you well.

Your answer also shows that you are uncompromising in your values. If this approach has made you happy and healthy, then you are being true to your deepest self. You know what you want and won't settle or be controlled. Good for you! But check to make sure that such a rigid decision is where you want to begin. Is there any room for negotiation before you begin to withdraw from the relationship? Some people are naturally timid and insecure; others have been hurt and scared. Depending on how much you love this person, it might serve you well to try to compromise or to have a few serious discussions on trust. You should never have to give up friends or mental freedom; but you may want to assure your lover that you are available for emergencies or anxious moments. Your lover's attitude is not healthy, but depending on other qualities, your mate may be worth a little work before you decide on a final break.

The secret rule that serves as the foundation for answer B finds a distrustful partner's actions acceptable: *A little jealousy among lovers is a natural and normal part of a relationship.* The next question, of course, is, "What's a *little* jealousy?" Does that mean you should give up friends, alter your lifestyle, and interrupt your work at any moment? You are patient and willing to put up with certain inconveniences, probably because you struggle with trust and jealousy a bit too. You have taken a compassionate stance and are willing to appease your lover. These are exceptional qualities, but if taken advantage of, they can bring you pain and loss of self.

Some insecurity is to be expected between partners. However, in this scenario, you are bordering on being dominated by a very demanding lover. Is that acceptable to you? Is there any point at which you would say, "Enough is enough"? Your hypothetical partner's efforts to socially isolate you and to keep your constant attention are quite unhealthy. Do not be afraid to maintain self-respect and a healthy independence.

Answer C's secret rule tries the "sneak around" approach: *I can best manage an insecure lover by using various deceptions.* After all, what we don't know can't hurt us, right? You feel that such a lover's requests are intrusive, but you still think you can make the relationship work. If you chose this secret rule, you have confidence in your moves and value your own skills as a manipulator. You like to think of yourself, however, as an "arranger" who bends the rules for the good of everyone. You are generally well-liked and have an ability to get others to believe in you as they have in the past.

It is certainly understandable that you don't want to be on call every hour of every day. Just consider how much energy you expend on deception. Do you sincerely believe a relationship can be healthy and true when based on deception? If your partner finds out, the trust that she lacked in the first place will now be even more difficult to attain. At some level, you might know that this is a losing battle, but you feel the need to try anyway. If that's what you have to do, then do it. But if you are going to suffer more in the long run, you might want to simply explain that you cannot live with constant distrust and jealousy. If your partner is still unwilling to step back, you might need to step away.

8. You have been dating your lover for about six months. You trust each other completely and have been enjoying a lot of fun. To top it all off, your lover is from the very same background as you; you share similar value systems and cultural practices. It seems perfect, except that your partner is becoming more and more critical. At the start, he would simply pick on small things, such as the color of your car or the way you make coffee. But it has escalated into a litany of complaints about your house, your appearance, your career, and even what wine is best to drink. All of these criticisms are apparently "for your own good," but they are making you feel sad and insecure. You have told your lover on more than one occasion that his corrections are hurtful and that they ruin your time together. Yet your requests are to no avail. What are you going to do with this critical but otherwise wonderful person?

A. If the relationship is good, I can take a little criticism. I'll just let it roll off my back.

B. I'm leaving this relationship right now. I have hit my breaking point and don't need to sacrifice my self-esteem for someone else.

C. One more warning. I will explain politely that, as much as I'm in love, I am not a project to be fixed. If things don't change, I will leave the relationship.

How do you deal with criticism from a loved one, especially when it is gratuitous? Choosing answer A signifies that you swallow criticism in order to maintain peace: *A love relationship involves some difficulties and unwarranted criticism that must be overlooked.* You approach love with your armor on, expecting arrows and tolerating them. Perhaps you have found a way to desensitize yourself. Are you content with this secret rule or do you feel the burning of anger deep inside?

The best way to learn whether this secret rule functions well in your life is to look at your self-esteem. Have your lover's remarks changed the way you look at yourself? Do you tend to believe such comments? You have an easy-going personality and like to accentuate the positives in your loved one. But you should consider protecting yourself as well. The "pleaser" rolls over and absorbs a barrage of needless criticism because she has learned that is acceptable in a relationship. Actually, as time goes on, her own self-worth diminishes instead of grows, as it would in a more healthy relationship. Are you a "pleaser"? If your secret rules allow you to love someone in spite of his critical nature, at the very least you must, in your own mind, decide when you will have reached the point of overload lest you damage your self-worth permanently.

Answer B's secret rule says the following: *I will not allow myself to be needlessly criticized just to maintain the relationship.* You respect all the good things about your lover, but you also know how destructive constant criticism can be. Therefore, you have drawn boundaries very quickly about what behavior is and is not acceptable to you. It seems you have a strong sense of your own value and won't allow yourself to be badgered even by someone you love very much. This is either a learned quality or one that someone reinforced in you. Have you been through this before? Have other relationships made you feel that someone was trying to put you down?

If you instinctively know that such a relationship will harm you, then follow your secret rule and get out quickly. However, if you feel that you often "jump ship" before making a strong effort to right things, you might want to consider doing more discussing before walking out. Only you know how sensitive you are and how effective you are at communicating what hurts you. Your partner might have grown up being criticized and doesn't realize what he is really doing to you. Much depends on whether your partner is willing to work on his problem and be more supportive. Also, much depends on how much you like to work on a problem before deciding it is irreparable.

The secret rule for answer C highlights that you are a tolerant and cautious person: *I should give my partner significant opportunities to change before I make a final judgement.* Your answer reveals that you have been working very hard on relationships for a long time. You have learned over time that people tend to get scared when they get close. So you chalk your partner's criticisms up to insecurities, attempts to make things perfect out of fear, and the like. You are a sensitive soul who gives ample opportunity for reconciliation. It may well be that your hypothetical lover is terribly scared of intimacy and covers it up with a barrage of criticism. But your lover might be arrogant and negative too. Have you truly developed the resolve to leave once you are pushed to a certain point?

There are individuals who like to fix other people, usually without a license to practice. Decide how much criticism you can really take and how much effort to give this guy. If he can't seem to change even with all your understanding and support, he may require more work than is warranted, and it might be better to take your wisdom and awareness where it is well appreciated.

9. You have fallen in love with someone who is everything and more. By your standards, your partner is much more attractive than you, has greater financial success, and is more highly regarded in the workplace. Despite these assets, your lover is kind and considerate, and seems to really love you. Even family and friends emphasize how fortunate you are. They say things like, "Your lover could have had anyone. Aren't you the lucky one!" What are your feelings regarding the future of this relationship?

A. I better enjoy all of this while I can, because it won't last.

B. Our differences mean nothing. Our love will continue indefinitely.

C. I'm not going to worry or make assumptions about the future. I'll simply enjoy the present.

Is there a "better half" in a love relationship? And if so, can you deal with being the lesser of the two—and still feel optimistic? You don't have much faith in a relationship that includes a significant difference between the two partners' attractiveness and success if you chose answer A. Your secret rule states, *Love lasts only when people are equal in most respects.* You may not like to hear that you are lucky because it implies that some unnatural force made a quirky mistake—and could take it back at any minute. While you are motivated and fun enough to make the most of the moment, you also are likely not to see yourself as something really worth keeping. Your self-worth is based almost entirely on what you have and what you can do.

If someone earns more or has a job of higher status, is that person more entitled to someone beautiful and successful? Do you believe that love is that logical or consistent? What do you suppose attracted this person to you in the first place? You must have something going for you. Outsiders don't often see the subtle gifts and sparks that make up a love relationship. Listen to your deepest self and hold onto the depth of this love, not the surface-level opinions of outsiders. If this secret rule has you feeling a little scared and inadequate, consider working to change it. Believe your worth is finite and you will reach only your limitations; believe your worth is limitless and there is no telling who you'll get.

Answer B's secret rule believes that love can conquer it all: *True love overrides any imbalance in the qualities that the individuals have.* From either good experience or good accounts from others, you have placed a tremendous amount of faith in the power of love. You see love as the great equalizer—partners do not need to match up evenly in every column of the "love checklist." You are really quite the romantic. There is much idealism in your rule, especially considering our ever-increasing materialistic world. But there is also much powerful optimism, and when you believe good things will happen, sometimes (if not often) they really do. Your healthy attitude will at least give your love the best chance to survive. It is for you, now, to show the way to cynics who understand love as an appropriate business transaction between two like companies.

It is one thing to hope that these things don't matter, but quite another to deeply believe that you are as adequate and desirable as another. If after an honest self-search, you still come to the conclusion that love can defeat all inequalities, then this secret rule is definitely for you. But if you find that your optimism is equivalent to one of those pained smiles that attempts to cover fears and tears, then you should reevaluate your opinion.

The secret rule behind answer C asserts the following: *Don't anticipate problems; take life and love one day at a time and let the future take care of itself.* We are often told to live each day as if it were our last; then we will get more out of it and be living more authentically. We all spend a lot more time thinking and worrying about the future than we need to. But if you chose answer C, you are making efforts to reduce anxiety in your life and appreciate each day as it comes. You try to live fully in the "now." That appreciation of the moment is a wonderful perspective to have. It will help you make the most out of every experience. Yet, there is more to your answer.

Beneath the surface of answer C, there is a subtle acceptance that a great stroke of "luck," if that's what you want to call it, might not be there tomorrow. Your partner might decide he *can* do better. This is much different from two soul mates who cling together because they have finally found their other half. One way to place your love at a disadvantage is to believe that, somehow, wealth, physical appearance, or prestige defines an individual. In some way, you are open to doubt. You might want to work on erasing that doubt, and instead look optimistically at the future, not just disregard it.

10. You and your fiancée are discussing how you will set up your life. You have discussed money, in-laws, and household chores. It seems like you agree on most things. Then your lover says that she has been independent for all of her adult life and has lots of friends and acquaintances of both sexes. Your sweetheart says that no matter how wonderful one person is to another, or how many similar interests a couple might have, one person cannot possibly fill all the needs of the other. Your lover promises to remain sexually faithful but insists that she has to fill certain emotional and intellectual needs through others. How much can or should a marital partner be able to meet the needs of the other?

A. Marriage is the main relationship, but other individuals are definitely necessary to achieve personal fulfillment. It is good for each person to have individual friends and time to be with them.

B. The spouse and the extended family are the basic unit; a person should not require much more.

C. A couple should, first and foremost, be best friends. They should also have other friends, but they should share them.

Can one person be all that you need? If you selected answer A, your secret rule tells you not to rely on one person for fulfillment: *One person, no matter how loving or special, cannot meet all the needs of the other.* You require more stimulation and diversity than one person can manage. You like the idea of having special friends for special interests, and that has developed your practical approach to love. This secret rule can be very effective, as long as the two partners agree. It can allow for a lot of independence and can make time together very exciting. And it exercises trust, which is important to the health of any relationship. Of course, if this rule comes with a "you just don't cut it" attitude, then there is something wrong.

You might have selected answer A because you are frustrated with your partner. Does your mate lack something that you desperately seek in others? Is there a hole in the relationship when it comes to discussions of good books, current events, or issues about your work? Does your partner lack emotional depth or intelligence? In any mature relationship, it is expected that each individual has personal friends. Just confirm that you are not fundamentally unsatisfied.

Answer B's secret rule puts the weight of the responsibility on family: *Virtually all needs should be met by the marriage partner and the family.* You believe that once you make a commitment to marriage or partnership, all that you need should come from that circle of individuals. If you chose this secret rule, you are selecting a fairly traditional arrangement. Does that mean that you shouldn't have individual friendships? Should they be limited in some way? Why would you expect that you could, in fact, meet all of your partner's needs?

If you favor ice fishing and your fiancée loves antiquing, should you now give up your hobbies because you don't share interests? Are you afraid that time spent away could lead to losing the person you love? Do you feel secure in the love that you have? For many couples, the extended family is all that is necessary for a contented life. But this is not always true. And if a relationship enjoys trust, then maintaining a few independent friendships will not be too jarring. There is no right way to be, But, if your secret rule expects closer family ties and less outside contacts, then very frank expression of those expectations may prevent a great deal of heartache later on. Also recognize the pressure you would put on a mate and family members, expecting them to fill all of your desires.

The secret rule for answer C argues the following: *A real love relationship means sharing everything, including all interests and friends.* You expect a lot of togetherness. You like the idea of having outside activities and friends, but you expect that you will do those things with your partner. If you chose this secret rule, you are requesting your lover to also be best friend and buddy. And there's nothing wrong with that. In fact, most would say it is ideal! You seem to feel that any needs that your partner has ought to be at least partially filled by you, and vice versa.

There are couples who share everything together, have a great deal in common, and don't tire of each other's company. Usually couples already have that kind of relationship before they marry and it grows with time. You are willing to try anything your partner likes just to be a good sport, and would function well in a close relationship. While some lovers might think it's great that you are willing to be part of anything, other partners might like the idea of time spent away and a little more personal space. Is there anything wrong with letting your lover do her own thing while you do yours? Part of your lover's needs may be time spent with others, period. Love is a special emotional state; it doesn't mandate a certain amount of time or shared activities. Because we all have different conceptions of love, it is your obligation to clearly define with your lover how much you expect to be doing together. To assume that things will fall into place because you love each other is bound to create unnecessary conflict that can be avoided with an honest discussion of needs.

CONCLUSION

You have made it through a challenging study of what love means to you. You have tackled some very difficult questions and possibly even probed into some painful memories. But you probably also experienced quite a few nods, smiles, and warm memories. And nods, smiles, and warm memories are some of the best parts of love. Now that you have gotten to know yourself a little better, take steps to create that exciting, life-giving, and passionate love that you have always dreamed about. If you already have it, do everything you can to nurture your treasure!

Conclusion

Before you opened the pages of this book, you may have thought that you were carefree, without a lot of rules regulating your behavior. If so, you were surely surprised to discover that you have so many rules! But we all need rules, and if we are unaware of the principles by which we operate in our daily lives, we too often are caught off guard or repeatedly make the same life mistakes.

Perhaps you read this book by yourself, without asking others what they thought or which answer they might have chosen. If you're like most people, though, curiosity got the best of you, and you asked the questions of others—perhaps as a subtle way of finding out what *they* thought about some very common life situations. If that was the case, you may have based your answers on what you thought was expected, rather than what you truly believed. It may have been important for you to sound more loyal, honest, or sexually conservative (or daring) than you actually are. In a group setting, there is often a tendency to agree with the majority rather than brave a response such as, "You would do *what*???" If you did review the questions with other people, to benefit most from this book, consider revisiting the questions now—especially those that you didn't answer quite honestly. Come up with answers that more accurately reflect your secret rules. You should reach a point where you can say to yourself, "That's how I feel and I don't care what anyone thinks." That's a good beginning.

You will also get more out of this book if you briefly look back at the questions and jot down some notes about your rules. For example, after working your way through Chapter 1, what did you discover about your rules regarding money? Are you more hungry than you thought, or are you truly content? And while you're considering your rules on money, figure out the importance of security in your life. You may, for instance, end up jotting down that fun and adventure waste money and endanger your goal of financial security. If the rule sounds good after your write it down, fine and dandy! If it rings a bit hollow, though, now is the time to change your course of action.

While money makes the world go around, most of us have to work for it. After reading Chapter 2, what did you learn about your work rules? How, for instance, do you keep work and play in balance? Take out your notepad and jot down your rule. What is the purpose of work? Restate your rule. And while you're thinking about it, consider where you got your rule. Was it from Dad? From Mom? How reliable was the source? Most important, ask yourself if your rule is making you happy and content, or if it's a bad rule—a rule that causes anxiety and conflict.

While your rules about money may be as old as the hills, chances are, your rules about men and women and their roles in society have changed over the years. If you are a man, you may be rethinking some of your old gender rules. And ladies, you need to make clear to the men in your life what the new rules are. Don't expect them to learn the rules intuitively by watching the sport's channel and polishing off a six pack. What is the rule that describes the role of a man in a romantic relationship? Can you have a relationship with a man who makes a fraction of the money you do, but has a heart of gold? Do you want respect or adoration? And what old stereotypes are you still carrying around? By knowing your secret rules about gender, as discussed in Chapter 3, you'll be able to catch up with the times—or realize that you're most happy with traditional roles and attitudes.

Chapter 4 deals with the area of power and control. During your reading of Chapter 4, did you find that you really don't want power, or did you discover that you'd like to control everything, from the stock market to the next presidential election? Most people err on one side or the other. That is, either they don't take advantage of the power they do have, or they attempt to control everyone around them. What are your rules about power and control, and how are they working in your life?

How many times have you heard someone say, "If I knew I was going to live this long, I would have taken better care of myself." Actually, this little joke is a big lie. In point of fact, most people never believe they are going to die until they get old and start to slow down, or they have the misfortune to watch people around them die. How important is it to you to stay alive—and not just alive, but healthy, too? In searching your soul for your secret rules about health in Chapter 5, you should have discovered what you will do to regain or maintain your well-being. Think about these rules, and see if they're right for you. Remember: Secrets are for treasure maps, *not* for staying healthy.

Who are you? Next time you meet someone at a party, ask them who they are. You will get some furrowed brows, but it might get people thinking about what they stand for and what they represent. Your ability to express yourself is an integral part of remaining alive and well. If you didn't quite get the message from Chapter 6, it may be summarized simply as "Do your thing." Cry when you're sad, laugh when you're happy, and be silly and funny as often as you can. Half of the mental health professionals would go out of business if individuals would just say, "This is who I am, and I'm proud of it." If you just discovered that you have a hard time with self-expression, congratulations! It is better to know this now than to find it out later. Learn your secret rules, and if they're keeping you from expressing yourself, make the necessary changes. Care about yourself and honor who you are. Besides being a whole lot happier, you will save a fortune on psychotherapy and antidepressants.

Friendship. What would life be without friendship? Of course, as you probably learned in kindergarten, to have a friend, you have to be a friend. Are you a friend? Do you understand what it takes to be a friend? Would you put yourself in jeopardy to help someone you cared about? Would you help a friend cheat? How much should you intervene if a friend is causing himself harm? As you learned in Chapter 7, all of these principles and more make up your secret rules about friendship. So if you want to be a good friend, learn your secret rules, and understand this important area of your life.

Of the many secret rules we hold, perhaps none is more personal than those regarding our spiritual beliefs—the topic of Chapter 8. Even those professing to share the same religion do not share the exact same beliefs about God, an afterlife, the soul, and other spiritual matters. Whether you spend countless hours contemplating the meaning of life or you never give it the slightest thought, you have very specific rules that govern your choices and your behavior. If you have always taken your spirituality lightly, close your eyes for a moment and listen to that still small voice. Don't let another day go by without understanding your secret rules.

If death and the world beyond is one of the least-discussed subjects of our day, certainly the most talked-about topic is that of sex, the subject of Chapter 9. We are told that a sexual revolution occurred some forty years ago. Maybe it started with the Beatles or the "pill" or the miniskirt, but somehow the world changed around us, and so did our most secret rules about sex. Are you freer now than you were earlier in life, or is it the other way around? Given a chance to live out your sexual fantasies, would you? Most important, are you happy with your secret rules? Have they led to a happy sex life, or have they left you feeling guilty, frustrated, or unsatisfied? If your rules are working for you, great. If not, consider starting a revolution of your own!

Love is a many splendored thing—or, at least, it should be. Your mission in Chapter 10 was to discover your innermost rules about love. Do you feel that sex is an essential part of romantic love, or is it the bonus— the cherry on top of the sundae? How much are you willing to trust the one you love? How much are you willing to sacrifice in the name of love? It is expected that with maturity and experience, we evolve healthy rules about love and romance. If not, hopefully, Chapter 10 has helped you formulate some new rules that will enable you to experience all the joy that love and romance have to offer.

If you opened this book thinking that it would supply you with easy answers to all your questions about money, work, spirituality, and more, you have found that it does not. But hopefully, this book *has* shown you that all the answers you want and need are already inside you in the form of your secret rules. Explore them, define them, follow them if they work for you, and change them if they don't. Understand your secret rules, and look forward to a life of greater calm, happiness, and satisfaction.

Index

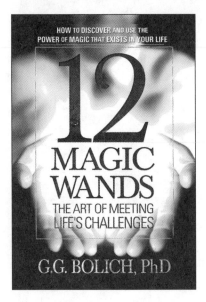